Commonsense Methods for Children with Special Educational Needs

In this era of inclusive education, it is essential that all teachers have a sound understanding of the nature of students' special educational needs and how these needs may best be met in the classroom. Not only must teachers understand and accept students with disabilities and learning problems, but they must also possess a wide range of teaching and management strategies. Similar knowledge and skills are also required by classroom assistants and other personnel working in a support role in schools.

This fully revised and updated sixth edition of *Commonsense Methods for Children with Special Educational Needs* offers sound practical advice on assessment and intervention based on the latest research evidence from the field. The practical advice the author gives throughout the book is embedded within a clear theoretical context supported by current research and classroom practice. Coverage includes:

general and specific learning difficulties
students with autism, intellectual, physical or sensory impairments
self-regulation
social skills
behaviour management
literacy and numeracy
curriculum adaptation and differentiation
teaching methods.

In addition, this seminal text includes for the first time a chapter on the characteristics and specific needs of gifted and talented students. The book also contains an extensive reference list, online resources, and recommendations for further reading, making it an invaluable resource for trainee and practising teachers as well as other key professionals working in schools, such as SENCOs, educational psychologists, guidance officers and school counsellors.

Peter Westwood has worked in education for many years as a teacher, educational psychologist and university lecturer. He has received awards for excellence in teaching from Flinders University in South Australia and from the University of Hong Kong.

Commonsense Methods for Children with Special Educational Needs

Sixth Edition

Peter Westwood

Routledge
Taylor & Francis Group
LONDON AND NEW YORK

KH

First published 1987
This sixth edition published 2011
by Routledge
2 Park Square, Milton Park, Abingdon, Oxon OX14 4RN

Simultaneously published in the USA and Canada
by Routledge
270 Madison Avenue, New York, NY 10016

Routledge is an imprint of the Taylor & Francis Group, an informa business

Typeset in Times New Roman & Gilsans by
Swales & Willis Ltd, Exeter, Devon
Printed and bound in Great Britain by
CPI Antony Rowe Ltd, Chippenham, Wiltshire

British Library Cataloguing in Publication Data
A catalogue record for this book is available
from the British Library

Library of Congress Cataloging-in-Publication Data
Westwood, Peter S.
  Commonsense methods for children with special
  educational needs/Peter Westwood. —6th ed.
  p. cm.
  Includes bibliographical references and index.
  1. Children with disabilities—Education.
  2. Mainstreaming in education. I. Title.
  LC4015.W44 2011
  371.9'043—dc22
                          2010022538

ISBN13: 978-0-415-58376-3 (hbk)
ISBN13: 978-0-415-58375-6 (pbk)
ISBN13: 978-0-203-83664-4 (ebk)

3/19/12

Contents

Introduction

This sixth edition of *Commonsense Methods for Children with Special Educationa. Needs* continues to be primarily about learning and teaching, rather than the philosophy and ideology of inclusive education. The material comes from my own experience as a teacher and educational psychologist, but I have also drawn extensively on recent international literature relating to classroom research and practice.

At the present time in Britain, Australia and the US, there has been public demand that teachers employ instructional methods that research has shown to be effective in advancing children's learning, rather than using untested approaches based on the latest fad or on teachers' own idiosyncratic styles. This call for evidence-based methods is reflected strongly in government reports dealing with the teaching of literacy, but similar pressure is now being felt in subject areas such as science and mathematics.

In this new edition, I have continued to provide generic information and practical advice that can be applied in any country and under any education system. I have avoided, as far as possible, relating the content closely to the special education administrative procedures, legal mandates, regulations, codes and terminology used in any one country. Where reference to a particular system has been necessary, I have usually compared the situation under discussion to similar situations in other countries, particularly Britain, Australia, and the US. Children with special needs, no matter where they are in the world, display remarkably similar learning characteristics and therefore require similar forms of effective evidence-based intervention. It is also my experience that high-quality teaching can be identified anywhere in the world by a set of generic competencies. It is of great interest to me that earlier editions of this book have been translated into Japanese and Chinese languages, thus supporting my view that practical ideas have international relevance and appeal.

I have retained the same scope and sequence of topics as in the previous edition, but a new chapter has been added on the special needs of gifted and talented students. The previous single chapter on physical and sensory disabilities has been significantly revised and is now presented as two separate chapters – the first dealing with physical disability and the other with sensory impairments (vision and hearing). All other chapters have been revised and updated to include the latest ideas and methods for teaching and managing children with special educational needs.

The extensive list of references at the end of the book, and the online resources listed at the end of each chapter, should be of value to teachers and researchers wishing to pursue any of the topics in greater depth. The updated further reading sections will also be of assistance.

I hope this new edition will continue to help all teachers understand their students' special educational needs, and at the same time increase teachers' repertoire of planning, management and instructional strategies.

Peter Westwood

Chapter 1

Special educational needs and learning difficulties

In Britain, the term *special educational needs* (SEN) was introduced more than thirty years ago. The desire at that time was to move away from older terminology such as 'handicapped children' to find a generic description that would more suitably embrace the increasingly diverse group of students with problems in learning. Prior to this time, there had been a preoccupation with categorizing students according to their disability or impairment, particularly for school placement purposes (Peterson and Hittie 2010). Using a categorical approach had never worked very effectively in practice for two main reasons. First, a small but significant number of children had more than one disability (or even multiple disabilities) requiring a combination of intensive services and defying any simple solution such as placement in a particular type of school. Second, very many children who experience difficulties in learning or adjustment in school have no identifiable disability, so could not be neatly categorized. While disability affects at most 9 per cent of school-age children, it is estimated that at least 20 per cent of children have some form of special educational need (Turnbull *et al.* 2010). These children tend to have a combination of personal, emotional, social, environmental and family problems, unrelated to disability, that cause them to be at risk of failure within the school system (Abrams 2010; Cadima *et al.* 2010). Children from poorer families, for example, are twice as likely to be officially diagnosed with special educational needs as other students in the UK (National Literacy Trust 2009a). It was felt, therefore, that rather than focusing on a child's disability it was more productive to focus on the nature and degree of a child's actual need for additional support, resources and special services.

The term *special educational needs* is also used widely now in other countries, particularly most parts of Europe, Australia and the Asia–Pacific region. In the US, policy documents frequently refer simply to 'students with special needs'. The omission of the qualifier 'educational' suggests, correctly, that special needs may extend well beyond those that are related directly to schooling and to accessing the curriculum. Special needs include those associated with the physical, personal, social, emotional and behavioural aspects of a child's development, in addition to those related to cognition and learning in school. It is now recognized also that *any* student may have 'additional educational needs' (AEN) arising from factors such as English as a second language, family difficulties, health problems or social disadvantage.

Educators in the US often use the description 'exceptional children', a term not widely applied in the UK or Australia. The notion of exceptionality embraces not only children with disabilities and learning difficulties but also those regarded as gifted or talented.

Delineating special educational needs

Children with special educational needs can be defined broadly as those with significantly greater difficulty learning and adjusting to school than other children of the same age. Some, but by no means all, of these students have a disability or disorder.

In the UK, the Special Educational Needs Information Act of 2008 resulted in the Department for Children, Schools and Families producing an annual report on the number of students with special educational needs (DCSF 2009a, 2009b). For statistical census purposes, these students are recorded under four categories: (i) *cognitive and learning difficulties* – which includes specific learning disability (SpLD) and intellectual disability (moderate, severe and profound/multiple); (ii) *behavioural, emotional and social difficulties*; (iii) *communication and interaction problems* – including speech and language disorders, autism spectrum disorders; and (iv) *sensory and/or physical impairments* – vision, hearing, physical disability, multiple disabilities (DCSF/TeacherNet 2009).

In the US, data are collected annually under rather more categories: specific learning disability; speech or language impairment; mental retardation (now classified as intellectual disability); emotional disturbance; multiple disabilities; hearing impairment; vision impairment; orthopedic impairment; autism; deaf-blindness; traumatic brain injury; and developmental delay (US Department of Education 2009).

In an attempt to clarify definitions and descriptions of students with special needs across various countries, the OECD (2007) created three convenient and meaningful categories:

*   students with identifiable disabilities and impairments;
*   students with behavioural and/or emotional disorders, or with specific difficulties in learning;
*   students with difficulties arising from socio-economic, cultural, or linguistic disadvantage.

For most children in all three categories (other than those with severe or complex disabilities) the worldwide trend is placement in mainstream classes rather than special schools. All teachers can expect to teach children with special educational needs in their regular classes, and all schools must strive to be inclusive by educating the full range of children from the local community. Adapting classroom programmes to facilitate this inclusion is discussed later in Chapter 14.

An important difference between the UK and other countries – including the US – is in the use of the term *learning disability*. In the UK, this term is applied now to students with *intellectual disability* (previously referred to as mental handicap or mental retardation) (RCP 2009). This is very different from current practice in most other countries, where 'learning disability' (LD) or 'specific learning disability' (SpLD) refers instead to children of normal intelligence who have major and ongoing difficulties in acquiring basic skills in literacy and numeracy. This inconsistent terminology gives rise to much confusion when reading the international research literature since the two groups of students are very different in terms of their characteristics and special needs. In this book, the term *intellectual disability* will be used exclusively to refer to students whose learning problems and special needs are primarily due to significant cognitive weaknesses. Students with intellectually disability are described fully in Chapter 2.

The term *general learning difficulties* will be used in this book when discussing students who may be of average or somewhat below average intelligence and are not in any way intellectually disabled. Often their difficulties in learning arise from social, emotional, motivational or behavioural problems, poor school attendance, or from some degree of socio-economic disadvantage (Friend and Bursuck 2009). In some cases, their problems are due to, or exacerbated by, poor quality or inappropriate teaching.

Finally, the term *specific learning disability* (SpLD) will be used in this book to refer to students of average or above intelligence with severe problems in learning. These students and their special needs are described more fully later in this chapter.

How many students have special educational needs?

The official estimate is that in Britain one in five children of school age has special educational needs (Clark 2009; DCSF 2009b). This estimate is similar to figures obtained in most other developed countries (OECD 2007).

Physical handicaps, vision impairment and hearing impairment are all regarded as fairly low incidence disabilities, together accounting for some 2 to 3 per cent of the school population. However, these disabilities comprise very important subgroups of children with special educational needs, as discussed fully in Chapter 3 and Chapter 4.

The prevalence of intellectual disability among children has remained fairly stable over the past decade at about 3 per cent. Many children of primary school age with mild intellectual disability (and a few with moderate disability) now attend mainstream schools rather than special schools or classes. At secondary school level, inclusion of students with mild and moderate intellectual disability becomes more problematic due to the increasing cognitive demands of the curriculum. However, some secondary schools with effective internal support services do manage to accommodate these students by drastically adapting the classroom programme.

Children with severe and complex disabilities – for example, deafness combined with blindness, or major physical impairments accompanying intellectual disability and a communication disorder – are regarded as very low incidence groups (less than 1 per cent of all children) (Howard *et al.* 2010). These individuals are usually catered for in special schools or units. Information on these children is also provided in Chapter 2.

In recent years, there have been increases in the numbers of children referred for speech and language problems, attention deficit hyperactivity disorder (ADHD) and for autism (DCSF 2009b). It is not clear whether this reflects a true increase in incidence for these conditions or simply an improvement in assessment and early identification procedures. Chapter 2 provides information on autism, and Chapter 7 addresses ADHD.

Significant emotional and behavioural difficulties are reported in approximately 9 per cent of the school population, with double that number of children judged to be at risk for developing such problems (Turnbull *et al.* 2010). The number of children with social, emotional and behavioural problems has increased very significantly in recent years (DCSF 2009a, 2009b). Chapters 6, 7 and 8 provide suggestions for working with these children.

Children with *general* learning difficulties (many of whom are not formally identified and recorded in official statistics on SEN) and those with social, emotional and behaviour problems comprise the two largest subgroups of children with special needs. The overall prevalence of general learning difficulties among school-age children is estimated to be between 12 and 16 per cent; but there is great variation across schools, with some schools reporting as many as 30 per cent of their students with learning problems. Many students with general learning difficulties also have significant emotional and behavioural problems. In some cases, these problems are the primary cause of the child's difficulties in learning, but in other cases the emotional problems stem mainly from frequent and ongoing experiences of failure in school.

Children with specific learning disability (SpLD) comprise a very much smaller group than those with general problems in learning. These students are usually of at least average intelligence but experience chronic problems in learning basic academic skills (Riddick 2010). This disability results in a marked discrepancy between a child's potential intellectual ability and actual academic achievement, and is characterized by a very slow response to remedial intervention. Based on international data, it is estimated conservatively that this group represents approximately 2 per cent of the school population (OECD 2007); but a much higher prevalence rate is claimed by advocacy groups that campaign for better recognition of the disability. In the UK, it is suggested that some 4 to 8 per cent of the school population has severe literacy problems that are due to SpLD (Rose 2009; Snowling 2008). In the US, more than 50 per cent of children identified as having special educational needs are currently being labelled as learning disabled (Moon *et al.* 2008); but it has been suggested that many of these students do not really meet the criterion of 'average intelligence'. Some may have general learning problems together with emotional and behavioural disorders, or they may simply not have received effective instruction. They are being categorized as learning disabled in order to attract funding for their schools and programmes. It is difficult to reach a consensus on the prevalence of SpLD because different countries and experts apply slightly different definitions and criteria. Children with general and specific learning difficulties are described in this chapter.

Children with learning difficulties

It is often argued that children with learning difficulties are not identified early enough in school and are simply considered to be immature, lazy or unmotivated. Unless provided with effective teaching, some of these children go on to develop serious social and emotional problems associated with constant failure in school, and some exhibit major behaviour problems (Hallahan *et al.* 2009). Early identification and effective intervention remain high priorities in improving the educational opportunities for these children.

Children with learning difficulties tend to fall into one of three possible subgroups – those with *general* learning difficulties, those with a *language-based specific learning disability* (SpLD) and those with a *non-verbal learning disability* (NLD). As stated above, children with general learning difficulties represent the largest group. There are far fewer children with specifically language-based learning difficulties, and fewer still with non-verbal difficulties. The learning characteristics of these three subgroups are rather different, but they all share a common need for systematic and direct teaching (Rose 2009; Wheldall 2009a). The main differences among the groups are delineated below.

General learning difficulties

The term *general learning difficulties* is often used widely and without much precision. The term should be applied only to students whose difficulties are not directly related to a specific intellectual, physical or sensory disability, or to an emotional disorder. Students who have been referred to in the past as 'slower learners', 'low achievers', or simply 'the hard to teach' certainly fall within this category. Some writers have referred to these students as having 'garden variety' learning difficulties, highlighting that their problems are fairly commonplace. Although not tied rigidly to a particular intelligence range, the IQs for this subgroup are typically reported to be between 70 and 100. In the case of children from disadvantaged backgrounds or with emotional or behavioural problems, IQs can sometimes be well above 100. Their learning difficulties most frequently manifest themselves as ongoing problems in acquiring adequate skills in literacy and numeracy. Serious weaknesses in these skills then impact adversely on the child's ability to learn in most subjects across the school curriculum. Constant failure undermines the child's confidence and self-esteem, and behavioural or emotional problems can occur. Over time, the child may regress to a state of learned helplessness, with a very significant decline in motivation and effort (Smith and Tyler 2010). Learned helplessness is the psychological state in which an individual never expects to succeed with any task he or she is given, and feels totally powerless to change this situation. Observation of young children suggests that, even at an early age, they can begin to regard themselves as failures in certain learning situations. This can lead to deliberate avoidance of the type of activity associated with failure, and sometimes even avoidance of any new or challenging situation. If students come to believe that they lack the ability ever to succeed, they may avoid participating in achievement-oriented activities simply to protect their feeling of self-worth. They believe that if they do not attempt the task, they will not be seen by others to have failed. Avoidance leads to lack of practice. Lack of practice ensures that the individual does not gain in proficiency or confidence while other children forge ahead. The effects of early failure are thus cumulative.

As indicated above, it is vitally important to identify as early as possible any students who are experiencing general problems in learning and to provide them with support and high-quality teaching. Kirby *et al.* (2005: 123) suggest that: 'There is evidence that difficulties experienced at school, if not addressed, may persist into adulthood with a greater risk of psychological problems such as anxiety, depression and lowered self-esteem.'

The cause of general learning difficulty usually cannot be attributed to a single factor. Most learning problems arise from a complex interaction among variables such as the learners' prior knowledge and experience, learners' cognitive ability, learners' confidence and expectation of success, teacher's instructional method, complexity of teachers' language, the perceived relevance and value of the curriculum content or task, and suitability of resource materials. Until recently, teaching methods and instructional materials were rarely investigated as possible causes of a learning difficulty. Now it is readily acknowledged that inappropriate teaching and inaccessible curriculum materials can present major barriers to learning (DfES 2004). Many additional factors also contribute to a failure to learn, such as distractions in the learning environment, the health or emotional state of the learner, socio-economic disadvantage, the interpersonal relationship between teacher and learner, and social relationships within the peer group.

Despite the many and varied causal factors associated with general learning difficulties, it seems that most teachers, psychologists and researchers still tend to focus almost exclusively on weaknesses within the learner to account for children's problems in coping successfully with the school curriculum. Even parents tend to assume that there is 'something wrong' with their child if school progress is unsatisfactory.

Many researchers have attempted to summarize characteristics of students with general learning difficulties (e.g. Olson *et al.* 2008) resulting in lists similar to the one below – often referred to as the 'deficit model' (Peterson and Hittie 2010). This construct suggests that learning problems can be due to:

- below average intelligence;
- limited attention span and high degree of distractibility;

- problems with visual and auditory perception;
- difficulties in understanding complex language;
- limited vocabulary, relative to age;
- low motivation;
- poor recall of previous learning;
- inability to generalize learning to new contexts;
- lack of effective learning strategies;
- deficient self-management skills;
- poor self-esteem;
- learned helplessness and diminished beliefs concerning self-efficacy;
- behavioural and emotional reactions to failure.

While these weaknesses do indeed exist in many children with learning difficulties, they should not be viewed as obstacles too difficult for teachers to overcome but rather as clear indications of the need for high-quality teaching. The deficit model does at least highlight specific areas of difficulty that must be taken into account when planning and implementing classroom programmes. But rather than focusing exclusively on deficits, it is usually much more productive to examine factors outside the child, such as quality and type of instruction, teacher's expectations, relevance of the curriculum, classroom environment, interpersonal dynamics within the class social group, and rapport with the teacher. These factors are much more amenable to modification than are factors within the child or within the child's family background or culture. Trying to identify how best to help a student with general learning difficulties involves finding the most significant and alterable factors that need to be addressed, and providing students with high-quality instruction. Teaching of this type typically involves clear presentation of information, skills and strategies by the teacher, direct explicit teaching, active engagement by the learners, guided practice with feedback, independent practice, and frequent reviews or revision (Bellert 2009; Wendling and Mather 2009). Later chapters in this book deal with explicit instruction in literacy and numeracy in more detail.

Language-based specific learning disability (SpLD)

The most comprehensive and widely accepted definition of SpLD comes from legislation in the US, where it is stated that:

> The term 'specific learning disability' means a disorder in one or more of the basic psychological processes involved in understanding or in using language, spoken or written, which disorder may manifest itself in imperfect ability to listen, think, speak, write, spell, or to do mathematical calculations. Such term includes such conditions as perceptual disabilities, brain injury, minimal brain dysfunction, dyslexia, and developmental aphasia. Such term does not include a learning problem that is primarily the result of visual, hear-

ing, or motor disabilities; of mental retardation; of emotional disturbance; or of environmental, cultural, or economic disadvantage.

(US Public Law 108–446, cited in Lerner and Kline 2006: 7)

Language-based difficulties affect mainly the acquisition of literacy skills (developing phonic decoding skills, vocabulary, comprehending text, writing, and spelling) and are classified as *dyslexia*. Some aspects of mathematics, such as solving word problems, can also be affected. Other forms of language-based learning disability described in the literature include *dysgraphia* (problems with writing), *dysorthographia* (problems with spelling) and *dysnomia* (inability to retrieve words, names, or symbols quickly from memory).

Dyslexia is the most common form of SpLD. It is a severe difficulty in learning to read and spell despite conventional instruction, adequate intelligence and appropriate opportunity. The oral reading performance of dyslexic students tends to be very slow and laboured, with maximum effort expended on identifying each individual word, leaving very little cognitive capacity for focusing on meaning. The student tires easily and avoids reading if possible. Rose (2009: 10) comments: 'Not surprisingly, young people with dyslexic difficulties generally do not read unless they have to; they are far less likely to read for pleasure or for information than other learners.' Lack of practice therefore exacerbates their problem.

Dyslexic students typically have great difficulty in:

- developing awareness of the phonological aspects of spoken language (e.g. understanding that words are composed of separate sounds);
- learning and applying phonic decoding skills;
- building a vocabulary of words recognized automatically by sight;
- making adequate use of contextual cues to assist word recognition;
- developing speed and fluency in reading;
- comprehending what has been read.

Over many years researchers have attempted to uncover the causes of language-based learning disability. Some authorities attribute the learning problem to neurological deficits or to developmental delay. However, the neurological perspective still remains somewhat controversial and has failed to produce any useful treatment strategies or effective interventions. Inefficient learning style is cited by others as a possible cause, because many children with dyslexia do not appear to have effective systems for decoding words, obtaining meaning from text, writing a story, or completing the steps in a mathematical problem. They are often referred to as 'non-strategic' learners (Smith and Tyler 2010). Their lack of effective task-approach strategies produces bewilderment, high error-rates, and rapid frustration. This in turn causes the children to disengage from important learning activities and to avoid participating productively in class.

An important weakness found in most students with reading and spelling problems is a lack of phonological awareness. This difficulty in identifying component sounds within words seriously impairs a child's ability to understand phonic principles and to apply a decoding strategy for reading. It is now believed that in the most severe cases of reading disability poor phonological awareness is often accompanied by a 'naming-speed' deficiency in which the student cannot quickly retrieve a word or a syllable or a letter-sound association from memory (*dysnomia*). These combined weaknesses create what is termed a 'double deficit' and together make it extremely difficult for the child to develop effective word recognition skills or become a fluent reader. It is now widely accepted that the foundation of any literacy intervention for children with SpLD must comprise the development of phonological awareness together with explicit teaching of let-ter-sound relationships. Phonic decoding is best taught using what is termed a 'synthetic phonics' approach, in which children are taught to use letter sounds to unlock the words they need to read and to build words they need to spell. Much more is said about intervention methods for literacy in Chapters 9 and 10.

Non-verbal learning disability

This category of learning difficulty is relatively new, having been identified as separate from other forms of learning disability in the late 1980s. To some extent, non-verbal learning disability shares some characteristics with a condition known as *dyspraxia,* although the two conditions are not the same.

Non-verbal learning difficulties are associated most obviously with problems in gross and fine motor coordination and spatial awareness (Foss 2001; McMurray *et al.* 2009). The child may appear to be unusually clumsy and poorly balanced. Fine motor skills such as handwriting, setting down columns of figures or drawing diagrams are particularly problematic. The child may have difficulties applying visual perception effectively in tasks such as interpreting details in a picture, dia-gram or table, or attending closely to signs and symbols in arithmetic. The com-bined coordination and visual perception problems cause particular difficulties with many classroom activities including writing, assembling puzzles and models, or handling equipment.

The measured verbal IQ of children with non-verbal learning disability is usu-ally very much higher that their non-verbal IQ. The child's oral verbal skills are usually within the normal range but he or she may have difficulty understanding non-verbal communication used by others (e.g. facial expression, stance, gesture). This difficulty can lead to problems with interpreting social situations and inter-acting easily with other children and adults. These students often need to be helped to interpret social situations more accurately in order to develop appropriate social behaviours.

Children with NLD can be helped significantly once their problem is identi-fied (Martin 2007). Speaking and listening are their best channels for learning. For example, teachers can use much more verbal mediation (i.e. clear verbal explanations) when presenting visual materials and teaching physical skills. More time can be given for students to complete work, and more advice, guidance and feedback can be provided. Often students with NLD will leave classroom tasks and bookwork unfinished. To overcome this tendency, they can be taught self-regulation strategies to enable them to approach classroom tasks systematically and see them through to completion (see Chapter 6). The students with very poor handwriting can be helped to develop an easier and more legible style. More than a usual amount of guidance may be needed to help these students set out their bookwork appropriately.

It should be noted that even a few gifted students have language-based or non-verbal learning disabilities. These disabilities tend to prevent the individual from reaching his or her potential. This issue is discussed further in Chapter 5.

Identification of specific learning disability

The traditional procedure for identifying SpLD has been to assess the student's level of intelligence using a standardized test of intelligence, and to compare the results with those obtained from standardized measures of attainment in reading, spelling and mathematics. Any marked discrepancy between level of intelligence and level of attainment (i.e. *under achievement*) might indicate the presence of a learning disability. In other words, it was the fact that the individual possessed adequate intelligence and was free from sensory or other impairments that differentiated specific learning disability from general learning difficulties. The issue has now become clouded, however, with recent reports (e.g. Rose 2009; Snowling 2008) suggesting that learning disabilities such as dyslexia can occur at any intelligence level.

While many educational psychologists still use IQ and attainment testing procedures to detect underachievement, a more recent identification model uses what is termed *response to intervention* (RTI) (IES 2009a, 2009b; Smith and Tyler 2010). Under this model all children beginning formal schooling receive a year of effective instruction in basic literacy and numeracy using systematic evidence-based teaching methods. This is termed Tier 1 or First Wave Teaching. During this period, any children who are not making adequate progress are given additional, regular, intensive tutoring in small groups (Tier 2 or Second Wave Teaching). Only those children who fail to respond within a reasonable period of time to this additional support are then considered to have a possible learning disability and are referred on to Tier 3 (Third Wave Teaching) for in-depth psycho-educational assessment and for even more intensive one-to-one tuition (Howard 2009).

According to Smith and Tyler (2010), the advantages of the RTI model are said to include:

- no long delay in providing intervention – the child does not have to wait to accumulate many months of failure before being identified and receiving support;
- effective evidence-based teaching methods are used at each tier;
- learning disability is distinguished from general learning difficulties not by measuring IQ, but by the child's response to additional support.

Teaching children with general and specific learning difficulties

It is fairly clear that the extensive study of SpLD over the years has not resulted in any major breakthrough in unique teaching methods or instructional resources for this subgroup of struggling learners. In terms of pedagogy, it is difficult to visualize that any teaching method found useful for children with general problems in learning to read, write or calculate would not also be highly relevant for other children identified as dyslexic – and vice versa. If one examines the vast literature on teaching methodology for children with SpLD (e.g. Martin 2009; Mercer and Pullen 2009; Strichart and Mangrum 2010), one usually finds not a unique methodology applicable only to SpLD students but a range of valuable teaching strategies that would be helpful to all learners. Those who have difficulty in learning to read, write and work with numbers are best served by teachers designing and delivering intensive high-quality instruction, rather than by sorting and classifying them with different labels according to IQ. This non-categorical approach to intervention is currently gaining much ground within the field of remedial intervention in Australia (e.g. Wheldall 2009a, 2009b). The approach dovetails well with the response to the intervention model.

There has been significant consensus reached across different countries in the matter of what constitutes high-quality instruction. Demands are growing worldwide for schools to adopt teaching methods that have been carefully evaluated for their efficacy – rather than employing methods based purely on teachers' personal intuition, style or preference (Moran 2004; Wendling and Mather 2009). This call for 'evidence-based instruction' has focused so far mainly on the teaching of literacy and numeracy skills, in response to concerns that the fairly informal child-centred approaches used in recent years have not been effective with some students.

Research evidence suggests that students with disabilities and learning problems usually do best in structured programmes in both literacy and numeracy where direct teaching methods and guided practice with feedback are employed (Bellert 2009; de Lemos 2005; Rowe 2006). In the past, many educators have suggested that child-centred methods such as whole language approach to literacy, activity mathematics, project work, and resource-based learning have most to offer children with special educational needs. These process-oriented approaches – which often seem to emphasize social interaction and emotional development rather than mastery of curriculum content – are thought to be more accommodating of student differences. However, during the first decade of the twenty-first century these methods have come under close scrutiny, due in no small part to the fact that in most developed countries too many students were failing to achieve adequate standards in basic skills. It is firmly believed now that the most effective teaching methods for developing these fundamental skills are those that provide a balance between, on the one hand, explicit instruction from the teacher to develop students' skills to a high level, and, on the other hand, independent application and practice (Ellis 2005). In general, effective teaching methods are those that provide students with the maximum opportunity to learn by increasing 'academic engaged time' and maintaining high levels of on-task behaviour. Academic engaged time refers to the proportion of instructional time in which students are actively focused on their work and are processing information successfully. This active involvement includes attending to instruction from the teacher, working independently or with a group on assigned academic tasks, and applying previously acquired knowledge and skills. Studies have shown that students who are receiving instruction directly from the teacher attend better to the content of the lesson than students who are expected to find out information independently. Effective lessons, particularly those covering academic skills, tend to have a clear structure, with effective use made of the available time (Brown and Colmar 2009). In learning basic skills in literacy and numeracy, for example, effective teaching provides carefully sequenced steps, adjusts the level of task difficulty to match students' abilities, and incorporates principles of overlearning and frequent review (Bellert 2009). Effective teaching of this type in the early years of primary school not only raises the attainment level of all students but also reduces significantly the prevalence of learning failure.

According to Foorman *et al.* (2006), the features most commonly found in effective classrooms that distinguish them from less effective classrooms in terms of student achievement include:

- teachers displaying good classroom management;
- more time devoted to instructional activities;
- students are more academically engaged;
- more active and explicit instruction is used;
- a good balance achieved between teacher-directed and student-centred activities;
- teachers providing support and 'scaffolding' to help students develop deeper understanding;
- tasks and activities are well matched to students' abilities;
- students are encouraged to become more independent and self-regulated in their learning.

Swanson (2000), using meta-analyses of learning outcomes from different types of teaching approach, drew the conclusion that the most effective approach for teaching students with learning difficulties combines the following features:

- carefully controlling and sequencing the curriculum content to be studied;
- providing abundant opportunities for practice and application of newly acquired knowledge and skills;
- ensuring high levels of participation and responding by the children (for example, answering the teacher's questions; staying on task);
- providing frequent feedback, correction and reinforcement;
- using interactive group teaching;

- clear demonstrations by the teacher of how best to attempt new learning tasks (direct strategy training);
- making appropriate use of technology (e.g. computer-assisted instruction);
- providing supplementary assistance (e.g. homework; parental tutoring, etc.).

In summary, explicit instruction appears to achieve most in the early stages of learning, and is highly appropriate for children at risk of failure. The use of direct teaching methods in no way precludes a student from ultimately developing independence in learning; indeed, direct teaching in the early stages facilitates greater confidence and independence in later stages. Over many decades, despite the popularity of student-centred approaches, clear evidence supports the value of appropriate direct teaching, often delivered through the medium of interactive whole-class lessons. Peterson and Hittie (2010: 74) sum up the situation very succinctly when they remark, 'Good teaching addresses many specific needs.' Good teaching also prevents many cases of failure. Much more information on teaching methods is contained in later chapters on literacy and numeracy, and is the main focus of Chapter 15.

Online resources

- Information on specific learning disabilities is available from *Help-Guide* at: www.helpguide.org/mental/learning_disabilities.htm (accessed 26 March 2010).
- Additional information can be found at *LD-online* website: www.ldonline. org/ldbasics/whatisld (accessed 26 March 2010).
- University of Warwick website provides useful information on learning difficulties and differences. Available online at: www2.warwick.ac.uk/services/ tutors/disability/splds/ (accessed 26 March 2010).
- Department of Education, Employment and Workplace Relations (Australia) presents helpful points on meeting the needs of students with learning difficulties. Available online at: www.dest.gov.au/sectors/school_education/ publications_resources/other_publications/successful_programs_strategies_ for_children.htm#Learning_difficulties_in_literacy_and_numeracy:__ What_seems_to_work_in_schools? (accessed 26 March 2010).
- For more on teaching approaches for students with learning difficulties visit the West Virginia University website at: www.as.wvu.edu/~scidis/learning. html (accessed 26 March 2010).

Further reading

Hoover, J.J. (2009) *Differentiating Learning Differences from Disabilities: Meeting Diverse Needs through Multi-tiered Response to Intervention*, Upper Saddle River, NJ: Pearson.
Jensen, E. (2010) *Different Brains, Different Learners: How to Reach the Hard to Teach*, Thousand Oaks, CA: Corwin Press.

Mastropieri, M.A. and Scruggs, T.E. (2010) *The Inclusive Classroom: Strategies for Effective Differentiated Instruction* (4th edn), Upper Saddle River, NJ: Merrill.

McDougal, J.L. Graney, S.B., Wright, J.A. and Ardoin, S.P. (2010) *TRI in Practice*, Hoboken, NJ: Wiley.

Riddick, B. (2010) *Living with Dyslexia: The Social and Emotional Consequences of Specific Learning Difficulties/Disabilities* (2nd edn), London: Routledge.

Strichart, S.S. and Mangrum, C.T. (2010) *Study Skills for Learning Disabled and Struggling Students, Grades 6–12* (4th edn), Upper Saddle River, NJ: Merrill.

Waber, D.P. (2010) *Rethinking Learning Disabilities: Understanding Children who Struggle in School,* New York: Guilford Press.

Chapter 2

Students with intellectual disability and autism

Teachers tend to find children with intellectual disability and with autism among the most difficult to include effectively in mainstream programmes. In order to receive the most appropriate education to meet their needs, many of these students with moderate to severe disability are still placed in special education facilities (Foreman 2009; Smith 2007). Others, particularly those with mild disability, are being placed successfully in mainstream schools, particularly in the early years. For this reason, all teachers need to have some knowledge of the effects of intellectual disability and autism on children's behaviour and capacity to learn. To assist these students in the mainstream, teachers usually need to make significant modifications to the teaching method, learning activities and content of the curriculum. In Chapter 14 strategies for carrying out such modifications are discussed in detail.

Intellectual disability

Intellectual (or cognitive) disability was previously referred to as mental handicap or mental retardation. The US was one of the last countries to replace the term *mental retardation* when, in 2006, the former American Association on Mental Retardation finally became the American Association on Intellectual and Developmental Disabilities. In Britain, the term *mental handicap* gave way to the use of *severe learning difficulty* (or severe learning disability), a confusing classification as explained in the previous chapter.

It is estimated that individuals with intellectual disability comprise some 3 per cent of the general population (Prater 2007). Children with this disability form a very heterogeneous group including a few very low-functioning individuals who require almost complete and continuous care and management, through to others (the majority) with only mild difficulties that are often not detected until the child is in school.

Children with intellectual disability can and will learn if provided with an appropriate instructional programme, teaching methods oriented to their individual needs, and adequate support (Howard *et al.* 2010). Peterson and Hittie (2010: 86) have remarked: 'When we use good teaching strategies, students with intellectual disabilities learn much more than anyone thought possible.'

Children with *mild* intellectual disability tend to be indistinguishable in many ways from those who have been described in the past as 'slow learners'. According to the National Dissemination Centre for Children with Disabilities (US) (2010) about 87 per cent of children with intellectual disability will only be a little slower than average in learning new information and skills.

Children with *moderate to severe* intellectual disability are more commonly accommodated in special schools or special classes – although in America, Britain, Canada, Australia and some parts of Europe there is a belief that children with even this degree of intellectual impairment should be integrated in mainstream schools (e.g. Downing 2008). In these countries, some students with moderate intellectual disability are already included, mainly in preschool and the early primary years. It is argued that this degree of disability should not act as a barrier to children attending their local schools, and should not be a reason for forcing them into segregated education.

Many individuals with severe intellectual disability may also have additional difficulties (physical, sensory, emotional, behavioural) and are frequently described as having 'high support needs' (Myrbakk and von Tetzchner 2008; Oeseburg *et al.* 2010). In particular, intellectual disability often results in significant limitations of development in the following areas:

- communication;
- self-care and daily living skills;
- social skills;
- basic academic skills (functional literacy and numeracy);
- self-regulation and self-direction;
- independent functioning in the community.

The list above also represents priorities within the curriculum for students with moderate to severe intellectual disability. The great dilemma facing those who wish to educate *all* children with severe disabilities in the mainstream is how to meet their basic needs for training in self-care, daily living skills and communication once they are placed in an environment where a standard academic curriculum prevails. Kauffman *et al.* (2005) have queried whether the potential benefits of socialization and normalization in the mainstream can outweigh all the problems involved in supporting these children in a curriculum that is not necessarily very relevant to them. Similarly, Dymond and Orelove (2001: 111) warned that, 'Functional skills, which were once widely accepted as the basis for curriculum development, have received limited attention as the field has moved to a more inclusive service delivery model.' For some students with disabilities, a special education setting may still offer the best environment to meet their needs. The purpose of having special schools and special classes was – and still is – to create an environment in which curriculum content, resources and methods of instruction can be geared appropriately to the students' needs and abilities.

Identification of intellectual disability

In the past, for an individual to be identified as having an intellectual disability he or she obtained a measured intelligence quotient (IQ) below 70 and exhibited delays in acquiring normal adaptive behaviours and independent functioning. In recent years attention in many countries has moved away from the rigid use of IQ for the identification of intellectual disability, and now the emphasis is on assessing how well the individual can function independently and the amount of additional support that is needed (Batshaw *et al.* 2007).

The most obvious characteristic of most individuals with intellectual disability is that they experience significant difficulty learning almost everything that others can learn with ease. From a practical viewpoint, intellectual disability presents itself as an inability to think as quickly, reason as deeply, remember as easily, or adapt as rapidly to new situations, when compared with so-called normal children. Children with intellectual disability usually appear to be much less mature than their age peers, exhibiting general behaviours typical of much younger children. Their behaviour patterns, skills and general knowledge are related more closely to their mental age than to their chronological age.

Learning characteristics of students with intellectual disability

Children who are developmentally delayed are slower at acquiring cognitive skills. For them, interpreting information, thinking, reasoning and problem solving are very difficult processes. In most aspects of conceptual development and reasoning, school-age children with mild to moderate intellectual disability tend to be functioning at what Piaget (1963) referred to as the 'concrete operational' level. They understand and remember best those things and situations that they can directly experience, so teaching for them must be *reality-based*. Students with severe to profound disability may be at an even early Piagetian cognitive stage of 'sensori-motor' or 'pre-operational'. It is generally accepted that children with intellectual disability pass through the same sequence of stages in cognitive development as other children (from sensori-motor, through pre-operational to concrete operational, and finally formal operational) but at a much slower rate. It is also clear that some intellectually disabled individuals never reach the highest level of formal operational thinking and reasoning, even as adults.

The main messages that educators need to note are these:

- cognitive development comes from action – students 'learn by doing';
- children need someone to interact with who will interpret (or *mediate*) learning experiences.

These principles must guide the teaching and design of curricula for students with intellectual disability, whether in special or mainstream schools.

Specific areas of difficulty

Attention

Individuals with intellectual disability appear often to have problems attending to the relevant aspects of a learning situation. For example, when a teacher is showing the student how to form the numeral 5 with a pencil, or how to use scissors to cut paper, the student is attracted perhaps to the ring on the teacher's finger or to a picture on the paper, rather than the task itself. This tendency to focus on irrelevant detail, or to be distracted easily from a learning task, is potentially a major problem for a child with intellectual disability when integrated into mainstream programmes without close supervision. The teacher will need to think of many ways of helping a child with intellectual disability to focus on a learning task. Without adequate attention control, any student will fail to learn or remember what the teacher is trying to teach. Gargiulo and Metcalf (2010) have remarked that attention and memory both increase when a learning task is interesting, involves action on the part of the student, and is paired with positive and corrective feedback.

Memory

Many students with intellectual disability also have difficulty storing information in long-term memory (Pickering and Gathercole 2004). This problem is linked, in part, with failure to attend closely to the learning task, as discussed above; but it is also due to the students' lack of any effective cognitive strategies for facilitating memorization. To overcome or minimize this memory problem, students with intellectual disability require much greater amounts of repetition and practice to ensure that important information and skills are eventually stored. Many opportunities must be provided in every area of the curriculum for abundant guided practice, independent practice, revision and overlearning.

Generalization

For any learner, the final and most difficult stage of acquiring new learning is that of *generalization*. A stage must be reached when a student can apply new learning in situations not directly linked with the context in which it was first taught. It is typical of most students with intellectual disability that they do not generalize what they learn (Turnbull *et al.* 2010; Westwood 2009a). They may learn a particular skill or strategy in one context but fail to transfer it to a different situation. It is recommended that teachers consider ways of facilitating generalization when planning lessons for students with special needs – for example, by re-teaching the same skills or strategies in different contexts, gradually increasing the range of contexts, challenging students to decide whether a skill or strategy could be used in a new situation, and reinforcing any evidence of students' spontaneous generalization of previous learning.

Language delay

Language ability is important for cognitive and social development. In particular, language serves the following functions:

- language enables an individual to make his or her needs, opinions and ideas known to others;
- language is important for cognitive development – without language one lacks much of the raw material with which to think and reason;
- concepts are more effectively stored in memory if they have a mental representation in words as well as in sensations and perceptions;
- language is the main medium through which school learning is mediated;
- positive social interactions with other persons are heavily dependent upon effective language and communication skills;
- inner language is important for regulating one's own behaviour and responses (self-talk).

One of the main characteristics of children with moderate and severe intellectual disability is the very slow rate at which many of them acquire speech and language (Haqberg *et al.* 2010). Even a child with mild intellectual disability is likely to be a little behind the normal milestones for language development and may exhibit a fairly limited vocabulary (Kroeger *et al.* 2009). A few individuals with severe and multiple disabilities never develop speech, so alternative methods of communication may need to be developed (e.g. sign language; picture or symbol communication systems) (Best *et al.* 2010).

Early intervention programs in the preschool years place heavy emphasis on developing children's communication skills. Foreman (2009) indicates that such interventions should also be family focused, involving parents and siblings as much as possible. The development of communication skills is given very high priority in special school curricula, and will be no less important for intellectually disabled students included in mainstream settings. Two obvious benefits of placing a child with intellectual disability in a mainstream class are immersion in a naturally enriched language environment, and the increased need for the student to communicate with others.

Language is best acquired naturally, through using it to express needs, obtain information and interact socially. Where possible, naturally occurring opportunities within the school day are used to teach and reinforce new vocabulary and language patterns. This 'milieu approach' is found to be more productive in terms of generalization and transfer of learning to everyday use than are the more clinical approaches to teaching language in isolation (Kaiser and Grim 2006).

Many students with intellectual disability require the services of a speech therapist (Hooper and Umansky 2009); but even with this help, improvement can be very slow. This is because the individual receiving help may not appreciate the need for it and may therefore have no motivation to practise what is taught. There is also the usual problem of lack of generalization – what is taught in a clinical setting does not necessarily transfer to the person's everyday speech.

Social development

For many individuals with intellectual disability the development of social competence presents many on-going difficulties (Seale and Nind 2010). The presence or absence of social skills in these students tends to be related to the extent to which they have had the opportunity to socialize in the home and other environments. Within the family, the social interactions between the child and others are likely to be mainly positive, but the same assumption cannot be made for contacts within the community and at school. Although community attitudes towards people with disabilities have become more positive and accepting, there is still likelihood that some children with intellectual disability will experience difficulty gaining acceptance and making friends – particularly if they have some irritating or challenging behaviours (Feeley and Jones 2008). Some students with intellectual disability are rejected and marginalized by their peers more often on the basis of their irritating behaviour than because they are disabled (Miller 2009). For example, the presence of inappropriate responses such as aggression, shouting, or temper tantrums makes it difficult for some of these children to be socially accepted. Intervention is needed to eliminate these negative behaviours and replace them with pro-social behaviours (Howard *et al.* 2010).

If the student with a disability is to make friends and be accepted in the peer group, social skills training may be needed (Peterson and Hittie 2010). Strategies for developing social skills are described in Chapter 8; but helping students with intellectual disability form lasting friendships with other children in the mainstream is actually very problematic (Shepherd 2010). Often mainstream students who start out with good intentions to socialize with a disabled peer quickly lose interest and fade away (Smith and Tyler 2010). In post-school years, socialization remains difficult for many individuals with intellectual disability and often they require regular and ongoing support from a social worker (Williams 2009).

While stressing the need to increase social interaction with others, students with intellectual disability (male and female) also need to be taught *protective behaviours* to reduce the possibility that they become the victims of financial or other forms of exploitation. The lack of social judgement of some teenagers and young adults with intellectual disability causes them to be rather naïve and trusting. There is also a risk of sexual abuse because they may not really comprehend right from wrong in matters of physical contact. For their own protection they need to be taught the danger of going anywhere with a stranger, accepting rides in a car, or taking gifts for favours. They need to know that some forms of touching are wrong, and they also need to know that they can tell some trusted adult if they feel they are at risk from some other person. These matters must be dealt with openly in schools and also reinforced by parents.

Self-regulation

In recent years, much emphasis has been placed on trying to increase self-regulation and self-monitoring strategies in students with intellectual disability by using cognitive methods and metacognitive training (Mitchell 2008; Dixon *et al*. 2004) (see Chapter 6). While this approach is proving useful for students with mild disabilities, it is very difficult indeed to employ cognitive training with low-functioning students for reasons that will be discussed later in connection with autism.

Self-determination

Decision-making and self-determination are areas currently attracting greater attention in the education of individuals with intellectual disability (McGuire 2010; Shepherd 2010). It is recognized now that too much of the life of a person with moderate or severe disability is typically determined by others; so in recent years educators and caregivers have been encouraged to find many more ways of ensuring that persons with disabilities have opportunities to exercise choice and make decisions. To facilitate this, clear objectives and goals for increasing independence and self-management must be included in the educational programme for all students with intellectual disability. Parents, paraprofessionals and volunteers may need to be reminded to allow the children with disabilities in their care to *do more for themselves*.

Teaching approaches for students with intellectual disability

The main priority in teaching children with intellectual disability is to make the curriculum *reality-based* and *relevant*. It has already been mentioned that for cognitive development and for the acquisition of skills, these children need to experience things at first hand and have others mediate (interpret) these experiences. For children at the concrete operational stage in terms of cognitive development, the principle of 'learning by doing' certainly applies. If they are to learn important number skills, for example, they should learn them not only from computer games and instructional materials but also from real situations such as shopping, stock-taking, measuring, estimating, counting, grouping, recording data and comparing quantities. Reading skills should be developed and practised using real books, real instruction cards, real recipes, real brochures and real comic books, as well as through graded readers, games and flashcards.

In addition to reality-based learning, children with intellectual disability also need some high-quality explicit instruction, with the content broken down into very simple steps to ensure high success rates (Peterson and Hittie 2010). Explicit instruction can be described as the teacher's intentional and direct delivery of information and skills to students. Guerin and Male (2006: 128) describe explicit instruction as involving: '(a) the teacher's modelling and demonstration of a skill or strategy, (b) substantial structured opportunity for students to practice and apply newly taught skills and knowledge under the teacher's direction and guidance, and (c) an opportunity for feedback'. It has been found that instruction using these principles is extremely effective for students with disabilities, particularly for teaching basic skills involved in literacy and numeracy (Carnine *et al.* 2004; Miller 2009; Turnbull *et al.* 2010). Lessons that employ explicit instruction aim to obtain many successful responses from students during the time available. Lessons are made enjoyable and there is heavy emphasis on practice and reinforcement. Direct explicit instruction is among the most extensively researched teaching methods and has consistently proved more effective for some types of learning than student-centred, independent learning approaches. The method is discussed fully in Chapter 15.

Other basic principles to consider when working with students with intellectual disability include the following:

- provide plentiful cues and prompts to enable learners to manage each step in a task;
- make all possible use of cooperative group work, and teach children the necessary group-working skills;
- frequently assess the learning that has taken place against the objectives in the curriculum;
- use additional helpers to assist with the teaching (aides, volunteers);
- involve parents in the educational programme whenever possible;
- most importantly, do not sell students short by expecting too little from them.

Preparation for work

Transition from school to work requires extremely careful planning for intellectually disabled students in the adolescent age range (McDonnell 2010). Appropriate training in work skills and routines, reliability and punctuality, together with regular opportunities to engage in work-experience are essential components of the curriculum for all senior students capable of gaining employment. In the past, senior special schools have usually risen to this challenge very well, with a strong emphasis on work experience. It is proving to be much more difficult to provide such authentic learning opportunities for senior intellectually disabled students in inclusive mainstream schools. This problem is yet to be resolved.

Approaches for individuals with severe and complex disabilities

A method known as '*intensive interaction*' has been developed for use with children who have severe and complex disabilities and who lack verbal communication (Firth 2009). The method has also been used with low-functioning autistic children.

The interactive approach tries to ensure that much of the teaching that takes place is based directly on a student's self-initiated actions and reactions, rather than on a preplanned curriculum imposed by an adult. In many ways, the method is similar to the natural approach used instinctively by mothers or fathers when responding to a baby's actions. For example, the parent may smile, reach out, touch, stroke, hug and speak. Something the child does spontaneously leads the adult to react, rather than the other way around. The adult responds, and by doing so reinforces the child and the behaviour. There is a vital ingredient of warm social interaction and communication involved. Often playing simple games or using sensory equipment will create a context for this to happen. For more information on intensive interaction, see Caldwell (2006) or visit the website at www.intensiveinteraction.co.uk.

Another approach that is currently emerging for students with severe disabilities – '*preference-based teaching*' – has fairly similar underpinnings to intensive interaction. It is based on the belief that students enjoy engaging in learning activities much more if the modes of teaching and the materials used are compatible with the individual's personal preferences – for example, using sand play rather than water play, or television rather than listening to a story. Attention is more effectively gained and maintained, and there are fewer behaviour problems.

In the case of young children with severe and multiple disabilities or with challenging behaviour, sensory stimulation is important. Great interest has been shown in an approach called *Snoezelen* developed in Holland (Cuvo *et al.* 2001). The approach provides both sensory stimulation and relaxation for severely or profoundly disabled individuals, and has been adopted in a number of special schools in Europe and Australasia. The approach is therapeutic and educational, using structured multisensory environments containing lights, textures, aromas, sounds and movement. Snoezelen is reported to have particular benefits for individuals who have emotional and behavioural problems combined with intellectual disability, and also for helping autistic children. In some cases Snoezelen has proved useful in reducing self-injurious behaviour (SIB) and self-stimulating behaviour (SSB). While Snoezelen rooms are unlikely to be developed in mainstream schools, teachers in preschools and special schools do need to note the potential value of sensory stimulation for young children with intellectual disability.

Students with autism spectrum disorders (ASD)

Children with autism are among the most difficult students to place successfully in mainstream classrooms (Turnbull *et al.* 2010). Those with severe autism are usually functioning intellectually at a level too low even to cope with the demands of an adapted mainstream curriculum. Coupled with lowered intellectual functioning are the added problems of poor social development and significant lack of communication skills. In US, Australasia and Britain only about 12 per cent of children with diagnosed autism receive their education in mainstream classes. However, most of the higher-functioning students with Asperger syndrome do attend mainstream schools.

Autism is a low-incidence disability with approximately 4 to 10 cases per 10,000 in the population. The lower figure represents the more severe cases; the upper figure includes those children with mild autistic tendencies. The ratio of males to females is 4 or 5 to 1. Autism is one of several disorders referred to under a general category of *Pervasive Developmental Disorders* (PDDs) – Asperger syndrome and Rett syndrome being other examples. Autistic children have been identified in all parts of the world and the disorder does not appear to be in any way culturally determined. Although autism has been found in individuals at all levels of intelligence, a degree of intellectual disability ranging from mild to severe retardation is found in many cases. As many as three-quarters of children with autistic disorders have IQ scores below 70, and on-going intensive special education is usually required to address their learning needs.

Characteristics of students with autism

Autism is a severe form of developmental disorder in which the most obvious characteristics are:

- major impairment of social interactions and lack of normal emotional relationships with others;
- impairment of communication;
- reduced ability to learn, particularly through incidental observation and imitation;
- the presence of stereotype behaviour patterns (e.g. rocking, hand flapping, spinning);
- obsessive interests, ritualized activities, and the desire to preserve 'sameness' in surroundings and daily routines;
- lack of imaginative and creative play.

Current thinking on the nature of autism embodies the notion of a *continuum* of autistic characteristics, implying that there is no clearly defined single syndrome. Included at the upper level within this continuum are all the atypical children who are difficult to diagnose and do not necessarily conform to the typical pattern of autism. Individuals with autism vary greatly – and a single child diagnosed as autistic may not show all the above characteristics. Some students with autistic tendencies are close to normal in many facets of their behaviour, while others are very low functioning in terms of cognition, self-regulation and social development. Some children with moderate to severe degrees of autism often sit for hours, engaging in unusual repetitive habits (*stereotypic behaviours*) such as spinning objects, head banging, flapping fingers in front of their eyes, or just staring at their hands. A few autistic children exhibit self-injurious behaviours, such as biting or scratching. These stereotypic behaviours need to be reduced as far as possible in order to make the child more available for new learning and to increase social acceptance by peers.

Diagnosis of autism

To be diagnosed as autistic, a child must show symptoms of abnormal social and interpersonal development before the age of three years, and must meet at least six of the twelve criteria listed in the *Diagnostic and Statistical Manual of Mental Disorders* (APA 2000). The list delineates in more detail the key areas of abnormal development typical of children with autistic spectrum disorders. The twelve diagnostic criteria are:

- marked impairment of non-verbal behaviours used in social interaction (e.g. eye contact, facial expression, posture, use of gestures, etc.);
- failure to develop peer relationships;
- no spontaneous interest in, or enjoyment of, other persons;
- no desire to return social or emotional contacts;
- delay (or total lack) of verbal communication skills;
- in individuals with speech, no obvious ability or desire to converse with others;
- the use of stereotyped and repetitive language (often echolalic);
- absence of imaginative play;
- preoccupation with one or more stereotyped patterns of behaviour or interest;
- inflexible adherence to specific rituals and routines;
- repetitive movements such as hand flapping, body rocking;
- obsessive preoccupation with tiny parts or details of objects.

Haqberg *et al.* (2010) suggest that one of the earliest signs predictive of possible autism is significantly delayed language development in the early years. Failure to develop language is often (but not always) associated with a lower IQ. These researchers suggest that any preschool child with delayed language should be assessed for possible signs of autism.

Interventions for autism

Many different approaches have been used to reduce the negative behaviours often associated with autism. These have included pharmacological treatments, diet control, psychotherapy, behaviour modification and cognitive self-management training. Of these approaches, behaviour modification (also known as applied behaviour analysis or ABA) has produced the best results (Ashcroft *et al.* 2010; Dempsey and Foreman 2001). Cognitive approaches are problematic with low-functioning children because their application requires a degree of metacognition and self-monitoring not usually found in severely autistic children.

Many other approaches have been tried, including sensory-integration training, music therapy, play therapy, holding therapy, Snoezelen, facilitated communication, speech and language training, and social skills coaching. Some treatments are regarded as highly controversial and of doubtful value (Levy and Hayman 2005).

Teaching and training approaches: general principles

Teaching, training and managing children with autism is almost always complex, on-going and multidisciplinary (Howard *et al.* 2010; Miller 2009). It has been said that, 'effective interventions are characterized by intense treatment, low adult–child ratios, and highly structured and individualized programs' (Ashcroft *et al.* 2010: 34). While some short-term gains from teaching programmes are reported in studies of autistic children, longer-term and lasting benefits seem more difficult to achieve. There is considerable variability in response to interventions, with some children making much more progress than others. Degree of progress seems to be related to the child's intelligence level (Howlin *et al.* 2009). Some children with the most severe forms of autism often appear to make minimal gains despite many hours of careful stimulation and teaching. However, the benefits reported for many children with autism are positive enough to make the investment of time and effort worthwhile.

There is general agreement that the focus of any intervention programme should attempt to:

- stimulate cognitive development;
- facilitate language acquisition;
- promote social interactions.

Teaching sessions for children with autism generally need to be implemented according to a predictable schedule. The classroom environment and daily routines must always be consistent (Friedlauder 2009; Howard *et al.* 2010). New information, skills or behaviours need to be taught in small increments through systematic and direct methods. Each child's programme is based on a very detailed appraisal of the child's current developmental level and existing skills and responses. It is essential to assess the strengths of each individual child and to set goals that will help build on these strengths. All teachers, parents and caregivers must know the precise goals of the programme and must collaborate closely on the methods to be used with the child. It is essential that parents also be trained in the teaching strategies to be used in any intervention programme because the child spends more time at home than at school (Howard *et al.* 2010).

Objectives are best achieved by using both direct instructional methods and by maximizing the naturally occurring opportunities in the child's daily life. The most effective interventions involve the child's family as well as teachers and therapists. Home-based intervention programmes (or programmes combining both school- or clinic-based intervention with home programmes) produce better results than purely clinic-based programmes.

For non-verbal autistic children, intensive use of alternative communication methods and visual cues (hand signing, pointing, pictures and symbol cards) are usually necessary in most teaching situations (Elliott 2009). Some programmes have been based on teaching a basic vocabulary of hand signs to autistic children who lack speech.

Specific programmes and methods

TEACCH

One approach that has become popular in recent years is TEACCH (meaning 'Treatment and Education of Autistic and Communication-handicapped Children') (Mesibov *et al.* 2005). This approach stresses the need for a high degree of structure in the autistic child's day and uses a combination of cognitive and behavioural-change strategies, coupled with direct teaching of specific skills. Importance is placed on training parents to work with their own children and to make effective use of support services. An important feature of the approach is that it tries to capitalize on autistic children's preference for a visual mode of communication rather than the auditory-verbal mode. Several studies have supported the value of using visual cues, prompts, and schedules to hold the child's attention and to represent information in a form that is easily interpreted (Kimball *et al.* 2004). Such systems can also operate at home. In general, TEACCH has proved to be of positive value in the education of autistic children (Simpson 2005).

Lovaas's 'Young Autism Program'

One very intensive programme for autistic children is that devised by Lovaas (Lovaas and Smith 2003). The programme begins with the child at age two years and involves language development, social behaviours and the stimulation of play activity. Emphasis is also given to the elimination of excessive ritualistic behaviour, temper tantrums and aggression. The second year of treatment focuses on higher levels of language stimulation, and on cooperative play and interaction with peers. Lovaas claims high success rates for the programme, including increases in IQ. He claims that almost half of the treated group of children reached 'normal' functioning levels. The fact that this programme takes 40 hours per week, using one-to-one teaching over two years, makes it very labour-intensive and expensive. While the general principles are undoubtedly sound, it is difficult if not impossible to replicate the approach in the average special preschool.

Pivotal response training

This approach, developed by Robert and Lynn Koegel and associates (2006), is based on the principle that intervention in autism should focus heavily on strengthening particular behaviours that will simultaneously have a beneficial effect on other associated behaviours. These 'pivotal behaviours' in a child's repertoire are those that have widespread positive effects leading to generalized improvement. An example of pivotal behaviour is the child's response to multiple stimuli. Training would seek to increase selective attention and improve the ability to combine information from different sources. Pivotal response training employs basic applied behaviour analysis techniques and has been used effectively in the areas of language skills, play and social behaviours.

SCERTS Model

Detailed information on SCERTS can be found in the two-volume manual by Prizant *et al*. (2006). The acronym SCERTS is derived from Social Communication (SC), Emotional Regulation (ER) and Transactional Support (TS); these are the areas of development prioritized within this approach. The designers of this trans-disciplinary and family-centred model stress that SCERTS is not intended to be exclusionary of other treatments or methods. It attempts to capitalize on naturally occurring opportunities for development that occur throughout a child's daily activities and across social partners, such as siblings, parents, caregivers and other children. The overriding goal of SCERTS is to help a child with autism become a more competent participant in social activities by enhancing his or her capacity for attention, reciprocity, expression of emotion, and understanding of others' emotions. In particular, SCERTS aims to help children become better communicators and to enhance their abilities for pretend play.

Social stories

A technique that appears helpful in developing autistic children's awareness of normal codes of behaviour is use of *social stories* (Quirmbach *et al*. 2009). Social stories are simple narratives, personalized to suit the child's own needs and behaviours, to which the child can relate. The theme and context of the story help the autistic child perceive, interpret and respond more appropriately to typical social situations – for example, sharing a toy, taking turns, or standing in line.

Asperger syndrome

Individuals with Asperger syndrome have some of the behavioural and social difficulties associated with other degrees of autism, but they tend to have language and cognitive skills in the average or even above average range. Some researchers argue that Asperger syndrome is simply a subgroup within the autistic disorders spectrum but others believe it is a different form of disability representing a discrete group of higher-functioning individuals with only a few autistic tendencies. Most students with this type of disorder are in mainstream schools. Their unusual behaviour patterns cause them to be regarded as strange (quirky) by peers and teachers, and they may have difficulty making friends.

Students with Asperger syndrome may exhibit the following characteristics:

- unusual features in their oral language (e.g. repeatedly asking the same question of the same person, even though it has been answered; using a strangely pedantic style of speech; the overuse of stereotypic phrases);

- a lack of common sense in their daily encounters with the physical environment;
- naïve and inappropriate social approaches to others;
- narrow, obsessive interests;
- some appear physically awkward and poorly coordinated.

A few high-functioning students with this syndrome may exhibit certain areas of very great talent or knowledge. The areas of outstanding performance have included such things as music, art, mental calculation and recall of factual information with amazing accuracy. Students with these highly developed special abilities are sometimes referred to as 'autistic savants'.

Teaching children with Asperger syndrome

The key educational considerations for these students include:

- strategic seating in the classroom so that they can be monitored closely and kept on task;
- clarity in explaining any task for the student to attempt;
- using direct, literal questioning, rather than open-ended questioning;
- avoiding the over-use of complex language that requires deeper interpretation (e.g. metaphors; idioms);
- establishing a reasonably predictable routine and structure to all lessons;
- using visual aids during lessons wherever possible;
- if necessary, using a student's obsessive interests as foci for schoolwork, but at the same time trying to extend and vary the student's range of interests over time.

Some students with Asperger syndrome may benefit from personal counselling that involves such issues as understanding the feelings of others, social interaction, dealing with their own problems, and how to avoid trouble with other students and with teachers. The student's own inability to understand the emotional world of others will not be overcome easily, but at least he or she can be taught some coping strategies. Children with Asperger syndrome are stronger candidates for social-skills training than are autistic children with intellectual disability (see Chapter 8).

Online resources

- Information on intellectual disability can be located on the *Merck Manual Online Medical Library* at: www.merck.com/mmpe/sec19/ch299/ch299e. html (accessed 27 March 2010).
- Practical advice on teaching children with mild intellectual disability can be found at *About.com: Special Education* website: http://specialed.about.com/od/handlingallbehaviortypes/a/MID.htm (accessed 27 March 2010).

- Additional strategies for teaching intellectually disabled students can be located at: www.as.wvu.edu/~scidis/intel.html (accessed 27 March 2010).
- A fact sheet on autism can be downloaded from the website of the National Institute of Neurological Disorders and Stroke at: www.ninds.nih.gov/disorders/autism/detail_autism.htm (accessed 27 March 2010).
- The National Autistic Society (UK) website provides comprehensive coverage of Asperger syndrome at: www.nas.org.uk/nas/jsp/polopoly.jsp?d=212 (accessed 27 March 2010).
- The website for Carolina Institute for Developmental Disabilities contains information on TEACCH approach at: www.cidd.unc.edu/About/TEACCH/ (accessed 27 March 2010).
- For information on the Lovaas Method visit the Lovaas Institute website at: www.lovaas.com/about.php (accessed 27 March 2010).
- Details of the SCERT approach for autistic children are available at: www.scerts.com/ (accessed 27 March 2010).
- SCERTS was reviewed positively by Landsman (2007) in *PsycCRITIQUES*, online at: www.barryprizant.com/TheSCERTSModel%20critique%20-%20APA%20psychcritiques.pdf (accessed 27 March 2010).
- *Snoezelen* multisensory environments can be seen at: www.rompa.com/cgi-bin/rompa.storefront (accessed 08 April 2010).

Further reading

Ashcroft, W., Argiro, S. and Keohane, J. (2010) *Success Strategies for Teaching Kids with Autism,* Waco, TX: Prufrock Press.

Downing, J.E. (2008) *Including Students with Severe and Multiple Disabilities in Typical Classrooms* (3rd edn), Baltimore, MD: Brookes.

Foreman, P. (2009) *Education of Students with an Intellectual Disability: Research and Practice*, Charlotte, NC: Information Age Publishing.

Odom, S.L., Horner, R.H. and Snell, M.E. (2009) *Handbook of Developmental Disabilities,* New York: Guilford Press.

Rhea, P. (2009) *Social Skills Development in School-age Children with High Functioning Autism Spectrum Disorders*, Rockville, MD: ASHA.

Smith, D.D. and Tyler, N.C. (2010) *Introduction to Special Education: Making a Difference* (7th edn), Upper Saddle River, NJ: Pearson-Allyn and Bacon.

Chapter 3

Students with physical disabilities

Unlike the disabilities described in the previous chapter, the difficulties considered here do not necessarily arise from impaired intellectual functioning. While some students with physical disabilities (particularly moderate to severe *cerebral palsy*) do have intellectual impairment, many with other forms of physical impairment will be of average or better than average intelligence. Physical disability is a relatively low incidence category of special educational needs. Most of these students can cope well with the mainstream curriculum if specific teaching approaches and assistive technology are used to motivate and support them. In the case of students with physical disabilities, their greatest need may be help in accessing normal learning environments, instructional resources and classroom experiences. The additional problem for severely disabled students who lack speech is to find ways of communicating with others in order to interact socially.

The impact of physical disability on learning and development

Students with physical disabilities comprise a relatively small but diverse group. Their disabilities range from those that have little or no influence on learning and development, through to other conditions that may involve neurological impairment affecting both fine and gross motor skills. It is important for teachers to realize that a physical disability does not automatically impair a student's ability to learn. It is true that some students with physical impairment do have learning problems, but assumptions should never be made about an individual's capacity to learn on the basis of a physical disability. Even severe types of physical impairment sometimes have no impact on intellectual ability, and the intelligence levels for students with physical disabilities cover the full range from gifted to severely intellectually disabled (Best *et al.* 2010).

The education of students with physical disabilities must focus on providing these individuals with opportunities to access the same range of social and learning experiences as those available to students without handicaps (Rouse 2009). This may require adaptations to be made to the environment, to the ways in which these students move (or are moved) around the environment, and to the teaching methods and instructional resources used (Best *et al.* 2010). In the case of students with milder forms of disability, and those with average or above average learning aptitude, there is usually no reason why they should not attend ordinary schools and access the mainstream curriculum. For those with more severe disabilities and high support needs, special schools may still offer the best placement (Kauffman *et al.* 2005). The special school can offer a curriculum, resources, methods of instruction and therapies tailored carefully to meet their specific needs.

When working with students with physical disabilities in special or in mainstream settings, it is usually necessary for teachers to undertake not only task analysis (to reduce a learning activity to simple steps) but also *situation analysis* relating to the learning environment (Best *et al.* 2010). It is important to consider any modifications that may be needed in the learning environment to enhance the students' opportunities to participate (e.g. seating arrangements, access and movement routes, use of available supports and resources).

It has been noted that some students with physical disabilities tend to lack confidence in their own self-efficacy, and they present as rather passive learners requiring more than the usual amount of extrinsic motivation (Konings *et al.* 2005). Teachers, tutors and classroom assistants should take this characteristic into account when providing support. These students often need to be encouraged to make extra effort, to see tasks through to completion, and to work steadily towards greater independence. Even those physically disabled students with good learning skills may need a great deal of encouragement in order to achieve their potential. They may also need to draw upon outside services that offer treatment, therapy and counselling in order to function successfully and to maintain a good quality of life.

It is beyond the scope of this book to provide details of each and every physical disability or health problem. Attention here will be devoted only to the most commonly occurring conditions, namely cerebral palsy (CP), spina bifida (SB), epilepsy, hydrocephalus, and traumatic brain injury (TBI).

Cerebral palsy

Cerebral palsy (CP) is a disorder of posture, muscle tone and movement resulting from damage to the motor areas of the brain occurring before, during or soon after birth (Howard *et al.* 2010). CP is one of the more frequently occurring physical disabilities, with a prevalence rate of approximately two cases per 1000 live births. There has been no significant decline in the prevalence rate of this disorder, even though there have been major advances in prenatal and antenatal care.

CP exists in several forms (*spasticity*, *athetosis*, *ataxia* and *mixed forms*) and at different levels of severity from mild to severe. Type and severity of the condition are related to the particular area or areas of the brain that have been damaged and the extent of that damage. CP is not curable, but its negative impact on the individual's physical coordination, mobility, learning capacity and communication skills can be reduced through appropriate intensive therapy, training and education.

Assistive technology (AT) plays a major role in the effective education of students with physical disabilities by enhancing movement, participation and communication, and facilitating access to the curriculum. AT ranges from 'very low tech' equipment such as adjustable slant-top desks, pencil grips, modified scissor grips, adapted or specially designed seating, pads and wedges to help position a child for optimum functioning, walking and standing frames, and head-pointers, through to 'high-tech' adaptations such as electric wheelchairs operated by head movements or by air pressure from breath control, modified computer keyboards, touch screens, and switching devices. The range of available assistive technology is described well by Best et al. (2010).

Students with CP often have additional disabilities. At least 10 to 16 per cent of cases have impaired hearing or vision. Major difficulties with eye-muscle control can lead to fatigue in close-focus tasks such as looking at pictures, typing, or reading print. Epilepsy is evident in up to 30 per cent of cases of CP and a significant number of the children are on regular medication to control seizures. Medication can often have the side effect of reducing the individual's level of alertness and span of attention, thus adding to potential problems in learning.

Some children with severe CP may not develop speech, although their receptive language and understanding may be quite normal. In their attempts to vocalize, they may produce unintelligible sounds and their laughter may be loud and harsh. In addition, they may exhibit other symptoms such as inability to control the tongue, jaw and face muscles, resulting in facial contortions or drooling. These physical problems are beyond the individual's control but can create potential barriers for easy social integration.

It is reported that approximately 60 per cent of individuals with moderate to severe CP also have some degree of intellectual disability, with 25 per cent exhibiting significant cognitive impairment and additional complications (Howard et al. 2010; Turnbull et al. 2010). It must be noted, however, that some persons with quite severe CP are highly intelligent; and there is a danger that the potential of some non-verbal CP students is not recognized because of their inability to communicate. One of the main priorities for these individuals is to be provided with an alternative method of communication (Heller and Bigge 2010).

Instructional needs of students with cerebral palsy

Academic instruction for children with CP will depend mainly upon their cognitive ability and their range of functional movement. Students with mild cerebral palsy and normal intelligence may simply be slower at completing assignments and will need more time. Allowance may need to be made for large and poorly coordinated handwriting. For some, adapted devices such as pencil grips and page-turners may be required, and papers may need to be taped firmly to the desktop. A few students may need to use a word-processor with modified keyboard for their assignments. Computers with adaptations such as touch panels rather than a keyboard or a mouse are useful for presenting academic work and as a medium for communication with others.

In addition to the problems with movement and speech, many children with CP tend to:

- tire easily and have difficulty attending to tasks for more than brief periods of time;
- take a very long time to perform basic physical actions (e.g. pointing at or picking up an object; eating);
- rely on the teacher or an aide to lift and move them;
- require physical placement in a particular position for work, with padded 'wedges' or cushions to enable them to apply their limited range of movements to best advantage, or be placed and supported in a 'standing frame' with desk-top attached;
- need to be fed and toileted by an aide.

There are many suggested treatments for CP, but few of these approaches have been subjected to really rigorous evaluation. Even 'conductive education' (Pawelski 2007), an approach originating from Hungary and once hailed as a major breakthrough, produces very mixed results (see online resources).

Spina bifida

Spina bifida (SB) is a congenital disorder, possibly of genetic origin, presenting with different degrees of severity. It affects approximately one child in every 1000 live births. The condition results from a failure of certain bones in the spine to close over before birth to protect the spinal cord. The milder forms of SB have no significant influence on learning and mobility, and it is estimated that approximately 80 per cent of individuals with spina bifida have intelligence within the normal range (Howard *et al.* 2010). However, learning difficulties are common in the remaining 20 per cent, with problems in attention, visuo-spatial ability, memory and number skills often reported. Difficulties in learning occur increasingly with severity of the disability. In some cases students with moderate to severe spina bifida may have learning difficulties due to a restricted range of experiences prior to schooling. This can contribute to their difficulty in understanding some aspects of the curriculum that rely on good background knowledge.

The most serious form of spina bifida, with the greatest impact on the individual's development, is *myelomeningocele*. In this condition, a small part of the spinal cord itself is exposed at birth and protrudes from a gap in the spine. The cord is usually damaged, and bodily functions below this point may be seriously disrupted, including use of lower limbs. The individual may need to use a wheelchair or leg braces. Control of bladder and bowel function may be impaired, necessitating the use of a catheter tube to drain the bladder and the implementation of a careful diet and bowel-emptying routine. The management of incontinence presents the greatest personal and social problem for individuals with SB.

Approximately 60 to 70 per cent of children with myelomeningocele may also have some degree of *hydrocephalus* (Howard *et al.* 2010). The normal circulation and drainage of cerebrospinal fluid within the skull is impaired, resulting in increased intracranial pressure. Treatment for hydrocephalus involves the surgical implanting of a catheter into a ventricle in the brain to drain the excess fluid to the abdominal cavity. A valve is implanted below the skin behind the child's ear to prevent any back flow of cerebrospinal fluid. Teachers need to be aware that shunts and valves can become blocked, or the site can become infected. If the child with treated hydrocephalus complains of headache or earache, or if he or she appears feverish and irritable, medical advice should be obtained.

Children with spina bifida and hydrocephalus tend to be hospitalized at regular intervals during their school lives for such events as replacing shunts and valves, treating urinary infections or controlling respiratory problems. This frequent hospitalization can significantly interrupt the child's schooling, with sequential subjects such as mathematics being most affected by lost instructional time. Many students in this situation require intensive remedial assistance with their schoolwork.

Traumatic brain injury

The term *traumatic brain injury* (TBI) is used to describe any acquired brain damage resulting from events such as car accidents, serious falls, blows to the head, unsuccessful suicide attempts, sports injury, the 'shaken infant syndrome' and recovery after drowning. An increasing number of school-age individuals acquire brain injury from falls, car accidents and partial drowning. Howard *et al.* (2010) suggest that head injuries now account for some 40 per cent of fatalities in pre-school children.

The detrimental effects of TBI can include:

- memory problems;
- attention difficulties;
- slowed information processing;
- inability to solve problems and plan strategies;
- speech and language functions disrupted temporarily or permanently;
- impairment of general motor patterns such as walking, balancing;
- onset of epilepsy;
- vision problems;
- severe headaches;
- unpredictable and irrational mood swings or behaviour (aggressive, restless, apathetic, depressed).

Students with TBI often improve dramatically in the first year following injury, but, after that, progress is often much slower. Turnbull *et al.* (2010) indicate that for some individuals with TBI there is a slight to moderate decline in functional intelligence, with skills such as reading comprehension and mathematical problem solving presenting areas of particular difficulty. Frequent problems with word and information retrieval (anomia) can slow down the individual's speech and cause great frustration. Many children with TBI express great irritation in knowing an answer to a question in class but being unable to retrieve the necessary words at the right time. Given the complexity of the problems that can occur with TBI, it is common to find that the individuals affected usually require ongoing personal counselling, as well as an adapted learning programme (Miller 2009).

The main challenges for the teacher are:

- finding ways of maximizing the individual's attention to a learning task by removing distractions, providing cues, limiting the amount of information presented and giving frequent feedback;
- keeping instructions clear and simple, and not overloading the student with information or tasks;
- breaking down lesson content into manageable units of work that are achievable within the individual's attention span;
- helping to compensate for memory loss by presenting visual cues to aid recall of information by encouraging visual imagery, rehearsing information more than would be necessary with other learners, teaching self-help strategies such as keeping reminder notes in your pocket, and regularly checking the daily schedule;
- helping the individual plan ahead by setting goals and then working towards them;
- understanding and accepting the student's poor ability to concentrate and to complete the work that is set.

Books by Best *et al.* (2010) and Turnbull *et al.* (2010) contain useful sections on teaching and management issues related to TBI in school-age children.

Augmentative and alternative communication

It has been mentioned that many students with severe and multiple disabilities, whether congenital or acquired, may have no oral–verbal method of communication. This can lead others to judge them, wrongly, as functioning at a low cognitive level. The priority need for severely disabled persons without speech is to develop an alternative method of communicating (Calculator 2009). The ultimate aim of any augmentative or alternative communication system is to allow the child to 'talk' about the same range of things that other children of that age would discuss.

Alternative communication modes include:

- sign language, finger-spelling and gesture;
- use of a picture and symbol system on a communication board or in a book that the person can access by pointing, or in some cases by eye glance;
- computer-aided communication.

The simplest form of alternative communication is a communication board comprising a small set of pictures or symbols that are personally relevant to the child's life and context. For example, the board may have pictures of a television set, a glass, a knife, fork and plate, a toilet, a toy, and a red cross for 'no' and a green tick for 'yes'. The child can communicate his or her wishes or basic needs by pointing to or looking at the appropriate picture. Other pictures and symbols are added as the child's range of experiences increases.

General points for mainstream teachers

- For students in wheelchairs or walking with leg-braces and sticks, it may be necessary to rearrange the classroom desks and chairs to give easier access and a wider corridor for movement.
- Some students with physical disabilities may have a high absence rate due to: (i) attending therapy or treatment appointments during school hours; (ii) frequent health problems. Frequent absence means that the teacher may need to provide the student with specific 'catch up' work to do at home, and may need to enlist the help of the support teacher or aide to provide some short-term remedial assistance for the student.
- Some students with physical disabilities (especially cerebral palsy) may also have epilepsy. To control the epilepsy the student may be on medication that tends to lower their level of responsiveness in class. If seizures appear to increase in severity or frequency, check that the student is actually taking the medication. Report all cases of seizure to parents.
- While applying all commonsense safety procedures, teachers should try not to overprotect students with physical disabilities. Whenever possible, these students should be encouraged to take part in the same activities enjoyed by other students. Teachers of PE and sport need to get practical advice on ways in which these physical activities can be adapted to include students with disabilities. Physically disabled students should never be left on the sidelines as mere spectators.
- Some students with physical disabilities will need to use modified desks or chairs. It is the teacher's responsibility to ensure that the student makes use of the equipment.
- Some secondary school students with physical disabilities will have great difficulty writing and taking notes. Their fine-motor movements may be slow and their coordination very poor and inaccurate. The teacher could establish a peer support network and allow the student to use a tape recorder to record lessons, or photocopy the notes of other students. Sometimes the teacher may

permit the student to use a scribe or submit an assignment as an audiotape rather than an essay.

Online resources

The website of the National Institute of Neurological Disorders and Stroke (NINDS) provides information on a number of physical disabilities.

- Cerebral palsy is located at: www.ninds.nih.gov/disorders/cerebral_palsy/cerebral_palsy.htm (accessed 27 March 2010).
- Spina bifida at: www.ninds.nih.gov/disorders/spina_bifida/spina_bifida.htm (accessed 27 March 2010).
- Traumatic brain injury at: www.ninds.nih.gov/disorders/tbi/tbi.htm (accessed 27 March 2010).
- Epilepsy at www.ninds.nih.gov/disorders/epilepsy/epilepsy.htm (accessed 27 March 2010).
- Information on conductive education can be found at: www.conductive-ed.org.uk/> (accessed 07 April 210).

Further reading

Aicardi, J., Bax, M. and Gillberg, C. (eds) (2009) *Diseases of the Nervous System in Childhood* (3rd edn), London: Mac Keith Press.

Best, S.J., Heller, K.W. and Bigge, J.L. (2010) *Teaching Individuals with Physical or Multiple Disabilities* (6th edn), Upper Saddle River, NJ: Pearson-Merrill-Prentice Hall.

Heller, K., Forney, P., Alberton, P., Best, S. and Schwartzman, M. (2009) *Understanding Physical, Health and Multiple Disabilities* (2nd edn), Upper Saddle River, NJ: Pearson Education-Merrill.

Kutscher, M.L. (2006) *Children with Seizures*, London: Jessica Kingsley.

Turnbull, A., Turnbull, R. and Wehmeyer, M.L. (2010) *Exceptional Lives* (6th edn), Upper Saddle River, NJ: Merrill.

Vagas, C.M. and Prelock, P.A. (2004) *Caring for Children with Neurodevelopmental Disabilities and their Families*, Mahwah, NJ: Erlbaum.

Chapter 4

Students with sensory impairments

Students with sensory impairments comprise a small but varied group within the population of children with special needs. Often they require additional teaching approaches and resources that differ somewhat from those normally available in mainstream schools. However, many students with sensory impairments are now included in regular classes and taught by mainstream teachers.

Vision impairment

In some countries the term *vision impairment* is replacing the older term *visually impaired*. When a child is described as vision impaired, it does not necessarily mean that he or she is blind, it means that the child has a serious defect of vision that cannot be corrected by wearing spectacles. In the population of children with impaired vision, there are those who are totally blind, those who are 'legally' blind and those with varying degrees of partial sight.

While impaired vision is a low incidence disability, it is important to note that it also occurs as a secondary handicap in many cases of severe and multiple disabilities. For example, many students with cerebral palsy also have serious problems with vision, as do some individuals with traumatic brain injury (Howard *et al.* 2010).

Impaired vision has multiple causes, including structural defects or damage to the retina, lens or optic nerve, inefficiency in the way the brain interprets and stores visual information, or an inability of the retina to transmit images to the brain. Some vision problems are inherited, including those associated with albinism, congenital cataracts and degeneration of the retina, while others may be due to disease or to medical conditions such as diabetes or tumours. Prematurity and very low birth weight can contribute to vision problems in childhood, with *retinopathy of prematurity* (ROP) being reported as one of the most common causes of impaired vision in very young children.

Special educational needs of children with impaired vision

Early years

Vision is important for developing gross and fine motor skills. Blind children and those with very weak vision may often be delayed in acquiring basic motor skills such as crawling, walking and feeding (Allen and Cowdrey 2009). Young children with impaired vision benefit from many physical activities that help them develop body awareness, depth perception, movement and coordination. These children need to be encouraged, within the realms of safety, to explore and interact with their immediate environment.

The absence of sight can also lead to delays in cognitive development and concept formation (Bardin and Lewis 2008). Early sensory stimulation is therefore vital for young children with seriously impaired vision, and needs to be accompanied by verbal interpretations by the parent or caregiver. Children with impaired vision are much less able to acquire knowledge and skills through observation and incidental learning (Turnbull *et al.* 2010), so the environment, and events happening within it, must be described through language to increase the child's awareness of things he or she cannot see. Parents and teachers need to provide a blind child with abundant verbal input while seizing many opportunities throughout the day to encourage the child's use of intact senses. For example, the child needs to be given different objects to explore through touch, and taught how to examine small objects and large objects in order to build relevant concepts. Auditory skills need to be encouraged through appropriate activities that involve careful listening.

Social development

Impaired vision can affect an individual's confidence and self-esteem (Bowen 2010) and this in turn can reduce that person's willingness to initiate social contacts. Teachers need to be proactive in helping blind and partially sighted students become involved in the social group (Smith and Tyler 2010).

For vision-impaired students who are able to cope with learning in the mainstream, inclusion in supportive mainstream classes can be extremely beneficial for overall social development. However, for some students the socialization process in the classroom and in the playground can often be problematic. This is partly due to lack of opportunity to mix and interact with other children from an early age, and thus observe and acquire social behaviours. It is also due to the fact that blind children can't see the many important non-verbal aspects of social interaction and communication such as nodding in agreement, looking surprised, smiling and respecting personal space when engaging in conversation (MacConville and Rhys-Davies 2007). Social development is further restricted if members of the peer group feel shy or are lacking in confidence when interacting with a person who is blind or partially sighted. It is sometimes helpful to foster better understanding in the peer group by discussing openly with the class the problems that a person with impaired vision may have in dealing with schoolwork and with the physical environment. Obviously, if such discussion is attempted, it should only be done with the student's agreement, and must be done with due sensitivity.

Accessing the curriculum and the environment

There are several areas in which blind children and those with seriously impaired vision need to be taught additional skills. These areas include mobility, orientation, the use of Braille and assistive technology (Smith and Tyler 2010).

Mobility

Blind students and those with very limited sight need to be taught mobility skills to enable them to move safely and purposefully in their environment. The skills include:

*   *self-protection techniques* – for example, in unfamiliar environments, holding the hand and forearm loosely in front of the face for protection while trailing the other hand along the wall or rail; checking for doorways, steps, stairs and obstacles; using auditory information to locate objects (e.g. air-conditioner, an open doorway; traffic noise);
*   *long-cane skills* – moving about the environment with the aid of a long cane swept lightly on the ground ahead to locate hazards and to check surface textures;
*   *using electronic travel aids* – for example, 'sonic spectacles' with a built-in device that emits a sound warning to indicate proximity to objects;
*   *using public transport* – an important part of training involves teaching the individual how to use and negotiate buses and trains.

The person with severely impaired vision needs sufficient mobility skills and confidence to negotiate the outside environment, including crossing the road, catching buses or trains, and locating shops. Increased mobility adds significantly to the quality of life for persons with impaired vision. While the classroom teacher and parents can certainly assist with the development of mobility skills, a mobility-training expert usually carries out the detailed planning and implementation of the programme.

Orientation

Orientation is the term used to indicate that a person with impaired vision is familiar with a particular environment and at any time knows his or her own position in relation to objects such as furniture, barriers, open doors or steps. Teachers should realize that for the safety and convenience of students with vision impairment, the physical classroom environment should remain fairly constant and predictable (Salisbury 2008). If furniture has to be moved or some new static object is introduced into the room, the blind student needs to be informed of that fact and given the opportunity to locate it in relation to other objects. In classrooms it is necessary to avoid hanging posters and other items at head height, and to make sure that equipment such as boxes and books are not left on the floor. Doors should not be left half open with a hard edge projecting into the room.

Mobility and orientation together are two of the primary goals in helping the blind student move towards increased independence. Without these skills the quality of life of the blind person is seriously restricted.

Braille

Braille is of tremendous value as an alternative communication medium for those students who are blind or whose remaining vision does not enable them to perceive enlarged print. Braille is a complex code, so its use with students who are below average in intelligence is not always successful. Obviously if an individual's cognitive level is such that he or she would experience difficulties in learning to read and write with conventional print, Braille is not going to be an easier code to master. The notion that all blind students use Braille is false. However, if a child's intelligence is adequate, the younger he or she begins to develop some Braille skills the better as this will prepare the child to benefit from later schooling. Braille 'readiness' activities are stressed during the pre-reading stage and include fingertip tactile sensitivity training.

A simplified system similar in principle to Braille is called Moon. It is reported to be easier to learn, particularly for children who have additional disabilities (Salisbury 2008). Moon uses only twenty-six raised shapes, based on lines and curves, to represent the standard alphabet, plus ten other symbols.

In recent years, debate has opened up around the issue of whether modern communications technology such as screen-to-speech and speech-to-text applications for computers, audio books, and audio newspapers has made touch systems such as Braille and Moon obsolete. Persons in the blind community have expressed varied opinions, but most believe that Braille is still important because it gives one an independent means of 'reading' (and, importantly, re-reading) information. This is deemed more effective for cognitive processing than purely transient audio input. Braille also provides the individual with a system for producing 'written' text.

Assistive technology

In the same way that students with physical disabilities can be helped to access the curriculum and participate more effectively in daily life through the use of assistive technology, children with impaired vision can also be assisted. Many devices have been designed to enable the partially sighted student to cope with the medium of print. *Low vision aids* are magnification devices or instruments that help the individual with some residual sight to work with maximum visual efficiency. The devices include a variety of hand-held or desktop magnifiers, and closed-circuit television or microfiche readers (both used to enlarge an image). For blind students, calculators and clocks with audio output, dictionaries with speech output, compressed speech recordings, and thermoform duplicators are used to reproduce Braille pages or embossed diagrams and maps.

Some students with impaired vision benefit from modified furniture such as desks with bookstands or angled tops to bring materials closer to the child's eyes without the need to lean over, or with lamp attachments for increased illumination of the page.

Teachers in mainstream classes should note that although assistive devices are of very great benefit to partially sighted students, many of these students will try to avoid using them in class because they feel that using them draws unwanted attention to their disability (MacConville and Rhys-Davies 2007). This emotional sensitivity to assistive technology as a marker of disability can begin in the primary school years, but occurs most frequently among vision-impaired students in mainstream secondary schools.

Teaching students with impaired vision

Teachers in the mainstream with no prior experience of vision-impaired children may tend to hold fairly low expectations of what these children can accomplish. Many teachers may not expect enough of the children and may assume that they cannot participate in certain activities. It is essential, however, to provide many new challenges for these students and encourage them to do as much as possible. Having a problem with vision should not exclude the children from access to normal classroom experiences, although significant modifications to materials and methods may need to be made (Supalo *et al.* 2008).

The following general advice may help mainstream teachers with vision-impaired students in their classes.

- Almost all students with impaired vision in mainstream classes will have partial sight rather than total or legal blindness. It is essential to encourage them to use their residual vision effectively because exercising the remaining vision is helpful, not harmful.
- Enlarge the font in all text, notes and handouts to one of the following point sizes:

24   36   48

- Use a photocopier when necessary to make enlarged versions of notes, diagrams and other handouts for the student.

- Seat the student in the most advantageous position to be able to see the whiteboard or screen.
- Ensure that your own material on whiteboard, PowerPoint, or screen is neat and clear, using larger script than usual. Keep the whiteboard surface clean to ensure clarity of text.
- Avoid overloading worksheets with too much information and heavy density of print.
- Allow partially sighted students to use a fibre-tip black ink pen that will produce clear, bold writing.
- When necessary, prepare exercise paper with darker ruled lines.
- Allow much more time for students with impaired vision to complete their work.
- Read written instructions aloud to students with impaired vision, to reduce the amount of time required to begin a task and to ensure that the work is understood.
- Use very clear descriptions and explanations, because verbal explanation must compensate for what the student cannot see.
- Train other students and the classroom aide to support the student with impaired vision when necessary – for example, by taking notes during the lesson, clarifying points, or repeating teacher's explanations.
- Call on blind students frequently by name during lessons to engage them fully in the group-learning processes. Acknowledge and value their contributions.
- Call upon other students clearly by name so that the blind student knows who is responding.
- Make sure that any specialized equipment is always at hand and in good order. If the student with impaired vision uses magnification or illumination aids or other devices, make sure that (i) you know when and how the equipment needs to be used, and (ii) you ensure that the student does not avoid using the equipment.
- Some forms of vision impairment respond well to brighter illumination, but in some other conditions bright light is undesirable. Obtain advice on illumination from support service personnel who are aware of the student's characteristics.
- If the student has extremely limited vision, make sure that any changes to the physical arrangement of the room are explained and experienced by the student to avoid accidents. The student needs to develop fresh orientation each time an environment is changed.
- Try to ensure that the student establishes a network of friends within the class. Social interaction is often not easily achieved without assistance.
- Obtain all the advice you can from the visiting support teacher and other advisory personnel. In the UK, there are now quality standards clearly specified for visiting support services (TeacherNet 2010).

Hearing impairment

Hearing impairment is a general term used to describe all degrees and types of hearing loss and deafness. Impaired hearing does not mean that an individual cannot detect any sounds. He or she may simply hear some frequencies of sound much more clearly than others. Individuals are usually referred to as *deaf* if they are unable to detect speech sounds and if their own oral language development is disordered. In some countries, those who can hear some sounds and can make reasonable use of their residual hearing are either termed *hard of hearing* or *partially hearing.*

Types and degrees of hearing loss

Most hearing loss can be classified as either *conductive* or *sensori-neural.* The key features of each type of are summarized below.

Conductive hearing loss

Conductive hearing loss occurs when sounds do not reach the middle ear or inner ear (cochlear) because of some physical malformation, blockage or damage. Common causes are excessive build-up of wax in the ear, abnormality of the ear canal, a ruptured eardrum, dislocation or damage to the tiny bones of the middle ear, or infection in the middle ear (*otitis media*). Hearing loss due to middle-ear infection is usually temporary and will improve when the infection is treated successfully. If infections are allowed to continue untreated, damage may be done to the middle ear resulting in permanent hearing loss. The use of a hearing aid may significantly help an individual with conductive hearing loss.

Sensori-neural loss

Sensori-neural hearing loss is related to the inner ear and the auditory nerve. The most serious hearing losses are often of this type. As well as being unable to hear many sounds, even those that are heard may be distorted. The problem of distortion means that the wearing of a hearing aid may not always help, because amplifying a distorted sound does not make it any clearer. Some individuals with sensori-neural loss are particularly sensitive to loud noises, perceiving them to be painfully loud.

Many students with impaired hearing have no other disability; but hearing impairment is often present as a secondary problem in children with intellectual disability, cerebral palsy, or language disorders.

Acuity of hearing is measured in units called decibels (dB). Zero dB is the point from which people with normal hearing can begin to detect the faintest sounds. Normal conversation is usually carried out at an overall sound level of between 40 and 50dB. Loss of hearing is expressed in terms of the amplification required before the individual can hear each sound. The greater the degree of impairment, the less likely it is that the child will develop normal speech and language, and the more likely it is that they will need special education services. Individuals with a hearing loss above 95dB are usually categorized as 'deaf' or 'profoundly deaf'. Other categories are:

- *slight loss*: 15–25dB*. Vowel sounds still heard clearly. Some consonants may be missed.
- *mild loss*: 25–40dB*. Can hear only loud speech. Usually requires hearing aid. May need speech therapy. Some difficulty with normal conversation.
- *moderate loss*: 40–65dB*. Misses almost all speech at normal conversational level. Requires hearing aid. Serious impact on language development. Speech therapy and special education often required.
- *severe loss*: 65–95dB*. Unable to hear normal speech. Major problems with language development. Hearing aid required (but may not help in some cases). Language training and other special services required.
- *profound loss*: above 95dB*. Cannot hear speech or other environmental sounds. Severe problems in language acquisition. Normal conversation impossible. Alternative forms of communication usually required (e.g. sign language). Special class placement often indicated.

Note: * The specific dB range varies slightly from country to country.

The difficulties experienced by children with slight to moderate hearing loss often remain undetected for several years, placing the child at risk of failure in school (DCSF 2009a). This is particularly the case if the hearing problem is intermittent and related, for example, to head colds or middle ear infections. Early detection of hearing loss must lead to appropriate early intervention.

Impact of deafness on learning and development

An inability to hear clearly places a young child at risk of delay in many areas, including the acquisition of spoken language, literacy skills and social development (Turnbull *et al.* 2010). For example, the speech of children with significantly impaired hearing often has very poor rhythm and phrasing, together with a flat and monotonous tone of voice. Many factors, including time of onset, severity, type of hearing loss and different instructional approaches used, all interact to produce large variations in spoken language performance. A priority goal in the education of all children with impaired hearing is to advance their language skills as much as possible. Any improvement in language will allow each child to make better use of his or her intellectual potential, understand much more of the curriculum, and develop socially.

Helping a deaf child acquire intelligible speech can be a long and difficult process. Early intervention and active parental involvement are essential elements in language stimulation (Smith and Tyler 2010). One well-respected programme for this purpose is the Ling Method (or Auditory Verbal Approach) (Ling and Ling 1978). In some cases, speech training and auditory training are also advocated for hearing-impaired students. Speech therapists or language teachers may, for example, use speech and articulation coaching based mainly on behavioural principles of modelling, imitation, reinforcement and shaping. In recent years, however, speech therapists and teachers have placed much more importance on trying to stimulate language development through the use of naturally occurring activities in the classroom ('milieu approach'). Such teaching is thought to result in better transfer and generalization of vocabulary and language patterns to the child's everyday life.

The inability to hear language from an early age not only creates a major problem in developing speech but can also have a negative impact on some aspects of intellectual development. It is often said that deaf students' limited vocabulary slows down development of cognitive skills necessary for learning in school. In recent years there has been some criticism of this viewpoint and it is now suggested that although deaf children may lack depth in *spoken* language, they still encode and store information and experience in other ways. They often have some other more visual representations of language such as signing or gesture that enable them to express their ideas.

Over the past two decades many hearing-impaired children have been included in mainstream classes. It is argued that they experience maximum social interaction and communication by mixing with other students using normal spoken language. They are exposed to more accurate language models than might be the case in a special class containing only hearing-impaired students. It is also hoped that students with normal hearing will develop improved understanding and tolerance for individuals who are slightly different from others in the peer group. Where deaf children are included in regular classes, some schools ensure that the hearing students are also taught basic sign language in order to promote communication.

Including students with significantly impaired hearing in mainstream classes relies fairly heavily on the availability of expert advice from visiting teachers and from regional hearing support services. In some countries where many schools are in country regions or in remote areas (e.g. Australia), providing this service can be problematic (Checker *et al.* 2009).

Basic academic skills

It is frequently reported that the academic attainment level of children with impaired hearing lags well behind that of their hearing peers (Evans 2009). Often this problem is due not only to difficulties in processing oral information from teachers but also to lack of adequate proficiency in basic literacy and numeracy skills. Careful attention must be given to the explicit teaching of reading and spelling skills to students with impaired hearing. It is typical of these students that as they progress through primary school they fall three to four years behind the peer group in terms of reading ability (Robertson 2009; Smith and Tyler 2010). For example, Trezek *et al.* (2010) indicate that by age 19 students with significant hearing loss typically read at the level of a 9-year-old child. This reading lag has a detrimental impact on their performance in all subjects across the curriculum.

Many of their difficulties in reading and spelling are thought to stem from their problem in accurately perceiving speech sounds. Limited phonemic awareness results in serious difficulty in learning decoding and encoding skills. At one time, it was believed that deaf and hard-of-hearing students need to learn to read by visual memory methods alone because they lack the underlying capacity to master decoding. It was thought, for example, that teaching printed words alongside their manual sign language equivalents would enable students to build up a meaningful sight vocabulary of words. However, such an approach is limited in the long term because it does not teach a system that would help a reader to unlock unfamiliar words. The visual approach used alone is no longer popular among educators and instructional methods now aim to help these students acquire an understanding of orthographic units (letters and letter groups) and their relation to speech (Diederichs 2009; Trezek and Malmgren 2005). The significant improvement in the quality of hearing aids in recent years has been beneficial in this respect by helping students detect speech sounds more accurately (Robertson 2009). While the beginning stages of reading instruction can focus on building a basic sight vocabulary by visual methods, later the teaching of word-analysis (decoding) skills must also be stressed for students with hearing loss. Without the phonic concept, their ability to read and spell unfamiliar words will remain seriously deficient. It is also essential when providing reading instruction for hearing-impaired children that due attention be given to developing comprehension strategies (Robertson 2009). A restricted vocabulary and limited awareness of complex sentence structures can cause major problems in fluency and comprehension (Trezek *et al.* 2010).

The written expression of deaf children is often reported to be problematic (Antia *et al.* 2005), with syntax and vocabulary the major weaknesses. Difficulties often include inaccurate sentence structure, incorrect verb tenses, difficulties representing plurals correctly, and inconsistencies in using correct pronouns. The written work of older deaf students has many of the characteristics of the writing of younger children, and may also contain 'deafisms' involving incorrect word order (e.g. 'She got black hair long', instead of 'She has long black hair').

Spelling instruction needs to be direct and systematic rather than incidental. For deaf children, it is likely that more than the usual amount of attention will need to be given to developing visual memory to enable them to spell and check words by eye as well as ear. The 'look-say-cover-write-check' strategy is particularly helpful and needs to be taught thoroughly (see Chapter 12).

Modes of communication

While listening and speaking remain the preferred methods of communication for students with mild and moderate degrees of impairment, for those who are severely to profoundly deaf alternative manual methods may be needed. These methods include gesture, sign language, cued speech, and finger-spelling.

Sign language

There are different forms of sign language (e.g. Signed English, Auslan, American Sign Language) sharing obvious characteristics in common but also having some unique features. Deaf children from deaf families will almost certainly have been exposed to, and become competent in, manual communication even before entering formal education. There is no strong evidence that early exposure to sign language has a detrimental effect on later oral communication skills, such as speech and lip reading (Meadow 2005).

Sign language remains a controversial issue in the field of deaf education. Often the use of sign language is the only thing that attracts the attention of others to the fact that a person is deaf. Many teachers, and some parents who are not deaf, feel that to encourage manual forms of communication will cause the child to be accepted only in the deaf community rather than in the wider community of hearing persons. They also believe that the use of signing will retard the development of speech, thus isolating the child even further. Experts suggest, however, that sign language should be respected as a language in its own right, with its own vocabulary, grammar and semantics, and it should be valued and encouraged as an effective mode of communication.

Oral–aural approach (oralism)

The belief underpinning *oralism* is that to be accepted and to succeed in a hearing world you need to be able to communicate through oral–verbal methods (Herer *et al.* 2007). The approach virtually places a ban on manual communication and stresses instead the use of residual hearing, supplemented by lip reading and speech training. Teachers should note, however, that hearing impaired students' ability to lip read is often greatly overestimated (MacConville and Palmer 2007). Attempting to interpret words from cues on the speaker's lips is an extremely difficult and inaccurate method of understanding the communication of others.

Total communication approach

The relative popularity of signing versus oralism ebbs and flows from decade to decade. In response, *total communication* (TC) or simultaneous communication (SC) deliberately combines signing and gesture with oral–aural methods to help deaf children comprehend and express ideas and opinions (Howard *et al.* 2010). A combination of oral and manual training at an early age appears to foster optimum communicative ability (Turnbull *et al.* 2010).

Assistive technology

Hearing aids

Hearing aids are of various types, including the typical 'behind the ear' or 'in the ear' aids and radio frequency (FM) aids. An audiologist assesses the specific needs of the child and a hearing aid is prescribed to suit the individual's sound-loss profile. The aid is adjusted as far as possible to give amplification of the specific frequency of sounds needed by the child. No hearing aid fully compensates for hearing loss, even when carefully tailored to the user's characteristics.

The great limitation of the conventional type of hearing aid is that it amplifies all sound, including background noise in the environment. The advantage of the radio frequency (FM) aid is that it allows the teacher's voice to be received with minimum interference from environmental noise. The teacher wears a small microphone and the child's hearing aid receives the sounds in the same way that a radio receives a broadcast transmission. The child can be anywhere in the classroom, and does not need to be near to or facing the teacher, as with the conventional aid.

Many hearing-impaired students do not like to be seen wearing a hearing aid, especially in mainstream situations and particularly in secondary schools. They will take every opportunity to hide it away and not use it. Some of these students report that they feel more socially at ease, and thus able to fit in more easily with their peers, if they do not wear the aid (MacConville and Palmer 2007). Teachers have a responsibility to make sure the hearing aid is used and is maintained in good order.

Cochlear implants

A cochlear implant is a device used to produce the sensation of sound by electrically stimulating the auditory nerve. The device has two main parts, the internal component (electrodes implanted into or on the cochlear) and an external receiver embedded in the temporal bone. Many developed countries are now carrying out the surgery required to implant this form of assistive device at a very young age.

Cochlear implants are normally recommended only for children who are profoundly deaf and cannot benefit at all from other forms of hearing aid. While the child can begin to perceive the electrical stimulation soon after surgery, it normally takes at least a year for gains in the child's language skills to become evident. The child's effective adaptation to the cochlear implant needs much support and encouragement from the parents. Many children with cochlear implants still rely on sign language to understand fully what is said. Smith and Tyler (2010: 347) have remarked, 'Teachers need to understand that students with cochlear implants may have speech that is difficult to understand, and they will be receiving intensive speech and language therapy.'

There is increasing evidence that integrating various forms of technology and software into teaching of students with impaired hearing can bring positive results. For example, CD-ROM-based packages, such as the auditory and language training program *Fast ForWord* (Scientific Learning Corporation) are showing some promise in helping children with mild hearing loss or with an auditory processing disorder to improve phonemic awareness and listening attention (Howard *et al.* 2010). In the domain of reading, Mueller and Hurtig (2010) describe a successful strategy for enhancing 'shared reading' activities (see Chapter 9) for deaf students by combining technology with sign language input.

Teaching students with impaired hearing

Using some of the following basic strategies for hearing-impaired students may also be helpful to students with other learning difficulties in the classroom. It is recommended that teachers:

- make greater use of visual methods of presenting information whenever possible;
- use clear and simple language when explaining new concepts, and teach all new vocabulary thoroughly;
- write new vocabulary on the whiteboard, ensuring that students with hearing impairment hear the word, see the word, and say the word;
- revise new vocabulary regularly; and revise new language patterns (e.g. 'Twice the size of . . .', 'Mix the ingredients . . .', 'Invert and multiply . . .');
- repeat instructions clearly while facing the class;
- do not give instructions while there is noise in the classroom;
- where possible, also write instructions as short statements on the whiteboard;
- attract the student's attention when you are about to ask a question or give out information;
- check frequently that the student is on task and has understood what he or she is required to do;
- where possible, provide the student with printed notes to ensure that key content from the lesson is made available;
- when group discussion is taking place, make sure a deaf student can see the other students who are speaking or answering questions;
- repeat the answer that another student has given if you think the hearing-impaired student may not have heard it;
- involve the student in the lesson as much as possible;
- ensure that the student has a partner for activities and assignments;
- encourage other students to assist the hearing-impaired student to complete any work that is set – *but* without doing the work for the student;
- do not talk while facing the whiteboard – a deaf student needs to see your mouth and facial expression;

- do not walk to the back of the room while talking and giving out important information;
- reduce background noise when listening activities are conducted;
- do not seat the student with impaired hearing near to sources of noise (e.g. fan, open window, generator);
- seat the student where he or she can see you easily, can see the whiteboard, and can observe the other students;
- make sure that you know how to check the student's hearing aid, and check it on a daily basis;
- seek advice regularly from the regional advisory service and from the visiting support teacher, and use such advice in your programme.

Online resources

- Information on blindness and vision impairment is available on the National Dissemination Centre for Children with Disabilities website at: www.nichcy. org/Disabilities/Specific/Pages/VisualImpairment.aspx (accessed 27 March 2010).
- Practical strategies for teaching children with impaired vision available at the Texas School for the Blind and Visually Impaired website: www.tsbvi. edu/Education/strategies.htm (accessed 27 March 2010).
- Practical strategies for teaching deaf and hearing-impaired students available at the Hearing, Speech and Deafness Centre website at: www.hsdc.org/News/ Audiology/teachers.htm (accessed 27 March 2010).

Further reading

Bishop, V.E. (2004) *Teaching Visually Impaired Children* (3rd edn), Springfield, IL: Thomas.

Hull, R.H. (ed.) (2010) *Introduction to Aural Rehabilitation*, San Diego, CA: Plural Publishing.

LeVenture, S. (2007) *A Parents' Guide to Special Education for Children with Visual Impairments*, New York: American Foundation for the Blind, AFB Press.

Niparko, J.K. (ed.) (2009) *Cochlear Implants: Principles and Practices* (2nd edn), Philadelphia, PA: Lippincott, Williams and Wilkins.

Nitttouer, S. (2010) *Early Development of Children with Hearing Loss*, San Diego, CA: Plural Publishing.

Salisbury, E. (ed.) (2008) *Teaching Pupils with Visual Impairment*, London: Routledge.

Trezek, B.J., Wang, Y. and Paul P.V. (2010) *Reading and Deafness: Theory, Research and Practice*, Clifton Park, NY: Delmar.

Chapter 5

Gifted and talented students

In the previous chapters, attention has been devoted to the characteristics and needs of students with various forms of learning difficulty or disability. This chapter explores the special needs of a group of students who are often assumed to have no problems in learning – namely those of high intellectual ability and those who possess specific talents. Piirto and Heward (2009: 496) are adamant that, 'Without doubt, advanced students have special educational needs.'

It is generally agreed that, based on intelligence, approximately 3 per cent to 5 per cent of the school population can be regarded as potentially intellectually gifted (Mastropieri and Scruggs 2010). Within this population there are degrees of giftedness ranging from 'moderate' to 'profound'. Less than one child in every 100,000 would be classed as profoundly gifted with an IQ above 180. Many intellectually gifted students – but by no means all – are also high achievers in most academic subjects in the school curriculum. Many – but by no means all – may also display exceptional ability and creativity in other areas such as art and design, technology, music, drama, dance, sports, gymnastics, interpersonal skills and leadership (Groth-Marnat 2009). In order for these exceptional students to reach their full potential, they need special attention and additional resources in school. Some important ways of meeting their needs are discussed in this chapter.

In addition to these intellectually and academically gifted students, there are also many others in our schools, not necessarily of above average intelligence, who develop exceptional talent in areas such as the manual arts, performing arts, technology, sport, social action, leadership and many other fields. These specifically 'talented' students also require special attention in our schools to enable their talents to develop to the full. Taken together, intellectually gifted students and other talented students comprise some 10 to 15 per cent of the school population (Piiro and Heward 2009). Unfortunately, the potential of some of these students is not always recognized in school and their particular needs are not met (Smith and Tyler 2010).

Bates and Munday (2005) argue strongly that every school should have a recognized and enacted policy that delineates how special provision will be made for gifted and talented students, and how teaching and learning within regular classrooms will be differentiated to meet their needs. At the moment we are still a long way from achieving that goal. The writers of the UK report *Providing for gifted and talented pupils* observe that, 'the essential need continues to be that schools examine and improve what they do for their high-ability pupils through the teaching of the mainstream curriculum, as well as through additional activities' (OfSTED 2001: 3). To facilitate such improvement, Geake (2009) recommends that there should be a much stronger focus on principles and practices of gifted education in all pre-service and in-service teacher education courses. Again, we are still a long way from training all teachers in strategies for identifying and working effectively with gifted and talented students. Some countries have attempted to address this problem by introducing specified training 'standards' for the professional preparation of teachers for work in this area (e.g. Kitano *et al.* 2008). All schools in the UK are now expected to appoint a member of staff with appropriate expertise in the role of Leading Teacher for promoting and monitoring gifted and talented education, in much the same way that schools are required to appoint a Coordinator for Special Educational Needs (SENCo). This is certainly a move in the right direction.

Defining giftedness and talent

For many years the terms *gifted* and *talented* have been used interchangeably as if the two are synonymous. However, in recent years debate has centred on essential differences in meaning between gifts and talents. The official line taken in Britain is that the two terms are not synonymous. The Department for Children, Schools and Families, for example, reserves the term *gifted* to describe learners who have the ability to excel *academically* in one or more school subjects. *Talented*, on the other hand, describes learners who have the ability to excel in *practical performances* such as sport, leadership, artistic ability, or in an applied skill.

The Canadian psychologist Françoys Gagné (2009) also views giftedness and talent as separate concepts, but arrives at this conclusion from a different perspective. Under Gagné's 'Differentiated Model of Giftedness and Talent' (DMGT), 'gifts' are regarded as outstanding *innate abilities or aptitudes* with which certain individuals are born. These innate abilities tend to relate to competencies within the intellectual, creative, social, socio-affective, physical and sensorimotor domains; and it is within these same domains that specific talents may be developed. However, an individual's talent will only develop through sustained personal effort and commitment. Gagné (2009: 33) states: 'The talent development process [involves] the progressive transformation, through long learning and training process, of outstanding natural abilities into high level competencies (knowledge and skills) in a particular field.' Under Gagné's model, 'giftedness' is thus regarded as innate potential from which a talent may or may not develop fully. The extent to which a talent may develop is influenced by:

- *educational opportunities* – such as high-quality and appropriate instruction, experiential learning and abundant practice;

- *environmental factors* – such as family support, availability of mentors, resources in the school;
- *intrapersonal factors* – such as the student's temperament, ambition, resilience and motivation.

From Gagné's (2009) perspective it is easy to understand that gifted students do not necessarily reach their full potential and do not necessarily develop their talents unless educational opportunities are optimum, environmental factors are positive, and intrapersonal factors are conducive to talent development.

Gagné's (2009) model has influenced thinking about gifted students in several countries, particularly Australia, where several states have based their definitions of giftedness and their educational policies for gifted and talented students on Gagné's differentiation between innate ability and performance.

The official view adopted in the US differs somewhat from that taken in Britain. The US federal definition, as contained within the Elementary and Secondary Education Act, tends to blur the distinction between giftedness and talent. It states therein that gifted students are 'children or youth who give evidence of high achievement capability in areas such as intellectual, creative, artistic, or leadership capacity, or in specific academic fields, and who need services and activities not ordinarily provided by the school in order to develop those capabilities fully' (cited in Stevens 2009: 17). Traditionally it is was common in the US to use the all-embracing term *gifted* to describe all students of superior (or potentially superior) ability in *any* field of endeavour. The current discourse in the US focuses on 'talent development' as being a principal goal in education for all students (Taylor *et al.* 2009; Treffinger *et al.* 2008), and the view is that outstanding potential ability exists anywhere within the school population. It is the responsibility of schools to identify such students and to provide appropriate education.

What is clear from developments over the past two decades is that theory and practice in gifted education have moved towards an increasingly dynamic and broader concept of giftedness and talent, influenced to no small degree by Gardner's (1983) theory of *multiple intelligences*. He suggests that individuals possess a range of special aptitudes ('intelligences') to a greater or lesser extent. These areas of intelligence are not limited only to cognitive ability but can also be identified in other domains such as linguistic, logical-mathematical, spatial, bodily-kinesthetic, musical, interpersonal and intrapersonal. Gardner's work continues to influence educators' views on the nature of students' abilities and how best to nurture their talents.

Creativity

A concept closely associated with giftedness and talent is *creativity*. Some definitions of giftedness even suggest that creativity is an essential component in all forms of giftedness. Renzulli (2003), for example, proposes that giftedness results from a positive interaction among three human traits – above average ability, a high degree of task commitment (motivation, persistence and effort) and creativity. Others have suggested that creativity, while clearly essential in fields such as visual and performing arts, literature, and many others, is not a necessary ingredient in *all* forms of outstanding ability or talent. Groth-Marnat (2009) points out that some studies have even suggested a fairly low correlation between measures of creativity and intelligence. Often intellectually and academically gifted students are not necessarily highly creative in the artistic or performance sense, although they may be extremely creative in areas such as problem solving and generating new ideas.

While the exact relationship between giftedness and creativity remains a topic for debate, it has become popular to argue that every student has some creative ability and that this attribute must be recognized, valued and encouraged in schools (Gargiulo 2009). This notion parallels the recommendation of Treffinger *et al.* (2008) that education should be concerned with developing the talents of *all* our students. There is concern expressed sometimes that current education reforms, particularly those concerned with standards and accountability, have caused the typical school curriculum to become too narrow, focusing almost exclusively on academic subjects and measurable outcomes. It is feared that this narrowing of fields of study may result over time in fewer opportunities for students to engage in a range of non-academic activities that foster creativity.

Identifying gifted, talented and creative students

Some gifted, talented and creative students are identified first by their parents during the preschool years. In terms of intellectual giftedness, indicators of potential ability in the early years include advanced language skills (vocabulary and sentence structure), exceptional memory for information and experiences, the ability to concentrate for long periods of time on the things that interests them, a tendency to ask many questions and to be curious about many things, the ability to read before the age of 4, and the ability to learn new information and skills rapidly with very few repetitions. Some talented children begin to reveal their specific talents and creativity through their artwork, models or other products, and through the quality of their imaginative play activities. Of course, some children who exhibit precocity in these areas during early childhood later turn out to be of average ability, rather than outstanding; but a significant number of children identified early by their parents are found by later testing and performance in school to be genuinely gifted (Gargiulo 2009). Parents are therefore of great value in the front line for identifying potential giftedness and talent. Early identification may, in some cases, lead to early enrolment in school.

In school, informal observation by teachers is still the major strategy used for identification of gifted and talented students. Many observation checklists exist to help teachers and others focus on specific behaviours and characteristics that are considered typical indicators of potential giftedness (e.g. Sword 2003; Webb *et al.* 2007). However, there is little evidence to suggest that these lists are widely used in schools. Instead, teachers typically use their own knowledge of child development and of age-appropriate standards of work, together with classroom test results, to identify their 'most able' or 'academically advanced' students. These individuals are recognized fairly easily by the quality of the work they produce. They may also exhibit exceptional ability in the quality and originality of their thinking – as revealed, for example, in the questions they ask in class and the responses they give to teachers' questions. Applying such criteria, teachers usually have no problem recognizing most of the intellectually gifted students who are doing very well in school. Studies have tended to suggest, however, that teachers' observations, if used alone, are not particularly accurate in identifying gifted students who are *underachieving* in school. Improving teachers' expertise in the identification of underachieving students therefore remains a high priority in pre-service and in-service teacher education (Commonwealth of Australia Senate Committee 2001; OfSTED 2001).

Testing of students' cognitive ability (intelligence) remains one of the more commonly used procedures for identifying students with high intellectual potential. The results from such testing can often reveal not only those who are doing well in school but also those who may be underachieving relative to their intellectual potential, and who might have been overlooked by teachers' informal observations. However, intelligence testing is thought to discriminate against gifted children from backgrounds where English is not the first language and against those from culturally disadvantaged families (Cartledge *et al.* 2009).

To summarize, a comprehensive approach to identification of gifted students usually involves a combination of methods including informal observation by parents and teachers, evaluating students' work samples and test results, formal assessments and discussions among relevant staff or outside experts (Piiro and Heward 2009).

Underachievement

Gifted underachievers may not be recognized as such by their teachers because they produce classroom work and test results that are satisfactory, but not outstanding. Their high potential remains unrecognized so nothing is done to vary their programme or provide additional support and motivation.

There are many reasons why certain high-ability students may underachieve in school. Among the most common reasons are:

- *Boredom* – the curriculum is not sufficiently challenging to hold the student's interest and attention. The average pace at which topics are covered in the programme may be much too slow for students who are able to learn at a fast rate. There may be too much time devoted to repeating or practising skills they have already mastered. Even in early childhood education settings there is evidence that in several countries the daily curriculum often contains too little substance and is lacking in intellectual challenge for young children of high ability, thus getting them off to a poor start (OECD 2006).

- *Personal or emotional problems* – the student may be experiencing difficulties at home or within the peer group. These problems can severely undermine students' motivation and can impair their ability to concentrate and devote effort to study. Other problems may stem from the very fact that the student is gifted. Phillipson and Cheung (2007: 215) remark that, 'When gifted students, consciously or unconsciously, know that they are different from their peers, they are actually more likely to suffer from emotional and social problems.' Some students of high ability are overly obsessed with producing results that are always perfect and are constantly fearful of failure (Webb *et al*. 2007). Some highly gifted individuals are thus prone to experience stress, anxiety and depression and often require personal counselling and support (Sisk 2009; Wood 2010)
- *Peer pressure* – a few students of high ability may conceal their talents from their classmates in order not to stand out as 'different'. For example, they may be reluctant to hand in work of a high standard or to speak out in class and ask or answer questions, even though they have much to contribute. Both boys and girls may deliberately underachieve so as not to be thought different and rejected by peers for being 'too smart'. This is especially true during adolescence (Webb *et al*. 2007).
- *Poorly developed work and study habits* – some gifted students are not naturally inclined to work hard, to set themselves goals, to make a commitment and to devote the necessary effort. Simply because an individual has high potential does not in any way ensure that he or she is motivated to develop that potential through hard work. In addition, a few gifted students have never been taught effective study strategies, so they do not always tackle assignments efficiently or successfully. Montgomery (2009: 225) comments that, 'The latest research on curriculum and learning needs has shown that the gifted need to be helped to develop study and research skills, reasoning capabilities and creative problem-solving.'
- *Learning disability* – a few students who are very talented and/or of high intelligence may also have a specific disability in areas such as reading, spelling, writing or mathematics, or may have attention deficit hyperactivity disorder (Assouline *et al*. 2010; Martin *et al*. 2010). Dyslexic students, for example, may be intellectually gifted but have major problems with writing assignments and reading fluently with good comprehension. Often the gifted student with these difficulties is thought by the teacher to be a low achiever, and may even be placed in a low-ability group. It must also be remembered that some students with severe physical or sensory disabilities may be gifted and talented, but their disability impedes their ability to reveal their potential.
- *English as a second language* – students whose first language is not English can have difficulty in performing to the best of their ability in schools where English is the medium of instruction (Allen and Cowdery 2009). The problem relates not only to difficulties with understanding spoken and written language but also to a reluctance (sometimes related also to cultural differences)

to ask and answer teachers' questions in class or to request additional help and explanations.

- *Socio-economic disadvantage* – some potentially gifted students may underachieve for a variety of reasons related to social disadvantage. For example, poverty leading to lack of resources in the home, dysfunctional family, low expectations and lack of support for learning are all factors associated with underachievement in school (Reed *et al.* 2009). In Britain, the document *Gifted and Talented Education: Guidance on Addressing Underachievement* suggests that improving outcomes in attainment, aspirations, motivation and self-esteem for the most disadvantaged students must be one of the key aims for gifted education (DCSF 2009c).

Meeting the needs of gifted and talented students

Phillipson and Cheung (2007) suggest that there are two ways to maximize progress for gifted students and to minimize underachievement. First, there must be early and accurate identification of giftedness. Second, there must be implementation of effective organizational and teaching strategies to meet gifted students' intellectual and affective needs (Miller 2009). Identification procedures have been described above. Organizational options may include, for example, allowing young gifted children to begin their schooling before the normal age of entry, creating part-time or full-time special groups (or 'cluster groups') containing only high-ability students, enrolling gifted students in separate specialist schools or 'academies' that cater for students with exceptional gifts and talents, 'grade skipping' (moving a student up to a higher age group for all or some subjects), early transfer to secondary school or to university, organizing a range of activities, training opportunities, clubs and competitions after school hours, enrolling students in special part-time programmes for gifted and talented learners, and establishing mentoring systems. These options will be described later.

The current policy of inclusive education now operating in most developed countries has called into question some of the organizational options described above. In particular, strategies that use ability grouping within mainstream schools, or methods that segregate high-ability students into specialist schools or classes for the gifted, tend now to be frowned upon because they separate gifted students from their age peers. Instead, it is argued that gifted students should remain in the mainstream and receive a suitably differentiated programme, matched to their abilities and talents (Gargiulo 2009; Smith and Tyler 2010). An ideally differentiated programme for a gifted student would set appropriate goals, provide relevant learning activities geared to ability level, allow for a faster pace of learning, spend less time on curriculum basics and revision, capitalize on the student's special interests and strengths, and monitor the student's progress closely (DEECD 2009). The gifted student's programme would simply be one of several alternative programmes operating together in a mixed-ability classroom under the system known as 'tiered instruction' (Piiro and Heward 2009). Tiered instruction usually provides appropriate activities for different groups of students at three or more levels of difficulty. The potential benefits claimed for the differentiated approach are that students of high ability remain as members of a mixed-ability class and are able to interact socially and intellectually with other students of differing abilities (Kostelnik *et al.* 2009). The high-achieving students may also act indirectly as role models for other students in the mainstream class in terms of study habits and motivation. The potential disadvantage of differentiation (and it is a serious disadvantage) is that many teachers find it almost impossible to plan, implement and sustain many different levels and types of activities operating at the same time within the same classroom (Hertberg-Davis 2009). The larger the class size, the more difficult the task becomes. Research has shown that very little differentiation of instruction typically occurs for gifted students in the average classroom; instead, these students tend to be given 'more of the same' or 'busywork' if they finish assignments quickly. According to Taylor *et al.* (2009: 5), 'Many gifted students are under served because their teachers do not know how to plan for them.'

In contrast to those who advocate inclusion in the mainstream for students of high ability, most educators, community groups and researchers working in the field of gifted education believe that grouping by ability, for at least part of the time, is necessary if gifted students are to reach their full potential (Gross 2004; National Association for Gifted Children (US) 2003; Piiro and Heward 2009). It is argued that teachers can be much more effective in providing challenging and rewarding curricula for students of high ability, and the pace of instruction can be much faster, if these students are grouped together for teaching and learning purposes (Gargiulo 2009; Gilman, 2008; Kulik 2004). Ability grouping can also be beneficial because it allows students of high ability to work closely and productively with others of similar ability (Gyles *et al.* 2009). Inclusion in mixed-ability classes, on the other hand, creates many serious difficulties for teachers in terms of planning, implementing, designing resources and sustaining differentiated instruction. Delisle (2006: 52) goes so far as to comment that, 'This error of inclusion and its ragtag "solutions" of differentiation and cooperative learning have done enormous harm to the appropriate education of gifted children.'

But regardless of where students of high ability are taught (segregated setting, or in the mainstream) there are three main approaches to meeting their instructional needs – acceleration, extension and enrichment. These approaches are not mutually exclusive and can be used in combination.

Acceleration

Acceleration refers to any method adopted to cater for the gifted student's faster pace of learning and to avoid students having to repeat material they already know. Colangelo and Assouline (2009) describe acceleration as a powerful and effective strategy. Studies have shown unequivocally that acceleration can contribute greatly to gifted students' motivation and academic achievement; and in most cases has no negative effect on their social adjustment (Kulik 2004; Rimm and

Lovance 2004). Acceleration can, of course, be a feature within a gifted student's differentiated programme in the regular classroom, or it can be achieved through some of the practices described below.

- *Grade skipping* – the gifted student works with an older group or class for certain lessons; or the student may be permanently promoted to a higher age group. Early admission to secondary school or university represents another example of this model. This form of acceleration, while useful for some exceptionally advanced students, does not necessarily suit all gifted children. Promotion to higher grade is also a difficult system to sustain over several years of schooling, particularly if a student changes schools. It should also be noted that acceleration will not help a gifted student at all if the programme or curriculum into which the student is promoted is of poor quality.
- *Curriculum compacting* – the teacher modifies assignments and omits certain topics, exercises or tasks in a course of study so that a student can skip work already known and achieve the learning objectives in a shorter period of time (Peterson and Hittie 2010). Piiro and Heward (2009) point out that a teacher needs to have a substantial understanding of curriculum content to be able to adapt and condense courses or to devise alternative assignments effectively in this way. It is not an easy option.
- *Independent learning contracts* – an individualized work plan is designed for the student of high ability, allowing him or her to work fairly independently or with a mentor for specific periods each week (Clark 2008; Smith and Tyler 2010). Such programmes usually involve the provision of more advanced learning resources (texts, computer software, DVDs, Internet connection) and more challenging learning objectives (Pletka 2007).

Extension

The strategy known as extension enables high achievers to go much more deeply into an area of study. This can be achieved in part by compacting the curriculum to save time and then using that time to work on more challenging assignments. Such extension activities often rely heavily on students' independent learning skills and self-management, so these students need first to receive direct teaching in the application of particular researching or data processing skills to enable them to go beyond the objectives set for most members of the class. The extension approach also tends to involve students in more first-hand investigation and problem solving, with an emphasis on development of critical and creative thinking.

Enrichment

Enrichment is the term used to describe an approach that seeks to broaden the field of study to include more applications and concepts (but not necessarily more difficult concepts) and to encourage creative or exploratory activities related to the central theme. It can be thought of as an expansion of the standard curriculum for those who are ready and able to go beyond the basic objectives (Turnbull *et al.* 2010). Enrichment is often achieved through the use of classroom learning centres, computer-assisted learning, project work, resource-based learning, and individual or cooperative study contracts. Enrichment is also the main function of the extra-curricular activities, clubs, competitions and summer schools that many schools organize. These activities often serve the additional purpose of encouraging specific talent development in areas other than the academic.

Both extension and enrichment can also be facilitated through *mentoring systems*. Mentoring makes use of adults or older students with special expertise in a particular area as tutors or guides for gifted students with an interest in, and aptitude for, that field. The area of study may be academic or may be related, for example, to the arts, recreation, sports or technology. Often mentoring sessions take place as extra-curricular activities.

The reality is that many teachers working with mixed-ability classes do not find it a simple matter to incorporate opportunities for acceleration, extension and enrichment into their everyday mainstream programmes. These approaches demand above-average creativity, organizational and managerial skills on the part of the teacher. In the case of acceleration, the approach also requires the full backing and ongoing support of the whole school. In 2001, an OfSTED report in the UK stated that most attempts to meet the needs of gifted students in mainstream schools have consisted of ad hoc activities intended to enrich students' learning experiences, but often these activities are not well integrated and purposeful and may result in very few lasting benefits. Similarly, Taylor *et al.* (2009) indicate that often enrichment activities, if provided at all, are added on as an afterthought, prepared and delivered only if the teacher has time. Webb *et al.* (2007) suggest that some enrichment attempts lack any academic rigor and substance. These points are made here not to suggest that adopting a differentiated approach for students with gifts and talents is not worthwhile but to indicate that strategies for acceleration, extension and enrichment require very careful planning, conscientious implementation, close monitoring and the support of the whole school community.

No matter whether gifted and talented students are taught within the mainstream or in cluster groups, Gilman (2008) suggests that there is a need to include the following components:

- individualized planning;
- access to advanced materials;
- faster pace of instruction;
- opportunities to reason and think critically;
- encouragement of free expression of ideas and disagreements;
- direct teaching of essential study skills and research strategies.

The Department of Education and Early Childhood Development (Victoria) (DEECD 2009) advocates the use of many open-ended, challenging and extended tasks with intellectually gifted students, requiring them to engage in high-level thinking, analysing, evaluating, synthesizing and creating new ideas. Turnbull *et al.* (2010) recommend increasing the amount of investigative work, problem-solving, and creative or expressive opportunities within any topic studied. It is also important to promote independence in learning and to encourage curiosity, persistence and confidence to talk through and share ideas. Gifted students also need to engage in self-evaluation and goal setting.

Specific programmes and models

Over the years, many different programmes, models and curricula have been devised to serve the needs of gifted and talented students. Coleman (2005) reports that these programmes can be very effective if well designed, efficiently delivered and sustained over time. A few of these models are described here, with others listed in the online resources at the end of the chapter.

Enrichment Triad Model

The Enrichment Triad Model (ETM) was developed by Joseph Renzulli (1976) and has undergone several modifications over the years. The model focuses on presenting students with a variety of activities that enable them to explore a topic from different perspectives and at different levels of challenge. It moves students of high ability beyond the regular curriculum and opens up new areas of interest. All students first engage in a range of introductory activities (Type I enrichment) to become conversant with the topic and to recognize interesting issues worthy of further investigation. All students are then taught any necessary investigative and data processing skills required to explore and report some of these issues in greater depth and breadth (e.g. online searches, note-taking, summarizing, diagramming, tabulation) (Type II enrichment). Finally, students can focus on one or more of the available subtopics and study these in much greater depth through applications, problem solving and independent or collaborative research (Type III enrichment). While Type III activities are available to all students in the class, they mainly serve to stretch and challenge fully the students of high ability.

Schoolwide Enrichment Model

Renzulli is also responsible for devising the Schoolwide Enrichment Model (SEM) (Renzulli and Reis 1997). The major goal of SEM is to strengthen a school's overall provision for gifted students and others by infusing enriched learning experiences and higher learning standards into the general curriculum. This is regarded as preferable to setting up special and separate programmes for students of high ability. The teaching approaches and activities recommended in the model have chiefly come from research evidence on effective pedagogy in the gifted education field. SEM has three main goals: (i) to develop talents in all children; (ii) to provide a broad range of advanced-level enrichment experiences for all students;

and (iii) to provide suitably challenging follow-up and extension opportunities for students, based on their strengths and interests.

Parallel Curriculum Model

The Parallel Curriculum Model (PCM) evolved from earlier work on curriculum adaptation by educators such as Carol Tomlinson in the US. PCM is based on the premise that every learner is somewhere on a path towards gaining expertise in a particular subject area. The parallel curriculum sets out to develop further the existing abilities of all students and to extend the specific talents of students who perform at advanced levels.

PCM offers four curriculum parallels that incorporate the element of ascending intellectual demand. The four parallels comprise: (i) a *Core Curriculum* of key knowledge, concepts and skills related to the subject; (ii) *Connections*, helping students connect new content with prior knowledge in this and other subject areas, and apply skills across disciplines; (iii) *Practice*, to help students function effectively in a particular discipline area; and (iv) *Identity*, helping students identify with the subject more deeply by connecting it with their own lives, interests and aspirations. These four curricular components can be used singly or in combination to help teachers plan and implement units of work around a central theme. Teachers must first determine each student's current performance level and from this information develop intellectual challenges that will move him or her along a continuum towards expertise (Tomlinson *et al.* 2008).

Autonomous Learner Model

The Autonomous Learner Model (ALM) has the stated aim of giving students the content, process and product knowledge that enables them to take responsibility for implementing and evaluating their own learning (Betts 1985). The model focuses on gifted and talented students in Grades 1 to 12. ALM has flexibility in that it can be used with students in the regular classroom, in small group settings, or as an individual course. Among the basic principles of the model are emphases on self-esteem, student interests and broad-based content topics. ALM consists of five major dimensions:

- *Orientation* – understanding giftedness, group building activities, self/personal development.
- *Individual development* – inter/intra personal understanding, learning skills, use of technology, university/career awareness, organizational and productivity skills.
- *Enrichment* – courses, explorations, investigations, cultural activities, community service, excursions, camps.
- *Seminars* – small group presentations of futuristic, problematic, controversial, general interest or advanced knowledge topics.

- *In-depth study* – individual projects, group projects, mentorship's, presentations, assessment of self and others.

To some extent, independent study of this type matches the preference of some high-ability students to work alone; but it must be noted that not all gifted students exhibit this preference (French and Shore 2009; Gyles *et al.* 2009).

Project *EXCITE*

Project EXCITE in the US targets African American and Hispanic students with high potential in Grades 3 to 8 and focuses on mathematics and science. A range of supplementary experiences are provided over a period of six school years to improve students' motivation and heighten self-esteem. Additional training is also given in relevant study skills to enable deeper and more extensive studies. EXCITE is operated under the auspices of the Centre for Talent Development at the Northwestern University, Illinois (Reed *et al.* 2009).

Online resources

- A copy of the report *National Excellence: A Case for Developing America's Talent* can be located online at: www.ed.gov/pubs/DevTalent/toc.html (accessed 27 March 2010).
- *Guidelines for an academic acceleration policy* (2009) is available online from the Institute for Research and Policy on Acceleration, University of Iowa. www.accelerationinstitute.org/resources/policy_guidelines/Accelerati on%20Guidelines.pdf (accessed 27 March 2010).
- The Department for Education and Skills in the UK prepared a guide titled *Effective provision for gifted and talented children in primary education.* In addition to information on identification, assessment and school organization, practical advice is also given on teaching methods. Available online at: www. standards.dfes.gov.uk/giftedandtalented/downloads/pdf/provision_g_and_t_ primary.pdf (accessed 27 March 2010).
- Department for Children, Schools and Families (2009) *The National Challenge: Raising Standards, Supporting Schools. Gifted and Talented Pilot Programme Element 3: Guidance on pedagogy for gifted and talented education.* This document can be downloaded from: http://nationalstrategies.stand-ards.dcsf.gov.uk/node/197372 (accessed 27 March 2010).
- In the UK, the *Young Gifted and Talented Programme (YG&T)* is funded by the Department for Children, Schools and Families and provides services (including online resources) for students in the age range 4 to 19 years. http:// ygt.dcsf.gov.uk/Primary/DynamicPage.aspx?pageId=8 (accessed 27 March 2010).
- *Selected Entry Accelerated Learning (SEAL)* programme operates in a number of secondary schools on the state of Victoria, Australia. Core subjects

are presented in an accelerated mode and time is available for in-depth study in specific areas. Website: www.education.vic.gov.au/studentlearning/programs/gifted/seal/default.htm (accessed 27 March 2010).

- A clear description of the Enrichment Triad Model can be found on the New Zealand Ministry of Education website at: www.tki.org.nz/r/gifted/handbook/stage2/prog_triad_e.php (accessed 27 March 2010).
- The Schoolwide Enrichment Model is explained fully on the University of Connecticut Centre for Gifted Education and Talent Development website at: www.gifted.uconn.edu/sem/semexec.html (accessed 27 March 2010).
- The Parallel Curriculum Model is explained, with examples, in a paper by Purcell, Burns and Leppien (2002) 'The Parallel Curriculum Model: The whole story,' *Teaching for High Potential*, 4, 1: 1–4. Available online at: www.nagc.org/uploadedFiles/Articles/THP%20new%20header.pdf (accessed 27 March 2010).
- The Autonomous Learner Model, and other approaches, are described online at: www.det.wa.edu.au/curriculumsupport/giftedandtalented/detcms/navigation/provision/teaching-learning-models/autonomous-learner-model/?oid=com.arsdigita.cms.contenttypes.ArticleSection-id-4601094&tab=Main (accesssed 27 March 2010).
- Routledge has published a useful series *Meeting the Needs of Your Most Able Pupils*, each book covering different areas of the curriculum. Similarly, Prufrock in the US has also produced a series titled *Practical Strategies in Gifted Education*.

Further reading

Balchin, T., Hymer, B. and Matthews, D.J. (eds) (2009) *Routledge International Companion to Gifted Education*, London: Routledge.
Davis, G., Rimm, S. and Siegle, D. (2011) *Education of the Gifted and Talented* (6th edn), Boston: Merrill.
Goodhew, G. (2009) *Meeting the Needs of Gifted and Talented Students*, London: Network Continuum.
Horowitz, F.D., Subotnik, R.F. and Mathews, D.J. (2009) *The Development of Giftedness and Talent Across the Life Span*, Washington, DC: American Psychological Association.
Montgomery, D. (ed.) (2009) *Able, Gifted and Talented Underachievers*, Chichester: Wiley-Backwell.
Sternberg, R.J. and Williams, W.M. (2010) *Educational Psychology* (2nd edn), Upper Saddle River, NJ: Merrill.
Vialle, W. and Rogers, K.B. (2009) *Educating the Gifted Learner*, Terrigal, NSW: Barlow Publishing.

Chapter 6

Self-management and self-regulation

One of the common observations concerning many students with learning problems is that they have become passive. They show little confidence in their own ability to bring about improvement through their own efforts or initiative. In contrast to this, studies over many years have yielded data indicating that self-regulated students tend to do well in school; they are more confident, diligent and resourceful. One of the goals of education must therefore be to help all students achieve this level of self-efficacy by teaching them *how to learn* and how to regulate and monitor their own performance in the classroom.

Self-regulation and self-management are essential competencies that children need to develop if they are to become autonomous learners. In the case of students with intellectual disability, emotional disturbance or learning disability, the skills and strategies involved in self-management and self-regulation may need to be explicitly taught (Polloway *et al.* 2008). When these children acquire adequate self-management, it is much easier for them to be accommodated effectively in inclusive classrooms.

Definition of terms

The terms self-regulation and self-management are often used interchangeably in educational discourse, but in the field of psychology each has its own precise meaning.

- *Self-regulation* is the term commonly used in relation to an individual's ability to monitor his or her own approach to learning tasks and to modify thinking processes or strategies as necessary (Mason *et al.* 2009). The concept also includes an ability to set personal goals and apply appropriate skills to achieve those goals (Abar and Loken 2010). Self-regulation in learning involves *metacognition* – the ability to monitor and control one's own cognitive processes such as attention, strategy application, rehearsal, recall, comprehension and self-correction. Self-regulation also includes the ability to manage one's emotions and to control anger or frustration (Levin and Nolan 2010). Self-regulation shares much in common with what some psychologists refer to as 'self-determination' (McGuire 2010), which in turn is related to feelings of 'self-efficacy'. Self-regulation in the context of classroom learning is discussed more fully later in the chapter.

• *Self-management* refers to an individual's ability to function independently in any given learning environment without the need for constant supervision, prompting or direction from others. In the classroom, for example, it relates to such behaviours as knowing how to organize one's materials, knowing what to do when work is completed, recognizing when to seek help from the teacher or a peer, understanding how to check one's own work for careless errors, how to maintain attention to task, how to observe the well-established routines such as ordering lunch, having sports equipment or books ready for a specific lesson, knowing when a change of lesson or room is to occur and so on.

Self-management in children

The specific self-management skills required by a child in school will tend to differ slightly from classroom to classroom according to a particular teacher's management style, routines and expectations, and according to the nature of the curriculum. For example, in some classrooms a premium is placed upon passive listening, note-taking and sustained on-task behaviour, while in other classrooms initiative, group-working skills and cooperation with others are essential prerequisites for success. The self-management skills required in an informal classroom setting tend to be very different from those needed in a more formal or highly structured setting. Knowing how to respond to the demands and constraints of different lessons or settings is an important aspect of a student's growth towards independence (Mercer and Pullen 2009).

The type of classroom learning environment created by the teacher, and the teacher's instructional approach, can both markedly influence the development of self-management and independence in children. Some teachers and tutors seem to operate with students in ways that foster their *dependence* rather than encourage their independence. For example, they may offer too much help and guidance for children with special needs in an attempt to prevent possible difficulties and failures. They may virtually spoon-feed the children using individualized support programmes that offer very few challenges and call for no initiative on the child's part. Too much of this support restricts the opportunities for a child to become autonomous.

The possession of self-management skills by a child with a disability or a learning difficulty seems to be one of the most important factors contributing to the successful inclusion in a regular classroom (Salend 2007). Some students, for example those with intellectual disability or with social, emotional or psychological disorders, frequently exhibit very poor self-management (Wehmeyer and Field 2007). Even students with milder forms of disability or learning difficulty often display ineffective self-management and need positive help to become more autonomous learners (Olson *et al.* 2008). It is essential, therefore, that all students with special needs, whether placed in special settings or in the regular classroom, be helped to develop adequate levels of independence in their work habits, self-control and readiness for learning. One of the major goals of intervention with such students is to increase their independence by improving their self-management.

Teaching self-management

When students are able to manage routines in the classroom and look after their own needs during a lesson, the teacher is able to devote much more time to teaching rather than managing the group. Evidence is accumulating to support the view that specific training in self-management and self-regulation can be effective in promoting students' independence. Intervention studies involving self-management and strategy training have suggested that there are very strong positive effects (e.g. Mooney *et al.* 2005).

To teach self-management, first teachers must recognize that such teaching is important and necessary. Second, teachers need to consider precisely which skills or behaviours are required in order to function independently in their particular classrooms – for example, staying on task without close supervision, self-monitoring, using resource materials appropriately, or seeking help from a peer. Third, students' current strengths and weaknesses in these skills must be assessed. Finally, any skills that are lacking must be explicitly taught using direct methods and corrective feedback.

Teaching self-management skills as part of an inclusive programme should have a high priority, particularly with young children and those with developmental delay. For students with special needs, a five-step procedure can be used to teach self-management.

*   *Explanation* – discuss with the student why a specific self-managing behaviour is important. Help the student recognize when other students are exhibiting the target behaviour.
*   *Demonstration* – the teacher or a peer models the behaviour.
*   *Role play* – the student practises the behaviour, with descriptive feedback.
*   *Cueing* – prompt the student when necessary to carry out the behaviour in the classroom.
*   *Maintenance* – praise examples of the student displaying the behaviour without prompting. Check at regular intervals to ensure that the student has maintained the behaviour over time.

It is important to teach the particular skills or behaviours to the point where the student no longer needs to be reminded or prompted. When teachers are constantly reminding the students of what to do, they are maintaining the students' dependence. Teachers may need to remind children with special needs rather more frequently than other students, and may have to reward them more frequently for their correct responses, but the long-term aim is to help these children function independently.

Locus of control

Self-management links quite closely with the personality construct known as *locus of control*. To understand locus of control one needs to recognize that individuals attribute what happens to them in a particular situation either to internal factors (e.g. their own ability, efforts, decisions or actions) or to external factors (e.g. luck, chance, things outside their control). Children with an internal locus of control recognize that they can influence events by their own actions and believe that they do to some extent control their own destiny. At classroom level, an example of internality might be when students recognize that if they concentrate on the task and work carefully, they get much better results. Appreciating the fact that outcomes are under one's personal control is a key component of one's feelings of 'self-efficacy' and a strong defence against learned-helplessness (Pajares and Urdan 2006).

Internalization of locus of control usually increases steadily with age if a child experiences normal success and reinforcement from his or her efforts in school and in daily life outside school. However, it has been found that many children with learning problems and with negative school experiences remain markedly external in their locus of control in relation to school learning, believing that their efforts have little impact on their progress and that they lack ability (Bender 2007). Young children enter school with highly positive views of their own capabilities, but this confidence rapidly erodes if they experience too many early failures and frustrations.

The child who remains largely external in locus of control is likely to be the child who fails to assume normal self-management in class and is prepared to be managed or controlled by powerful others such as the teacher, parent, teacher's aide or more confident peers. There exists a vicious circle wherein the child feels inadequate, is not prepared to take a risk, seems to require support, gets it, and develops even more dependence upon others. The teacher's task is one of breaking into this circle and causing the child to recognize the extent to which he or she has control over events and can influence outcomes. It is natural for a teacher, tutor or aide to wish to help and support a child with special needs, but it should not be done to the extent that all challenge and possibility of failure are eliminated. Failure must be possible and children must be helped to see the causal relationship between their own efforts and the outcomes. Children will become more internal in their locus of control, and much more involved in learning tasks, when they recognize that effort and persistence can overcome failure.

It is important that teachers and parents publicly acknowledge and praise children's positive efforts, rather than emphasizing lack of effort or difficulties. Teachers' use of praise has been well researched. Praise seems particularly important for low-ability, anxious, dependent students, provided that it is genuine and deserved, and that the praiseworthy aspects of the performance are specified. A child should know precisely why he or she is being praised if appropriate connections are to be made in the child's mind between effort and outcome. Trivial or redundant praise is very quickly detected by children and serves no useful purpose. *Descriptive* praise, however, can be extremely helpful; for example: 'Good work, David! You used your own words instead of simply copying from the reference book.'

In general, teachers' use of descriptive praise has a strong positive influence on children's beliefs about their own ability and the importance of effort. When praise is perceived by children to be genuine and credible, it appears to enhance their motivation and feelings of control.

Attribution retraining

A markedly external locus of control usually has a negative impact upon a student's willingness to persist in the face of a difficult task. It is easier for the child to give up and develop avoidance strategies rather than persist if the expectation of failure is high. In the intervention approach known as *attribution retraining* (McInerney and McInerney 2009), students are taught to appraise carefully the results of their own efforts when a task is completed. They are encouraged to verbalize their conclusions aloud: 'I did that well because I took my time and read the question twice', 'I listened carefully and I asked myself questions'. The main purpose in getting students to verbalize such attribution statements is to change their perception of the cause of their successes or failures in schoolwork. Verbalizing helps children focus their attention on the real relationship between their efforts and the observed outcomes. In most cases, attribution retraining seems to have maximum value when it is combined with the direct teaching of effective cognitive strategies necessary for accomplishing particular tasks.

Teaching cognitive strategies

Some teachers exacerbate students' learning problems by failing to demonstrate the most effective ways of approaching each new task. Often, appropriate skills and strategies needed for approaching a task are not taught explicitly and may therefore remain obscure to many students. Teachers should always provide a clear model of how to tackle new learning tasks efficiently to maximize the chances of early success. A teacher who says, 'Watch and listen. This is how I do it – and this is what I say to myself as I do it', is providing the learner with a secure starting point. The teacher who simply says, 'Here is the task. Get on with it', is often providing an invitation to failure and frustration.

It was noted in Chapter 1 that many students with general or specific learning difficulties appear to lack appropriate skills and strategies for tackling schoolwork. They do not seem to understand that these tasks can be carried out effectively if approached with a suitable plan of action in mind. For example, attempting to solve a routine word problem in mathematics usually requires careful reading of the problem, identification of what one is required to find out, recognition of the relevant data to use, selection of the appropriate process, completion of the calculation and a final checking of the reasonableness of the answer. This approach to solving the mathematical problem involves application of a *strategy* (an overall plan of action) and utilization of *procedural knowledge* (knowing how to carry out the steps in a specific calculation).

Cognitive strategies are mental plans that help students complete learning tasks, solve problems and self-regulate (University of Kansas 2010; Wolsey and Fisher 2009). A typical strategy includes both cognitive (thinking) and behavioural (action) elements that guide and monitor the individual's engagement in the task. Strategy training involves teaching students to apply effective step-by-step procedures and self-monitoring when approaching and completing a particular task or problem (Waters and Schneider 2010). The typical teaching procedure for establishing effective strategies usually follows this sequence:

*   *Modelling* – the teacher performs the task or carries out the new process while thinking aloud. This involves self-questioning, giving self-directions, making overt decisions and evaluating the results.
*   *Overt external guidance* – the students copy the teacher's model and complete a similar task, with the teacher still providing verbal directions and exercising some control.
*   *Overt self-guidance* – the students repeat the performance while using self-talk.
*   *Covert self-instruction* – the students perform several similar tasks while guiding their responses and decisions using inner speech.

Typical self-questions, statements and directions a student might use when attempting to solve a problem in mathematics would include: *What do I have to do? Where do I start? I will have to think carefully about this. I must look at only one problem at a time. Don't rush. OK, I need to multiply these two numbers and then subtract the answer from 100. That's good. I know that answer is correct. I'll need to come back and check this part. Does this make sense? I think I made a mistake here, but I can come back and work it again. I can correct it.* These self-monitoring statements cover problem definition, focusing attention, planning, checking, self-reinforcement, self-appraisal, error detection and self-correction. They are applicable across a fairly wide range of academic tasks. Sometimes the steps involved in tackling a specific task are printed on a cue card displayed on the students' desks while the lesson is in progress. The students may also need to be taught a method for remembering the steps for implementation (e.g. a mnemonic). Examples of mnemonics are provided later in the chapters on literacy and numeracy.

Maintenance and generalization

Maintenance and generalization of strategy training have always been problematic, particularly for students with learning difficulties. Students may learn successfully how to apply a given strategy to a specific task but not recognize how the same approach could be used more widely in other contexts. To help students overcome this problem, teachers might:

- provide strategy training that makes use of a variety of different authentic tasks from across the curriculum;
- discuss different situations in which a particular strategy could be applied;
- involve students as much as possible in creating or adapting strategies to the demands of particular tasks.

More effective use of strategies within the curriculum can be fostered by direct teaching, abundant practice, discussions about the value of strategies, and how and when to apply them. Cooperative learning activities, peer tutoring, sharing views on how problems can be solved or tasks accomplished, can also help to foster, generalize and maintain strategy use.

It is important to ensure that the specific strategies taught to students are actually needed in the daily curriculum to facilitate their immediate application. Students will find most relevance in strategies they can use to complete classroom assignments and homework more successfully. Strategies should be taught that focus particularly on tasks the students usually find too difficult. Students with learning problems tend to take very much longer than other students to accept and adopt new learning strategies, so the teaching process needs to be sustained until independent use is finally established.

Metacognition

Effective strategy training incorporates elements of self-regulation training together with cognitive and metacognitive instruction (Waters and Schneider 2010). It is essential that students not only complete tasks independently but also monitor, reflect upon and control their own performance. Metacognitive instruction focuses on tactics that require a learner to monitor the appropriateness of his or her thoughts and responses, and to weigh up whether or not a particular strategy needs to be applied in full, in part, or not at all in a given situation. This self-regulation of thought and action includes mental activities such as pre-planning, monitoring, regulating, evaluating, self-correcting or modifying a response. It is considered that metacognition helps a learner recognize that he or she is either doing well or is having difficulty understanding the task. A learner who is monitoring his or her own on-going performance will detect the need to pause, double-check, perhaps begin again before moving on, weigh up possible alternatives, or seek outside help. It is essential that teachers encourage students to think about their own thinking and the quality of their own performance in a variety of learning situations.

Metacognition involves inner verbal self-instruction and self-questioning (self-talk) in order to focus, reflect, control or review. The scaffolding that teachers provide should therefore include modelling this self-talk to help students develop their own inner language. Effective use of self-talk is vital for better self-regulation in both learning and classroom behaviour (see *cognitive behaviour modification* below).

Reading comprehension, written expression and mathematics problem solving are examples of academic areas that can be improved by cognitive and metacognitive strategy training (Brissiaud and Sander 2010; Coyne *et al.* 2009). Students can be taught how to approach printed information and mathematical problems strategically, and then given abundant opportunities to practise the application of the strategies on a wide variety of texts, tasks and problems. It is said that, 'Strategy instruction is the only instructional method that has been shown through research to enable students with disabilities and other at-risk students to meet the complex learning demands of secondary and post-secondary education. Through strategy instruction, they become able to find, study, and express information independently' (University of Kansas 2010). Several examples of cognitive strategies are provided in later chapters.

The Centre for Research on Learning at the University of Kansas (2010) has explored most facets of strategy training and has produced helpful information for teachers. The online resources listed at the end of this chapter include reference to the Kansas Strategic Instruction Model (SIM).

Cognitive behaviour modification

Cognitive behaviour modification (CBM) is closely related to metacognitive strategy training. It involves procedures to help students gain better independent control over their own behaviour by using inner self-talk to guide their thoughts and actions. CBM is different from other forms of behaviour management in that the students themselves, rather than teachers or powerful others are the agents for change.

Typically, students with a behaviour problem in class are taught to memorize and use a mental 'script' that enables them to monitor their behaviour in a particular situation and then make appropriate decisions. An example might be a student who has great difficulty in staying on task and who often gets out of her seat to wander around during the lesson. A small timing device with a beeper might be placed on her desk and she would be taught to monitor her own on-task behaviour every time the beeper sounds. If she is on task, she praises herself: 'Good! I am working. I am finishing the task. I must keep working. I have remained in my seat.' At the end of each lesson the teacher may reward the student in some way if she has remained seated and on task.

Training in self-control techniques of this type is considered to be particularly useful for improving the self-management of students with mild intellectual disability, Asperger syndrome, and attention deficit hyperactivity disorder (ADHD). The application of cognitive behaviour modification in cases of behaviour disorder is discussed in the next chapter.

Online resources

- University of Kansas (2010) provides information on learning strategies. Available online from the Centre for Research on Learning at: www.ku-crl. org/sim/strategies.shtml (accessed 28 March 2010).
- A clear description of metacognition can be found at North Central Regional Education Laboratory at: www.ncrel.org/sdrs/areas/issues/students/learning/lr1metn.htm> (accessed 28 March 2010).
- Locus of control is explained fully at: http://wilderdom.com/psychology/loc/LocusOfControlWhatIs.html (accessed 28 March 2010).
- Kid Source Online provides more information on attribution retraining with students with learning difficulties at: www.kidsource.com/kidsource/content5/fail.syndrome.ed.html (accessed 28 March 2010).

Further reading

Dawson, P. and Guare, R. (2010) *Executive Skills in Children and Adolescents* (2nd edn), New York: Guilford Press.

Meltzer, L. (2010) *Promoting Executive Functioning in the Classroom*, New York: Guilford Press.

Reid, R. and Lienemann, T. (2006) *Strategy Training for Students with Learning Disabilities*, New York: Guilford Press.

Waters, H.S. and Schneider, W. (eds) (2010) *Metacognition, Strategy Use and Instruction*, New York: Guilford Press.

Wolsey, T.D. and Fisher, D. (2010) *Learning to Predict and Predicting to Learn: Cognitive Strategies and Instructional Routines*, Boston: Pearson-Allyn and Bacon.

Chapter 7

Managing classroom behaviour

Teachers in primary and secondary schools place great importance on students' ability to control their own behaviour and to work cooperatively with others (Larrivee 2009). Many teachers report that one of their main concerns in the regular classroom is the child who disrupts lessons, seeks too much attention from teacher or peers, and who fails to cooperate when attempts are made to provide extra help (Levin and Nolan 2010). The teachers feel that although they know what the child needs in terms of basic instruction and support, it proves impossible to deliver appropriate teaching because the child is unreceptive. Turnbull *et al.* (2010) suggest that some 9 per cent of school-age students present with intense behaviour problems, while another 15 per cent are at risk for developing such problems unless taught effective ways of self-control. In recent official reports, it has been highlighted that, 'The quality of learning, teaching and behaviour in school are inseparable issues, and the responsibility of all staff' (Steer 2009: 3).

Teachers with emotionally disturbed or behaviourally disordered children in their classes need the personal and professional support of their colleagues. In particular they need acknowledgement and understanding from colleagues that the student's behaviour is not due to their own inability to exercise effective classroom control. Unless a school adopts a collaborative approach to the management of difficult and disruptive behaviour, certain problems tend to arise. These problems include:

- individual teachers feeling that they are isolated and unsupported by their colleagues;
- teachers feeling increasingly stressed by the daily conflict with some students;
- the problem becoming worse over time.

This chapter presents an overview of some of the approaches for preventing or reducing behaviour problems in school through effective use of proactive strategies.

Preventing behaviour problems

Shepherd (2010: 134) has written, 'Behaviour management provides students with a safe and secure environment in which learning can take place, teaches students the necessity of having rules and consequences, and helps students develop self-discipline and self-control.' The underlying principle of behaviour management practices in schools today is 'being positive rather than punative' (Wheeler and Richey 2010: 108). Teachers are encouraged now, under a positive and preventive approach, to catch students being good and to praise them for appropriate behaviour, rather than waiting to reacting to bad behaviour (Yell *et al.* 2009).

It is generally agreed that the first step in preventing problem behaviour at the classroom level is to have a well organized, predictable and supportive learning environment, an interesting curriculum, effective teaching methods, and well-established routines (Lindberg *et al.* 2009; Steer 2009; Wheeler and Richey 2010). The next step, at whole-school level, is to have a clear policy on behaviour management issues. The policy will describe ways in which individual teachers and all school staff should approach general matters of discipline and classroom control. The policy may also make specific reference to the management of students with significant emotional or behavioural disorders, and to students with disabilities. A clear school policy is the basis for consistent implementation and practice by all staff (Steer 2009).

A school-level policy document must be much more than a set of rules and consequences. A good policy will make clear to students, teachers, parents and administrators that schools should be safe, friendly and supportive environments in which to work. In many ways, a school policy on student behaviour should be seen as dealing more with matters of welfare, safety and social harmony rather than procedures for punishment and enforcing discipline. The heart of any behaviour management policy should be the stated aim of teaching all students responsible and effective ways of managing their own behaviour and making appropriate choices (Larrivee 2009). A good policy in action will protect not only teachers' rights to teach and students' rights to feel safe and to learn, but will also help students recognize the personal and group benefits that self-control and responsible behaviour can bring.

In the case of a child with serious behaviour problems, it is essential to involve the child's parents fully in the implementation of any behaviour change programme (Hue and Li 2008). The parents and school staff should together agree on the goals and strategies for such intervention, and be consistent in applying the same management strategies in school and at home (Wheeler and Richey 2010).

Positive Behaviour Support

The typical approach to behaviour problems in schools has always tended to be reactive and aversive rather than preventive. The Positive Behaviour Support (PBS) model attempts instead to be proactive and reduce the likelihood that serious problems will arise (Chitiyo and Wheeler 2009; Shepherd 2010). For example, a student who frequently gets into fights with other students while waiting for the school bus to arrive at the end of each day is given an important job to do in the classroom instead of waiting in line. When the bus arrives, he quickly joins the other students.

PBS intervention strategies include:

*   modifying or eliminating classroom conditions that increase the probability of challenging behaviour arising (for example, reducing group size, arranging seating differently, changing teaching method, eliminating interruptions and distractions);
*   teaching students self-control strategies;
*   using positive reinforcement, rather than reprimands;
*   providing active and supportive supervision;
*   discussing behaviour codes and personal rights and responsibilities with students;
*   explicitly teaching students the behaviours they need to display.

To facilitate this pro-active approach at the whole-school level, it is recommended that *behaviour support teams* of teachers and assistants in the school should be established (Lane *et al.* 2009). These teams have the role of implementing behaviour policy, encouraging positive approaches to classroom management, helping to solve specific problems related to behaviour and learning, and assisting with staff development. In the US this approach is referred to as Schoolwide Positive Behaviour Support (SWPBS) (Lane *et al.* 2009; Turnbull *et al.* 2010).

Behaviour support teams also operate at regional level, serving a number of different schools. For example, in the UK, multi-agency *Behaviour and Education Support Teams* (BESTs) have been established in many areas to work closely with schools and families to address the needs of children and young people with emotional, behavioural and school attendance problems. Schools drawing on the services of BESTs include those with high proportions of students with, or at risk of developing, behavioural problems and poor attendance. Services offered to schools by BESTs range from work with individual students, family therapy, case conferences, parent support groups and whole-school behaviour improvement interventions. Similar support teams now operate in most states in Australia and the US.

Two recent initiatives targeting behaviour and truancy in Britain include the *Partnership to Improve Behaviour and Tackle Persistent Absence* and *Behaviour Challenge*. The latter is an initiative to help all schools – particularly those with poor standards of behaviour – make necessary improvements. This initiative stemmed from recommendations in the report *Learning Behaviour: Lessons Learned* (Steer 2009). This document reported findings from a comprehensive review of behaviour standards and practices in schools in the UK (see online resources). Also relevant for practical purposes in creating a safe and supportive school environment is the initiative called *Social and Emotional Aspects of Learning (SEAL)*. *SEAL* provides valuable curriculum resources and deals with many relevant topics such as bullying and conflict resolution.

Classroom behaviour

While it is true that some students exhibit behaviour problems in school that are a reflection of stresses or difficulties outside school, it is also evident that disruptive behaviour can result from factors within the learning environment. For example, an unsuitable curriculum or inappropriate teaching methods quickly lead to poor behaviour because students who are bored or frustrated may well become troublesome (Swainston 2007). In addition, research has shown that class size, grouping, and seating arrangements are factors influencing behaviour.

One of the factors adding to a student's problems in secondary school is the frequent change of teachers for different subjects. Within the course of one day a student may encounter quite different and inconsistent management styles, ranging from authoritarian to permissive. This lack of consistency can have an unsettling effect on students who have emotional or behavioural difficulties. When cases of disruptive or challenging behaviour are reported, it is important to consult with other teachers to discover whether the student also has a problem when in their classes. All teachers who have contact with the student will need to get together to agree upon a consistent approach to be used when dealing with the behaviour. There has to be recognition at whole-school level that behaviour problems are best dealt with from a shared perspective and tackled with a team approach.

Occasionally of course it is necessary to seek outside expert advice when a child's behaviour does not respond to standard forms of effective management; but in many cases behaviour can be modified successfully within the school setting. A sound starting point is the establishment of positive classroom rules (Yell *et al.* 2009), building upon sound principles as set out in the school policy.

Classroom rules

Classroom rules are essential for the smooth running of any lesson and should be negotiated by the children and teacher early in the school year. Students should appreciate why rules are necessary, and must agree on appropriate consequences if a rule is broken. For example, the first time a rule is broken the teacher will give a warning in the form of a rule reminder. The second time a student violates the rule he or she may be given 'time out' for five minutes.

Rules should be clear, consistent, expressed in positive terms (what the students *will do*, rather than *must not do*), few in number and displayed where all students can see them. Basically, rules should be based on personal rights and responsibilities, and on respecting the rights of others. While the actual rights and the rules that protect them are important, the process by which they are developed is just as important. Students should feel ownership of rules through contributing to their formulation. Rules might include matters related to noise level during lessons, movement within the classroom, seeking assistance, making your opinions heard, safety, personal property, sharing of equipment and respect for the ideas of others.

Classroom-based research on the management style of teachers has indicated that the most effective teachers establish rules and procedures as a top priority at the beginning of the year. They discuss and create the rules with the students and apply them systematically and fairly. These teachers are also more vigilant in the classroom, use more eye contact, are more proactive to prevent behaviour problems arising, set appropriate and achievable tasks for students to attempt, avoid 'dead spots' in lessons, keep track of student progress, check work regularly and provide feedback to the whole class and to individuals.

Classroom procedures

Swainston (2007) suggests that all teachers should develop their own *discipline plan* to enable them to know in advance what to do when classroom behaviour is disruptive. The plan gives a teacher confidence when the pressure is on. Corrective actions a teacher might decide to use include:

- tactical ignoring of the student and the behaviour (for low-level disruptions);
- simple directions ('Ann, get back to work please');
- positive reinforcement ('Good, Ann');
- question and feedback ('What are you doing, Mark? OK, I'll come and help you');
- rule reminders ('David, you know our rule about noise. Please work quietly');
- simple choices ('Excuse me, Joanne. You can either work quietly with Susan, or I will have to move you to a different seat – OK?');
- isolation from peers (take the student aside and discuss the problem, then place him or her in a quiet area to do the work);
- removal from class (time out under supervision in a different room).

Teachers may also use strategies such as deflection and diffusion to take the heat out of a potential confrontation. Teacher: 'Sally, I can see you're upset. Cool off now and we'll talk about it later; but I want you to start work please.' The judicious use of humour can also help to defuse a situation without putting the student down. Sometimes it is appropriate to ask senior students to write a self-reflection about an incident of inappropriate behaviour in which they have been involved. They must say what they did, what they should have done and what they are going to do to remedy the situation. This reflection might then become the basis of a discussion with the teacher or school counsellor, and could be used as a starting point from which to formulate a plan of action for behaviour change.

One approach that never works is to lecture students endlessly about their perceived misdemeanors. Swainston (2007: 32) remarks:

> Young people are just like adults. If they think they are being told something obvious, by someone who is using a mountain of words to explain it, they will feel they are being spoken to in a condescending way. Less is more in terms of giving guidance to students.

Identifying the problem

According to Levin and Nolan (2010) a discipline problem exists whenever an incident interrupts the teaching process, interferes with the rights of others to learn and results in lost instructional time. Children who are constantly seeking attention, interrupting the flow of a lesson and distracting other children are very troubling to teachers. Naturally, teachers feel professionally threatened by children who constantly challenge their discipline (Etscheidt and Clopton 2008). The feeling of threat can cause the situation to get out of hand, and a teacher can get trapped into confrontations with a child rather than looking for possible solutions that will provide responsible choices and save face for the child and the teacher.

All too often teachers react overtly to undesirable behaviour, thus reinforcing it. Many behaviour problems in the classroom, particularly disruptive and attention-seeking behaviours, are rewarded by the adult's constant reaction to them. For example, the teacher who spends a lot of time reprimanding children is in fact giving them a lot of individual attention at a time when they are behaving in a deviant manner. This amounts to a misapplication of social reinforcement, and the teacher unintentionally encourages what he or she is trying to prevent. Some control techniques used by teachers (e.g. public rebuke) can have the effect of strengthening a child's tough image and status in the peer group.

If a teacher has a student who often displays inappropriate behaviour in the classroom, it is useful to analyse possible reasons for this behaviour. The following questions may be helpful when teachers attempt to analyse a case of disruptive behaviour:

- How frequently is the behaviour occurring?
- In which lesson is the behaviour less frequent (e.g. the more highly structured sessions, or the freer activities)?
- At what time of day does the behaviour tend to occur (a.m. or p.m.)?
- How is the class organized at the time (groups, individual assignments, etc.)?
- What am I (the teacher) doing at the time?
- How is the child occupied at the time?
- What is my immediate response to the behaviour?
- What is the child's initial reaction to my response?
- How do other children respond to the situation?

- What strategies have I used in the past to deal successfully with a similar problem?

The analysis deals with issues that are observable in the classroom. Behaviour analysis does not need to examine the child's past history or search for deep-seated psychological problems as causal explanations for the child's behaviour.

A simple plan for setting up a behaviour-change intervention might follow this sequence (Etscheidt and Clopton 2008):

- identify precisely the target behaviour to be changed;
- observe and record the current frequency and duration of this behaviour;
- set attainable objectives, involving the student in this process if possible;
- select teaching procedures such as modelling, prompting, role play;
- identify potential reinforcers by observing what this student finds rewarding;
- have the child rehearse the target behaviour;
- implement and monitor the programme, providing reinforcement and feedback to the child;
- ensure the new behaviour is maintained over time, and help the child generalize the behaviour to different settings and contexts.

It should be understood that changing a student's behaviour is often difficult. Sometimes the behaviour we regard as inappropriate has proved to be quite effective for the child in attaining certain personal goals. It has been practised frequently and has become very well established. In order for a positive behaviour change to occur, the child must first *desire* to change. The responsibility of the teacher is then to help the child understand exactly *how* to bring about and maintain the change.

Lane *et al.* (2009) suggest that there are four key elements to a behaviour change programme in school:

- any new behaviour to be established should be recognized as valuable by the student;
- methods to be used to eliminate an undesirable behaviour and teach a new behaviour should be evidence-based (i.e. of proven efficacy);
- close monitoring of progress towards the goal is essential;
- administrative processes and structures existing within the school should be such that behaviour change methods can be implemented consistently by all personnel involved and across all contexts.

Behaviour modification

One approach that is commonly used to bring about change is referred to as *behaviour modification*. It is based on principles of applied behaviour analysis

(ABA) (Alberto and Troutman 2009; Christian 2008). In this approach three assumptions are made:

- all behaviour is learned;
- behaviour can be changed by altering its consequences;
- factors in the environment (in this case the classroom) can be engineered to reward and maintain specific behaviours.

Using ABA, problematic behaviour is observed and analysed to identify factors that are causing and maintaining the behaviour. A programme is devised to reshape this behaviour into something more acceptable through a consistent system of rewards (reinforcement), ignoring, or punishment.

In cases of very persistent negative behaviour, such as aggression or severe disruption, positive reinforcement procedures alone may not be sufficient to bring about change. In such cases it may be necessary to introduce negative consequences and reductive procedures, such as loss of privileges, loss of points, or time out. Attention must also be given to improving the student's own self-monitoring and decision-making in order to increase his or her self-control over the problem behaviour.

Criticism is sometimes levelled at behaviour modification approaches on the basis that the control is exercised by powerful others from outside the individual. It is suggested that the manipulation of the individual's behaviour is somehow out of keeping with humanistic views on the value of interpersonal relationships, the social nature of learning and the need for personal autonomy. However, the very precise planning and management of a behaviour modification programme requires careful observation of how the child, the teacher and other children are interacting with one another and influencing each other's behaviour. Far from being impersonal, the techniques used to bring about and maintain change are usually highly interpersonal.

Regardless of criticisms that have been made, the behavioural approach has proved its efficacy in an impressive number of research studies over a long period of time; there can be no doubting the power of behaviour modification techniques in changing students' behaviour and enhancing learning (Christian 2008). In particular, ABA techniques are of great practical value to parents, carers and teachers working with students who have severe disabilities, autism, emotional disorders and challenging behaviour.

Strategies for reducing disruptive behaviour

Levin and Nolan (2010) define disruptive behaviour as the upsetting of the orderly conduct of teaching. Disruptions often prevent a teacher from achieving the objectives for a particular lesson and may also impair the quality of personal and social interaction within the group. Frequent disruptions have a ripple effect and can cause major reduction in the overall quality of learning and teaching occurring in that classroom, as well as destroying a positive classroom atmosphere. Teachers can lose almost half of their teaching time in some classrooms due to students' disruptive behaviour.

Sometimes simple changes such as modifying the seating arrangements, restructuring the working groups, reducing noise level and monitoring more closely the work in progress will significantly reduce the occurrence of disruptive behaviour. The following strategies are also recommended.

Tactical ignoring

If a child begins some form of disruptive behaviour (e.g. shouting to gain attention), the teacher ignores that child's response, and instead turns away and gives attention to another student who is responding appropriately. When the first student is acting appropriately, the teacher will ensure that he or she is noticed and called upon.

Clearly it is not sufficient merely to ignore disruptive behaviour. It is essential that planned ignoring be combined with a deliberate effort to praise descriptively and reinforce the child for appropriate behaviours at other times in the lesson – 'catch the child being good'. It is a golden rule to be much more positive and encouraging than to be critical and negative in interactions with students.

Signal interference

Many teachers use the strategy of signal interference to indicate to a student that his or her behaviour is becoming inappropriate (Levin and Nolan 2010). The use of non-verbal indicators such as staring hard at the student, frowning, or shaking the head are often sufficient to bring that student back on task without disrupting the attention of others in the class (Li 2008).

Proximity interference

Proximity interference refers to the common strategy of moving much closer to the student and giving him your undivided attention. This usually has the effect of redirecting the student's efforts back on the lesson, again without affecting the attention of the other students.

Reinforcement and rewards

In order to modify behaviour according to ABA principles, particularly in young or immature children, it may be necessary to introduce a reward system. If social reinforcers such as praise, smiles and overt approval are not effective, it will be necessary to apply more tangible rewards, selected according to students' personal preferences. Children differ, and what one child may find rewarding another may not.

For students with special needs, some teachers use tokens to reinforce behaviour or work in class. Tokens are simply a means of providing an immediate concrete reward. Tokens are usually effective because of their immediacy and students can see them accumulating on the desk as visible evidence of achievement. Tokens can be traded later for back-up reinforcers such as time on a preferred activity, being dismissed early, or receiving a positive report to take home to parents. While not themselves sensitive to individual preferences for particular types of reinforcement, tokens can be exchanged for what is personally reinforcing.

Most textbooks on educational psychology provide some general rules for using reinforcement. It is worth repeating them here.

- Reinforcement must be given immediately after the desired behaviour is shown and at first must be given at very frequent intervals.
- Once the desired behaviours are established, reinforcement should be given only at carefully spaced intervals.
- The teacher must gradually shift to unpredictable reinforcement so that the newly acquired behaviour can be sustained for longer and longer periods of time without reward.

Time out

Time out refers to the removal of a student completely from the social group situation to a different part of the room, or even to a separate but safe setting for short periods of isolation. While time out may appear to be directly punishing, it is really an extreme form of ignoring. The procedure ensures that the child is not being socially reinforced for misbehaviour.

If the time out technique is being used, it is important that every instance of the child's disruptive behaviour be followed by social isolation. The appropriate behaviour will not be established if sometimes the inappropriate behaviour is tolerated, sometimes punished, and at other times the child is removed from the group. It is essential to be consistent.

Cooling off

Explosive situations may develop with some disturbed children, and a cooling-off period is necessary. A set place should be nominated for this (e.g. a corner of the school library where worksheets may be stored for use by the student). The student should be under supervision for all the time spent out of the classroom. The student will not return to that particular lesson until he or she is in a fit emotional state to be reasoned with and some form of behaviour contract can be entered into between teacher and student (Friend and Bursuck 2009). Following a period of time out it is usually beneficial to have the child participate in a debriefing session in which he or she is encouraged to discuss the incident, reflect upon the behaviour, identify behaviour that might have been more effective and set a goal for improvement.

Behaviour contracts

A behavioural contract is a written agreement signed by all parties involved in a behaviour-change programme. After rational discussion and negotiation, the student agrees to behave in certain ways and carry out certain obligations. The staff and parents agree to do certain things in return. For example, a student may agree to arrive on time for lessons and not disrupt the class. In return the teacher will sign the student's contract sheet indicating that he or she has met the requirement in that particular lesson, and add positive comments. The contract sheet accompanies the student to each lesson throughout the day. At the end of each day and the end of each week, progress is monitored and any necessary changes are made to the agreement. If possible, the school negotiates parental involvement in the implementation of the contract, and the parents agree to provide some specific privileges if the goals are met for two consecutive weeks, or loss of privileges if it is broken. When behaviour contracts are to be set up, it is essential that all teachers and school support staff are kept fully informed of the details.

Punishment

Punishment represents yet another way of eliminating undesirable behaviours – but the use of punishment in schools is a contentious issue. The principal objection to punishment, or *aversive control*, is that while it may temporarily suppress certain behaviours, it may also evoke a variety of undesirable outcomes (fear, a feeling of alienation, resentment, an association between punishment and schooling, a breakdown in the relationship between teacher and student). Punishment may also suppress a child's general responsiveness in a classroom situation as well as eliminating the negative behaviour.

If it is absolutely necessary to punish a child, the punishment should be administered immediately after the unacceptable behaviour is exhibited. Delayed punishment is virtually useless. Punishment also needs always to be combined with positive reinforcement and other tactics to rebuild the child's self-esteem. The goal of intervention should be to help students gain control over their own emotions and behaviour, but this goal will not be achieved if aversive control is the only method implemented.

Aggressive behaviour

Teachers are bothered most by aggressive behaviour in children (Etscheidt and Clopton 2008). Increases in work-related stress among teachers are related in part to increases in acting-out and aggressive behaviour among students. Teachers should be trained in simple strategies for dealing with students' anger.

There is evidence that a *cognitive behavioural approach* can be effective in helping students understand and control their own anger – although the students must genuinely want to change their own behaviour if the approach is to work.

Humphrey and Brooks (2006) report positive outcomes from the use of six one-hour intervention sessions over a period of four weeks. During the sessions participants explored the following issues:

- what anger is, and why we need it;
- when anger becomes a problem;
- things that trigger our anger;
- how we can take control by recognizing that we are becoming angry;
- how to use self-instruction and relaxation strategies.

Similarly, Cullen-Powell *et al.* (2005) reported some benefits for students in upper primary and secondary school from a sixteen-session 'self-discovery programme' (three modules over one school year) to teach relaxation and self-control strategies that students can implement when feeling anxious or stressed. Larrivee (2009) suggests that there is value in teaching all students (and particularly those with aggressive tendencies) to apply 'conflict resolution' strategies so that they can control threatening situations by negotiation and compromise.

It is reported that less aggression is found in schools where a caring and supportive environment has been nurtured and where curricular demands are realistic. Schools where there is constant frustration and discouragement seem to breed disaffection and stimulate more aggressive and anti-social behaviour in students (Levin and Nolan 2010). Effective schools honour their responsibility of meeting students' emotional needs.

Bullying

It is crucial not to ignore bullying in schools as this problem will not cease of its own accord. The lives of too many children are made miserable when they become the victims of bullying (Urbanski and Permuth 2009). For the victim, bullying is known to cause absenteeism, psychosomatic illnesses, low self-esteem, impaired social skills, feelings of isolation, learning problems, depression and, in extreme cases, suicidal tendencies (Henley 2010). From the number of adults who report the impact that bullying had on them, it is clear that the experience frequently has long-lasting effects.

Some estimates put the prevalence of bullying at about one child in every ten; but self-report studies reveal many more students who later indicate that they were bullied when they were at school but did not report it. Both boys and girls are involved in bullying other children.

Bullying may take several different forms – direct physical attacks, verbal attacks, or indirect attacks such as spreading hurtful rumours or by excluding someone from a social group. Physical bullying is different from generally aggressive behaviour because bullies pick their targets very selectively (Swainston 2007). There are often characteristics of victims that make them targets for bullies – for example, they may appear to be vulnerable, weaker, shy, nervous, overweight, of different ethnic background, or 'teacher's pet'. There is some evidence that students with intellectual disability are sometimes subjected to teasing and bullying in both mainstream and special school settings (Norwich and Kelly 2004). Unpopular children and those with behaviour disorders or poor personal and social skills are more likely than others to be victimized (Henley 2010).

Bullies are often older or more physically advanced than their victims. Four out of five bullies come from homes where physical or emotional abuse is used frequently, and are therefore victims themselves to some degree. They appear to have less empathy than non-bullies. When bullying is carried out by gangs of students, factors come into play such as the importance of roles and status within the group. Some individuals feel that they are demonstrating their power by repressing the victim. Even those who are not themselves bullies get carried along with the behaviour and do not object to it or report it. Few would ever intervene to help the victim.

Within a school's behaviour management policy there should be agreed procedures for handling incidents of bullying so that all staff approach the problem with similar strategies. Much bullying occurs in the schoolyard, particularly if supervision is poor. Increased supervision is one intervention that schools can introduce to reduce bullying. Obviously the behaviour of the bully or the gang members needs to be addressed with direct intervention; but, in addition, the issues of consideration and respect for others and the right of every student to feel safe also need to be discussed.

Recent data from several countries suggest an alarming increase in 'cyber bullying' – the student becomes the target for derogatory comments, malicious gossip and lies posted on social networking websites, instant messaging, emails and by mobile phone (Tomazin 2009). With older adolescents, the bullying can also take the form of sending embarrassing photographs involving the victim. Unfortunately, as with other forms of bullying, children tend not to report such bullying to their parents. Levin and Nolan (2010: 60) comment that, 'The effects [of cyber bullying] include lower grades, lower self-esteem, lost interests, depression, and in extreme cases suicide. In one study 30 per cent of cyber-bullied victims reported being very or extremely upset and 19 per cent very or extremely afraid.'

In his advice to parents, Beane (2008) suggests that signs of cyber bullying to watch for include the child seeming to be constantly upset, anxious or secretive, particularly after spending time on the computer or mobile phone, and spending more time than usual in online chat rooms. Beane's book also provides a number of helpful hints for parents and teachers on how to monitor a child's use of information and communication technology and how to deal with problems of cyber bullying. Teachers should, if necessary, discuss with their classes at an appropriate time what cyber bullying is and its effect on the person targeted.

It is suggested that issues of bullying and aggressive behaviour should become the focus of attention within the school curriculum – perhaps under the general heading 'human relationships.'

Cognitive approaches for self-control

The main goal of any type of behaviour-change intervention should be the eventual handing-over of control to the individual concerned so that he or she is responsible for managing the behaviour. One way of achieving this is to employ the cognitive behaviour modification (CBM) approach described in Chapter 6. The teacher or trainer provides coaching in the use of self-talk to help the student monitor his or her own reactions to challenging situations. The self-talk enables the student to process aspects of the situation rationally and enables him or her to manage responses more effectively. A key ingredient in the approach is teaching the student to use self-talk statements that serve to inhibit impulsive and inappropriate thoughts or responses, allowing time for substitution of more acceptable responses – for example, to be assertive but not aggressive; to approach another student in a friendly rather than confrontational manner.

The intervention must help the student analyse the inappropriate behaviour and understand that lashing out at others or arguing with staff, for example, is not helping them in any way. Next the student is helped to establish both a *desire to change* and the *goals* to be aimed for over the following week (i.e. to stop doing the negative behaviour and to start doing the more positive behaviour). Over a number of sessions the student is helped to change negative thoughts and beliefs to more appropriate positive perspectives.

Social stories

Another cognitive approach to behaviour change is the use of 'social stories'. The use of stories with autistic children was discussed in Chapter 2. Social stories can also be used with young or intellectually disabled students to help them discriminate between appropriate and inappropriate patterns of behaviour. Haggerty *et al.* (2005) explain that social stories, with pictures of the children engaging in desirable and undesirable behaviour, can be used to help the children observe and reflect upon their own behaviour and the reaction it gets from others. For example, a first picture might show the children lining up in front of a cake stall at the school Open Day. One child is pushing another out of the line in order to take his place. The children on each side are looking very unhappy. In the next picture two of the other children are beginning to push the naughty child away from the line and a fight starts. In the third picture the lady in charge of the cake stall is telling the children that she will stop selling the cakes unless children line up in a neat queue. The final picture shows a neat queue of children with happy faces, each paying in turn for a cake. The story can be prepared, read and discussed with several children in a small group, but social stories are most frequently used to target the negative behaviour of one particular child. In such cases the story is personalized with the child's own name and the activity conducted individually. The story approach can also be used to help children who are shy or lacking in social skills.

Attention deficit hyperactivity disorder

A few children in our schools display chronic and extreme problems in maintaining attention to any task. They may also exhibit hyperactive and impulsive behaviours. These children are generally classified now as having attention deficit hyperactivity disorder (ADHD). This disorder has three subtypes: (i) a subtype in which the symptoms are predominantly associated with poor attention and distractibility; (ii) a subtype in which the symptoms are predominantly those of hyperactive and impulsive behaviours; and (iii) a subtype in which the symptoms combine both of the above problems (Humphrey 2009). Children with ADHD may also be diagnosed with 'conduct disorders' – defined as a pattern of persistent and repetitive violations of the rights of others or a disregard for age-appropriate social norms and rules (Glanzman and Blum 2007). ADHD can accompany certain other disabilities (e.g. cerebral palsy, traumatic brain injury, autism, specific learning disability and emotional disturbance) (Heward 2009; Smith and Tyler 2010).

Reviews of the extensive literature available now on ADHD seem to suggest that some 5 to 10 per cent of school-age children may present with symptoms of ADD or ADHD (Wright et al. 2009). In the past ten years there has certainly been an increase in the number of students diagnosed with ADHD and these children now represent some 26 per cent of all referrals for psycho-educational assessment.

To be formally diagnosed as ADHD, the child must exhibit six or more of the nine symptoms described under 'inattention' and 'hyperactivity' sections in the *Diagnostic and Statistical Manual of Mental Disorder, DSM IV-TR* (APA 2000). Of course, no test or checklist exists that can lead to certain identification; usually information from several sources is combined to help the doctor or psychologist reach a conclusion.

No single cause for ADHD has been identified, although the following have all been put forward as possible explanations (Dybdahl and Ryan 2009; Wheeler and Richey 2010): genetic influences, central nervous system dysfunction (perhaps due to slow maturation of the motor cortex of the brain), subtle forms of brain damage too slight to be confirmed by neurological testing, allergy to specific substances (e.g. food additives), adverse reactions to environmental stimuli (e.g. fluorescent lighting), maternal alcohol consumption during pregnancy, and inappropriate management of the child at home or school. Most authorities now agree that the ADHD syndrome represents a neuro-behavioural disorder with multiple possible causes.

ADHD children, while not necessarily below average in intelligence, usually exhibit poor achievement in most school subjects. Impaired concentration and restlessness associated with ADHD have usually impaired the child's learning during the important early years of schooling. Many ADHD students also have problems with peer relationships and in developing social competence. Some of these students seem to lack an understanding of the emotional reactions and feelings of others, resulting in many negative confrontations and other inappropriate social interactions (Kats-Gold and Priel 2009).

Interventions for ADHD

Because of the possibility that ADHD is caused by different factors in different individuals, it is not surprising to find that quite different forms of treatment are advocated; and what works for one child may not work for another. Treatments have included diet control, medication, psychotherapy, behaviour modification and cognitive behaviour modification. There have also been other 'alternative' therapies which, as Wright *et al.* (2009) point out, are of doubtful value. Any approach to the treatment of ADHD needs to attend to *all* factors that may be causing and maintaining the behaviour. The most effective treatment requires effective teaching strategies to be integrated with a behaviour management plan, parent counselling, home management programme and (often) medication.

There is strong agreement among experts that children with ADHD need structure and predictability in the learning environment. Effective teaching strategies must be used to arouse and hold the child's interest. Children with ADHD need to be engaged as much as possible in interesting work, at an appropriate level, in a stable environment. Enhancing the learning of children with ADHD will also involve:

*   providing strong visual input to hold attention;
*   using computer-assisted learning (CAL);
*   teaching the students better self-management and organizational skills;
*   monitoring them closely during lessons and finding many opportunities to praise and reinforce them descriptively when they are on task and productive.

The use of medication in the management of ADHD remains a controversial issue. In the US, almost 60 per cent of students with ADHD are taking medication such as Ritalin or Adderal to reduce their hyperactivity and to help them focus attention more effectively on schoolwork. In Britain and Australia, the use of medication as a first resort is a little less common, with the focus being more on behavioural interventions. While medication does appear to have a positive impact on students' activity level, attention and school achievement (Scheffler *et al.* 2009), it is not without side effects such as loss of appetite, drowsiness, insomnia, headaches and increased nervousness.

Online resources

*   A document outlining the *Behaviour Challenge* initiative in Britain can be downloaded from http://publications.teachernet.gov.uk/eOrderingDownload/ DCSF-00961-2009.pdf (accessed 28 March 2010).
*   The TeacherNet website provides information on *Partnerships to Improve*

Behaviour and Persistent Absence at: www.teachernet.gov.uk/wholeschool/behaviour/collaboration/guidance/ (accessed 28 March 2010).

* The curriculum outline for *Social and Emotional Aspects of Learning (SEAL)*, from the Department for Children, Schools and Families in UK, can be found online at: http://nationalstrategies.standards.dcsf.gov.uk/inclusion/behaviourattendanceandseal/seal (accessed 28 March 2010).

* Steer, A. (2009) *Learning behaviour: Lessons Learned*, Annesley: DCSF Publications. Online. Available HTTP. http://publications.teachernet.gov.uk/eOrderingDownload/DCSF-Learning-Behaviour.pdf (accessed 28 March 2010).

* Classroom material for teachers and students is available from *Behaviour Online* at: www.behaviouronline.com/ (accessed 28 March 2010).

* A pamphlet titled *School Discipline: Your Powers and Rights as a Teacher*, published by Department for Children, Schools and Families (2009) can be downloaded from: www.teachernet.gov.uk/_doc/13516/8209-DCSF-School%20Discipline%20DL.pdf (accessed 28 March 2010).

* Detailed information on ADHD can be located at the National Institute of Mental Health website www.nimh.nih.gov/health/publications/attention-deficit-hyperactivity-disorder/complete-index.shtml (accessed 28 March 2010).

Further reading

Alberto, P.A. and Troutman, A.C. (2009) *Applied Behavior Analysis for Teachers* (8th edn), Upper Saddle River, NJ: Pearson-Merrill.

Crone, D.A., Hawken, L.S. and Horner, R.H. (2010) *Responding to Problem Behavior in Schools* (2nd edn), New York: Guilford Press.

Kerr, M.M. (2010) *Strategies for Addressings Behavior Problems in the Classroom*, Boston: Pearson.

Levin, J. and Nolan, J.F. (2010) *Principles of Classroom Management* (6th edn), Upper Saddle River, NJ: Pearson Education.

Shepherd, T.L. (2010) *Working with Students with Emotional and Behavior Disorders: Characteristics and Teaching Strategies*, Upper Saddle River, NJ: Merrill.

Swearer, S.M., Espelage, D.L. and Napolitano, S.A. (2009) *Bullying Prevention and Intervention: Realistic Strategies for Schools*, New York: Guilford Press.

Wheeler, J.J. (2010) *Behavior Management: Principles and Practices of Positive Behavior Supports*, Boston: Pearson.

Chapter 8

Social skills and peer group acceptance

Social competence is often lacking in children with learning difficulties and with disabilities. Mercer and Pullen (2009) remark that many experts now believe that problems in achieving acceptance in a social group are just as debilitating as academic failure for these students. They feel socially isolated and unsupported in class and tend to disengage from learning (Pletka 2007). Even students without disabilities are at risk in school if they lack social skills and are rejected or victimized by others. It is for this reason that establishing good social relationships with other children has been described as one of the most important social goals for education.

It is evident that poor peer relationships during the school years can have a lasting detrimental impact on social and personal competence in later years. Shepherd (2010: 155) has observed that:

> The importance of social skills cannot be underestimated. Children with deficits in social skills are at risk for unemployment, aggressive interactions in the community, juvenile delinquency, and adult mental health problems.

There is obviously an urgent need to enhance the social acceptance and social competence of children with special needs when they are placed in regular classrooms (Mannix 2009). This applies to many children with intellectual disability, physical or sensory impairments, learning disabilities and emotional problems. Children with autism and those with ADHD are particularly at risk (Cotugno 2009; Leaf *et al.* 2009).

Inclusive education settings create a potential opportunity for these children to engage in more positive social interaction with their peers – but social acceptance of students with special needs does not occur spontaneously (Friend and Bursuck 2009; Hooper and Umansky 2009). The results of most studies of inclusion give no support at all to the belief that merely placing a child with a disability in the mainstream will automatically lead to his or her social integration into the peer group. The situation is most problematic for children who have an emotional or behavioural disorder, and there is a danger that such children become marginalized, ignored or even openly rejected by classmates.

Opportunities for social interaction

At least three conditions must be present for positive social interaction and development of friendships among children with and without disabilities. These conditions include:

- *Opportunity* – being within proximity of other children frequently enough for meaningful contacts to be made. Inclusive schooling provides proximity and frequency of contact. It creates the best possible chances for children with disabilities to interact with their peers, and also to observe and imitate the social behaviours of others (Ross and Roberts-Pacchione 2007; Shepherd 2010).
- *Continuity* – being involved with the same group of children over a reasonable period of time; and also seeing some of the same children in their own neighbourhood out of school hours.
- *Support* – being helped to make contact with other children in order to work and play with them; and if possible being directly supported in maintaining friendships beyond school. In this matter, it is important for parents to be encouraged to nurture their child's peer friendships outside of school hours (Court and Givon 2007).

When students with disabilities are placed in regular settings without adequate preparation or on-going support, three problems may become evident:

- children without disabilities do not readily demonstrate easy acceptance of those with disabilities;
- children with disabilities, contrary to popular belief, do not automatically observe and copy the positive social models that are around them;
- some teachers do not intervene to promote positive social interaction.

It is necessary for teachers to identify as soon as possible any children in their classes who appear to be without friends at recess and lunch breaks and who seem unable to relate closely with classmates during lessons (Court and Givon 2007).

Creating a supportive environment

A positive and supportive school environment is, of course, important for the social development of all children (Mastropieri and Scruggs 2010). To facilitate social interaction for children with special needs in regular classrooms three conditions are necessary:

- the general attitude of the teacher and the peer group towards students with special needs must be as positive and accepting as possible;
- the environment should be arranged so that the child with a disability has the maximum opportunity to spend time socially involved in group or pair activities both in the classroom and at recess;

- children with special needs must be taught the specific skills that may enhance social interaction with peers.

Creating classroom environments where competition is not a dominant element is the first step in facilitating social development. Cooperation, rather than competition, needs to be encouraged. Students must be involved frequently in group activities that encourage social cooperation, collaboration and mutual support. In addition, the class activity called *Circle Time* can be used to advantage as an opportunity for children to discuss aspects of social behaviour such as helping one another, preventing bullying or teasing, building self-esteem, looking for strengths in other people and showing interest in the ideas of others. Circle Time is often associated with kindergarten and early primary years, but the value of having students coming together in a relaxed situation in which they can voice their opinions can extend easily into secondary schools.

Facilitating social interaction

The following strategies can be used to increase the chances of positive social interaction for students with disabilities.

- Make more frequent use of non-academic tasks (e.g. games, model-making, painting) because these place the child with special needs in a situation where he or she can more easily fit in and contribute.
- 'Peer tutoring' and 'buddy systems' have been found effective. Several versions of these exist, including Classwide Peer Tutoring (CWPT). Research over two decades has confirmed the effectiveness of peer tutoring for improving learning and social outcomes for students at all age and ability levels (McMaster *et al.* 2006).
- Make a particular topic – for example, 'friends' or 'working together' – the basis for class discussion. 'If you want someone to play with you at lunchtime how would you make that happen?' 'If you saw two children in the schoolyard who had just started at the school today, how would you make them feel accepted?'
- Peer-group members can be encouraged to maintain and reinforce social interactions with less-able or less-popular children. Often they are unaware of the ways in which they can help. They, too, may need to be shown how to initiate contact, how to invite the child with special needs to join in an activity, or how to help that classmate with particular school assignments.

Circle of Friends is a peer-group support strategy to help children with special educational needs who have difficulty finding a friend or coping in class (Friend and Bursuck 2009; Howarth 2008). The system operates by involving some of a child's classmates as natural supporters to help the child acquire more positive behaviours and self-management. Any improvements in these areas will help make the child more socially acceptable and successful. Specific members of the support group are detailed to greet the child each day, to be friendly and helpful at all times, to assist with routines at lunch and break times, to make sure the child is counted in for all activities, and to help the child solve any problems that may arise. The role of the teacher is to facilitate and encourage this process. This approach originated in Canada but is now used in US, UK and Australia as one way to foster social inclusion for students with special needs.

It must be noted that if the peer support element in Circle of Friends is poorly implemented, it may encourage passivity in the child being supported. Peers should be aware that the goal is to help the child become more competent and assertive, not to do everything for him or her or to remove all challenges (MacConville and Rhys-Davies 2007).

Another difficulty that can arise with this type of direct support is that some students with special needs actually resent any obvious intervention by a teacher to 'fix them up' with a friend. This is particularly the case with adolescents who are ultra sensitive to peer group opinion. They prefer to solve their social and other problems themselves (Friend and Bursuck 2009). The reality is that teachers cannot really 'force' friendships to be established between students with special needs and others; they can only hope to establish the conditions under which this may occur spontaneously (Smith and Tyler 2010).

Importance of group work

The regular use of group work in the classroom is one of the main ways of providing children with opportunities to develop social skills through collaborating with others (Olson *et al.* 2008; Peterson and Hittie 2010). Careful planning is required if group work is to achieve the desired educational and social outcomes. The success of collaborative group work depends on the composition of the working groups and the nature of the tasks set for the students.

When utilizing group work as an organizational strategy, it is important to consider the following basic principles.

- Initially there is merit in having groups of children working cooperatively on the *same task* at the same time. This procedure makes it much easier to prepare resources and to manage time effectively. When each of several groups is undertaking quite different tasks, it can become a major management problem for the teacher.
- Choice of tasks for group work is very important. Tasks have to be selected which *require* collaboration and teamwork. Children are sometimes seated in groups in the classroom but are actually expected to work on individual assignments. Not only does this negate the opportunities for collaboration, it also creates difficulties for individuals in terms of interruptions and distractions.
- It is not enough merely to establish groups and to set them to work. Group members may have to be taught how to work efficiently together. They may

need to be shown behaviours that encourage or enable cooperation – listening to the views of others, sharing, praising each other and offering help. If the task involves the learning of specific curriculum content, teach the children how to rehearse and test one another on the material.

- The way in which individual tasks are allotted (division of labour) should be carefully planned. Each child needs to understand clearly his area of responsibility – for example, 'John, you can help Craig with his writing, then he can help you with the lettering for your title board.' Contingent praise for interacting with others should be descriptive: 'Good, Sue. You are taking turns and working very well with Sharon.'
- Teachers should monitor closely what is going on during group activities and must intervene when necessary to provide suggestions, encourage the sharing of a task, praise examples of cooperation and teamwork, and model cooperative behaviour themselves. Many groups can be helped to function efficiently if the teacher (or classroom assistant or a parent helper) works as a group member without dominating or controlling the activity.
- The size of the group is important. Often children working in pairs is a good starting point. Select the composition of the group carefully to avoid obvious incompatibility among students' personalities. At times a teacher needs to intervene to help a particular child gain entry to a group activity or to work with a carefully chosen partner.
- When groups contain students with special needs, it is vital that the specific tasks and duties to be undertaken by these students are clearly delineated. It can be useful to establish a system whereby the results of the *group's* efforts are rewarded by the way in which they have worked together positively and supportively. Under this structure, group members have a vested interest in ensuring that all members learn, because the group's success depends on the achievement of all. Helping each other, sharing and tutoring within the group are behaviours that must be modelled and supported.
- Talking should be encouraged during group activities. It is interesting to note that sub-grouping in the class has the effect of increasing transactional talk (talk specifically directed to another person and requiring a reply) by almost three times the level present under whole-class conditions.
- Seating and work arrangements are important. Group members should be in close proximity but still have space to work on materials without getting in each other's way.
- Group work must be used frequently enough for the children to learn the skills and routines. Infrequent group work results in children taking too long to settle down.

Group work can become chaotic if the tasks are poorly defined or too complex. Other problems arise if the students are not well versed in group-working skills, or if the room is not set up to facilitate easy access to resources. It is essential that all tasks have a very clear structure and purposes that are understood by all. There is great value in discussing openly with a class the best ways of making group work effective, and identifying the skills necessary to cooperate productively with others.

In the case of children displaying extreme withdrawal or rejection, simply relying on group work opportunities to increase social interaction is not sufficient. Sometimes it is necessary for a child to be coached intensively in a particular social skill before that skill can be applied in the peer group setting.

Social skills training

Social skills are the specific behaviours an individual uses to maintain effective interpersonal communication and interaction. Social skills comprise a set of competencies that allow individuals to initiate and maintain positive social interactions with others and cope effectively within the social environment.

While some students with disabilities are very popular with classmates in the mainstream, particularly if they have a pleasant personality, others with similar disabilities or with emotional and behavioural difficulties are particularly at risk of social isolation (Fisher and Haufe 2009). One of the main reasons why certain children are unpopular is that they lack appropriate social skills that might make them more acceptable. They are in a Catch-22 situation, since friendless students have fewer opportunities to practise social skills, and those who do not develop adequate social skills are unable to form friendships. It is argued that these children need social skills training.

Early training in social skills can be instrumental in reducing or preventing problem behaviour in later years. Cartledge (2005) recommends that social skill instruction should begin in the preschool years or the early primary grades, when children are most receptive to behaviour change. Such instruction should be embedded in the context of events that occur naturally within the children's social environment. Research shows that there is very limited transfer or maintenance of social skills when they are taught in contrived exercises unrelated to real situations. The most meaningful settings in which to enhance the child's skills are usually the classroom and schoolyard.

The teaching of social skills usually involves establishing some or all of the following behaviours:

• making eye contact;
• greeting others by name;
• gaining attention in appropriate ways;
• talking in a tone of voice that is acceptable;
• knowing when to talk, what to talk about and when to hold back;
• initiating a conversation;
• maintaining conversations;
• answering questions;
• listening to others and showing interest;

- sharing with others;
- saying 'please' and 'thank you';
- helping someone;
- making apologies when necessary;
- being able to collaborate in a group activity;
- taking one's turn;
- smiling;
- accepting praise;
- giving praise;
- accepting correction without anger;
- coping with frustration;
- managing conflict.

The basic list above is similar to that found in published programmes for social skills training. Each skill should be considered relative to the particular child's age and specific needs; it is pointless to teach skills that are not immediately useful in the child's regular environment. For example, the conversational skills needed to function adequately in an adolescent peer group are obviously far more complex and subtle than those required by the young child just starting school. Similarly, skills needed to deal with conflict situations become more complex as a child gets older. In each individual case, the first step is to decide what the priorities are for this child in terms of specific skills and behaviours to be taught. The skills to be targeted need to be of immediate functional value to the child in the setting in which he or she operates.

Studies suggest that, to be effective, social skills training needs to: (i) target the precise skills and knowledge an individual lacks; (ii) be intensive and long term in nature; and (iii) promote maintenance, generalization and transfer of new skills into the individual's daily life. Training of social skills is based on a combination of modelling, coaching, role playing, rehearsing, feedback and counselling. At times, video recordings are also used effectively to provide examples of social behaviours to discuss and imitate, or to provide a child with feedback on his or her own performance or role play (Wang and Spillane 2009). The use of Social Stories (see Chapter 2 and Chapter 7) has also proved to be effective in encouraging children's awareness of social skills (Shepherd 2010).

These are the typical steps in coaching social skills.

- *Definition* – describe the skill to be taught and indicate how its use helps social interactions to occur. Illustrate the skill in action by pointing out examples happening in the peer group. Key points can be reinforced using video, pictures, cartoons, or a simulation using puppets. The teacher may say, 'Look at the two girls sharing the puzzle. Tell me what they might be saying to each other.'
- *Model the skill* – break the skill down into simple components and demonstrate these clearly yourself, or get a selected child to do this.

- *Imitation and rehearsal* –the child tries out the same skill in a structured situation. For this to occur successfully, the child must be motivated to perform the skill and must attend carefully and retain what has been demonstrated.
- *Feedback* – this should be informative. 'You've not quite got it yet. You need to look at her while you speak to her. Try it again.' 'That's better! You looked and smiled. Well done.' Feedback via a video recording may be appropriate in some situations.
- *Provide opportunity for the skill to be used* – depending upon the skill being taught, use small group work or pair activities to allow the skill to be applied and generalized to the classroom or other natural setting.
- *Intermittent reinforcement* – watch for instances of the child applying the skill without prompting at other times in the day and later in the week. Provide descriptive praise and reward. Aim for maintenance of the skill once it is acquired.

To a large extent, social skills, once established, are likely to be maintained by natural consequences – that is, by more satisfying interactions with peers. Individuals with acceptable social skills are less likely to engage in problem behaviour, are better at making friends, are able to resolve conflicts peacefully, and have effective ways of dealing with persons in authority.

As well as having appropriate positive pro-social skills, a socially competent individual must also *avoid* having negative behavioural characteristics that prevent easy acceptance by others – for example, high levels of irritating behaviour (interrupting, poking, or shouting), impulsive and unpredictable reactions, temper tantrums, abusive language, or cheating at games. In many cases these undesirable behaviours need to be eliminated by behaviour modification or through cognitive self-management. Training in social skills is not a matter simply of teaching a child something that is missing from his or her repertoire of behaviours but may also involve *replacing* an undesirable behaviour that is already strongly established with a new alternative behaviour. The negative behaviours we often take as indicative of lack of social skill in some children (e.g. aggression, non-compliance, verbal abuse) may actually be very rewarding behaviours for the individuals concerned and represent more powerful and effective forces than the new pro-social skills we attempt to teach. This residual influence of pre-existing behaviours is one of the reasons why skills taught during training are often not maintained – they are competing with powerful behaviours that have already proved to work well for the child.

Is social skills training effective?

Some researchers warn against over-optimism in regard to the long-term efficacy of social skills training (e.g. Olson *et al.* 2008). While most social skills training produces positive short-term effects, there are usually major problems with maintenance and generalization. In particular, it is suggested that social training appears to have limited effect when applied to children with serious behaviour disorders and others with chronic relationship difficulties. Yell *et al.* (2009) suggest that such training rarely has lasting effects if it is the only form of intervention used with the child. It needs to be one component in a more comprehensive programme.

It must also be noted that even when children with disabilities are specifically trained in social skills, some may still not find it any easier to make friends. Students with intellectual disability or with non-verbal learning disabilities often report on-going loneliness even after successfully participating in a social skills programme (Court and Givon 2007). Unexpected outcomes may also occur – for example, some students may feel *less* socially competent after training because the training has made them more acutely aware of their own deficiencies.

Poor scholastic achievement seems to be one factor contributing to poor social acceptance, even after social skills have been taught. Unless achievement within the curriculum can also be increased, acceptance may remain a problem for some children. With this fact in mind, attention is focused in the following chapters on approaches for teaching basic academic skills to students with special needs.

Online resources

- Additional information on social skills training for children with disabilities can be found on the *Encyclopedia of Mental Disorders* website at: www.minddisorders.com/Py-Z/Social-skills-training.html (accessed 28 March 2010).
- Additional information on *Circle of Friends* can be obtained from: www.circleofriends.org/ (accessed 28 March 2010).
- Several useful resources such as lesson plans and curricula for social development and social skills can be found on *About.com: Special Education* website at: http://specialed.about.com/od/characterbuilding/Character_Building_Character_Education.htm (accessed 28 March 2010).
- University of Kansas (2010) website has suggestions for *'Strategies for effectively interacting with others'*. Available online from the Centre for Research on Learning at: www.ku-crl.org/sim/strategies.shtml (accessed 28 March 2010).

Further reading

Csoti, M. (2009) *Developing Children's Social, Emotional and Behavioural Skills,* London: Continuum.

Gutteridge, D. and Smith, V. (2010) *Creating an Emotionally Healthy Classroom*, London: Routledge.

Kostelnik, M.J., Whiren, A.P., Soderman, A.K. and Gregory, K.M. (2009) *Guiding Children's Social Development and Learning* (6th edn), Clifton Park, NY: Delmar.

Mannix, D. (2009) *Social Skills Activities for Secondary Students with Special Needs* (2nd edn), San Francisco, CA: Jossey-Bass.

Merrell, K.W. and Gueldner, B.A. (2010) *Social and Emotional Learning in the Classroom,* New York: Guilford Press.

Rapoport, E.M. (2009) *ADHD and Social Skills: A Step-by-Step Guide for Teachers and Parents,* Lanham, MD: Rowman and Littlefield.

Shepherd, T.L. (2010) *Working With Students With Emotional and Behavior Disorders,* Upper Saddle River, NJ: Merrill.

Chapter 9

Reading and reading difficulties

The ability to read is among the most important skills that students need to learn because reading provides the key to acquiring new information in all areas of the curriculum. It is therefore the main means by which children become independent learners. Even in this technological age, reading still represents the main method of obtaining information and is also used for recreation and enjoyment. Reading can stimulate a child's imagination and emotions. In life beyond school, people with good literacy skills are more able to take advantage of opportunities that life may offer them and are likely to have higher self-esteem, better jobs and higher wages than those with poor literacy skills (National Literacy Trust [UK] 2009b).

Failure to learn to read with adequate proficiency places any child at risk of failing in most school subjects. Unfortunately, many children with special educational needs have major difficulties learning to read; and without effective intervention they fall increasingly behind their age peers in school achievement (Coltheart and Prior 2007). On-going failure undermines any child's confidence and motivation, leading eventually to disengagement from learning and the belief that learning to read is simply too difficult. Early intervention is therefore absolutely essential so that a child is helped to make good progress before detrimental feelings of helplessness set in.

Reading difficulties can affect the progress of up to 30 per cent of children in some schools, and the problem is not confined to children with disabilities or with other identified special needs (Lonigan and Shanahan 2008). Even a few students regarded as gifted sometimes exhibit problems with reading. Weakness in reading remains the principal reason for the high number of referrals for psycho-educational assessment and additional support in schools. It is obvious, therefore, that schools must adopt the most effective initial teaching methods to prevent this problem and ensure that almost every child gets off to a smooth start in reading.

The most effective, evidence-based methods for teaching reading have been the focus of attention in several countries in recent years − for example, Australia (DEST 2005), UK (House of Commons Education and Skills Committee 2005; Rose 2005), and the US (National Reading Panel 2000). The main purpose of these reports has been to identify methods that are supported by research data proving their efficacy, rather than advocating methods that are simply based on teachers' personal whims, preferences and idiosyncratic styles. Attention in the reports has been given particularly to how best to teach the beginning stages of reading.

A sound start

The Response to Intervention (RTI) model, referred to in Chapter 1, is predicated on the assumption that at Tier 1 (beginning stage) all children in the first year of schooling will receive high-quality instruction that maximizes their opportunity to learn. The overwhelming consensus emerging from research in recent years is that Tier 1 instruction in reading for all children aged 5 to 6 years should be direct, explicit, systematic and aimed primarily at developing efficient decoding skills, word recognition and comprehension (IES 2009a; Lonigan and Shanahan 2008; Wheldall 2009b). The ability to decode unfamiliar words using knowledge of letter-to-sound relationships (phonics) leads to optimum progress in reading for most children. In the earliest stages of learning to read, children have not yet built up a large vocabulary of words they know instantly by sight, so they must use knowledge of letters and groups of letters to help them identify unfamiliar words. Children cannot really become independent readers unless they master the alphabetic code. It is now generally accepted that explicit instruction in phonic principles needs to be a key component in all early reading programmes.

This view differs very significantly from that held by educators in the period from 1980 to 2000. At that time, the importance of phonic skills was de-emphasized, and primary school teachers encouraged children to read by attending almost entirely to context and meaning in order to guess most of the words on the page – the so-called 'whole language approach'. Only as a last resort would a teacher tell a child to 'sound out' a word. During this period, very little direct teaching of phonic knowledge occurred in the crucial early years of schooling, and many trainee teachers had no instruction at all in teaching children to decode. Fortunately, some children discovered the alphabetic principle for themselves and became good readers; but many others, including most of the students with general and specific learning difficulties, did not. When a child with difficulties was referred for diagnostic assessment during this period, it was common to find that the problem was an almost total lack of phonic knowledge and no confidence in decoding – often the result of inappropriate or insufficient teaching.

While decoding ability and word recognition are clearly essential foundations for reading, children must also be able to process with understanding the information they are reading in a text. For this reason, a balanced early reading programme contains not only explicit teaching and practice in phonic decoding but also instruction in comprehension strategies (Coyne et al. 2009). A balanced approach also incorporates many aural and oral language enrichment activities to encourage careful listening, build oral vocabulary, establish familiarity with language patterns, and introduce books and materials that foster children's interest in reading.

The simple view of reading

It is now considered that the process of reading comprises two complementary abilities: (i) decoding, and (ii) language comprehension. This belief has become widely known as the 'simple view of reading' (Hoover and Gough 1990). This simple view has gained popularity with cognitive psychologists and educators who favour a skills-based approach to teaching (e.g. Catts *et al.* 2003; Tan *et al.* 2007; Westwood 2009b) and with some government education systems (e.g. DCSF [UK] 2006; DET [NSW] 2009). In the United Kingdom, the 'simple view of reading' has been adopted officially within the *National Literacy Strategy* to provide the framework for teaching and evaluating reading in primary schools. In the strategy it is stated that:

> Learning to read . . . involves setting up processes by which the words on the page can be recognized and understood, and continuing to develop the language processes that underlie both spoken and written language comprehension. Both sets of processes are necessary for reading; but neither is sufficient on its own.
>
> (DCSF 2006: 2)

The simple view of reading is not without its critics. Some educators and reading experts suggest that it is *too* simple and that reading is a much more complex process that draws on many other sub-skills and domains of knowledge (e.g. Dombey 2009). In particular, it is suggested that the simple view overlooks the vital importance of *fluency* in reading – fluency being the ultimate outcome from effortless decoding, rapid word recognition and reading with understanding (O'Connor 2007).

Regardless of any minor criticisms of the simple view of reading, the focus it places on decoding and language comprehension provides teachers with a strong sense of direction for most teaching purposes in the beginning stages of literacy (Stainthorp and Stuart 2008). The simple view of reading underpins the remaining material in this chapter.

The role of phonemic awareness

Before a child can understand the principle and operation of the alphabetic code, he or she must first understand that spoken words are made up of separate sound units (*phonemes*). For example, the word *tree* actually comprises the sounds /t/ /r/ /ee/ (or /tr/ /ee/) and the word *tin* contains the phonemes /t/ /i/ /n/. The ability to identify these sounds in spoken words is termed *phonemic awareness*. If a child lacks phonemic awareness, it is impossible for him or her to understand that a letter, or group of letters, in print represents a unit of sound within a word, and that these sound units can be identified and put together to build the word. A child cannot acquire functional phonic skills without first understanding how to break down spoken words into component sounds (a process referred to as *segmenting*) and how to put sound units together to build a word (referred to as *blending*). While some children discover for themselves that spoken words are made up of sounds and that sounds can be manipulated mentally to construct words when reading and spelling, it should never be assumed that all children can reach this understanding unaided. Studies have shown that students with reading difficulties or with language disorders are frequently very slow indeed to acquire phonemic awareness and it is the main underlying cause of their problem (Fielding-Barnsley and Twaddell 2009). Activities to develop phonemic awareness are therefore essential components in all beginning language and reading programmes.

Specific training in phonemic awareness is not required by every child; some will have discovered for themselves during their preschool years the existence of phonemes in words through everyday activities that involve listening, rhyming and playing with words. Teachers need to appraise their youngest students' levels of phonemic awareness in order to identify individuals needing explicit teaching and additional practice. It is often useful to inspect children's early attempts at spelling as these can reveal the extent to which they have developed phonemic awareness and letter knowledge. The same is true of older students with learning difficulties.

For young children, the skill of segmenting words can be taught explicitly by spending a little time taking words apart into their component sounds and syllables. For example: 'What's in this picture, Jackie? Yes. It's a frog. Listen. Let's say frog very slowly. Let's stretch the word out . . . /FR/–/O/–/G/. You try it.' The child could also be asked to count and clap the number of sounds heard in the word. Analysing a few target words each day in this way can be one of many follow-up activities used in approaches such as shared-book and language-experience, described later.

Children can be helped to understand how even single-syllable words may be taken apart by using what are termed onset-rime activities. For example, in the word 'stick', /st/ is the *onset* and /ick/ is the *rime*. Being able to break simple words into onset and rime units provides a good foundation for more demanding word analysis and segmentation later.

Teachers and tutors can also create activities that will help children gain more experience in blending sounds to build words. For example, using the simple 'I Spy' game: 'I spy with my little eye a picture of a /CL/ – /O/ – /CK/. What can I see?' Blending skill should also be applied and practised in every context when the student is reading aloud and needs to sound out a particular word.

Teaching letter-to-sound correspondences

Once a child is able to perform oral and aural activities that involve segmenting and blending (and some children can already do this on entry to school), it is opportune to teach directly the common letter-to-sound correspondences – the most basic building blocks of phonic skills. Studies have indicated clearly that teaching phonics early and systematically produces superior results to those obtained by whole-language approach or the whole-word recognition method (Torgerson *et al.* 2006). Current evidence suggests that the method known as *synthetic phonics* (learning to identify words in print by building them from their component sounds) produces the best results (DET [NSW] 2009). Synthetic phonics helps children acquire a word-analysis technique that they can continue to develop and apply independently for themselves.

In contrast to the synthetic phonics approach, the method called *analytic phonics* teaches children essential letter-sound relationships by analysing words they can already recognize in print. For example, the sound of letter /t/ is taught from words such as '*tin, top, tap, tip*'. Or, the consonant blend /cl/ might be taught from the words '*class, clap, clip*' and so forth. Analytic phonics is favoured as a method by some teachers because it moves in the direction from whole to part, rather than part to whole. However, research has not shown it to be more effective than synthetic phonics. Since 2006 all schools in England have been required to use the synthetic phonics approach when teaching early reading.

Reading experts differ in their views on exactly how letter-sound correspondences should be introduced. As a general principle, all agree that phonic knowledge and decoding skills should not be taught and practised totally out of context. Letter knowledge is only useful if it helps with the reading and writing of meaningful text. While students do need specific time devoted to mastering phonic units and working with word families, every effort must be made to ensure that this learning is quickly applied to meaningful reading and writing. Much phonic knowledge can be taught or reinforced from the words children are already meeting in storybooks their teachers are sharing with them every day. However, simply embedding some occasional and incidental instruction in decoding within a whole-language programme is totally inadequate for many children. This unsystematic approach to phonics lacks intensity and does not ensure that young children master decoding ability to the necessary level of automaticity. By way of contrast, evidence suggests that 10 to 20 minutes a day spent in enjoyable word study in the early years enables young children to master the fundamental relationships among letters and sounds and how to apply this knowledge (DET [NSW] 2009).

It is reasonable to ask if there is any prescribed order in which to introduce the common associations between letters (graphemes) and sounds (phonemes). The consensus view is that there is no single best order. In practice the order is often dictated by the nature of the reading materials or programme the children are using. However, when working with children who have reading difficulties, it is useful to consider how the task of learning letter–sound correspondences might be organized into a logical sequence. One systematic approach begins by selecting highly contrastive sounds such as /m/, /k/, /v/, and avoiding confusable sounds such as /m/ and /n/, or /p/ and /b/. It is also helpful to teach first the most consistent letter–sound associations. The following consonants often provide a useful starting point because they represent only one sound, regardless of the letter or letters coming after them in a word: j, k, l, m, n, p, b, h, r, v, w. Identifying initial consonants can be made the focus within many of the general language activities in the classroom.

Obviously, to enable children to engage in meaningful decoding, vowel sounds and their letters must be taught very early. Vowel sounds are far less consistent than consonants in their letter-to-sound relationships. After first establishing the most common vowel sound associations (/a/ as in apple, /e/ as in egg, /i/ as in ink, /o/ as in orange and /u/ as in up) these can be used in simple word building and spelling activities with consonant-vowel-consonant (CVC) words. More complicated variations involving vowels are best tackled much later in combination with other letters when words containing these units are encountered in word families and in text (e.g. -ar-, -aw-, -ie-, -ee-, -ea-, -ai-, etc.).

With the least able children it is likely that much more time and attention will need to be devoted to mastery of letter-to-sound correspondences. This can be achieved not only through direct teaching and daily practice but also through games and activities (McDougall *et al.* 2009). There are also many programmes designed to teach basic phonic knowledge in a very systematic way. For example, THRASS (*Teaching Handwriting, Reading and Spelling Skills*: Davies 2006) is designed to teach students how specific letters and letter groups represent the forty-four phonemes in the English language. The programme has many supplementary teaching materials for practice and reinforcement. Approaches such as THRASS, using direct teaching and synthetic phonics, are highly appropriate for students with learning difficulties who otherwise remain confused about the fact that some of the same sound units in English can be represented by different orthographic units (e.g. /-ight/ and /-ite/) and how the same orthographic pattern can represent different sounds (e.g. /ow/ as in flower or /ow/ as in snow). Other examples of successful programmes are *Jolly Phonics* (Lloyd and Lib 2000) and *Letterland* (Wendon 2006). *Jolly Phonics* sets out to teach forty-two basic sound-to-letter correspondences, taught in seven groupings using a multisensory and synthetic phonics approach. *Letterland* uses a story approach with pictograms representing the characters involved. Alliteration in the characters' names (e.g. Golden Girl, Robber Red, Hairy Hatman, Munching Mike) helps to reinforce the learning of letter-to-sound relationships. Both programmes are supported fully by a wide range of teaching materials.

Simple word-building experiences

It is important that word-building activities involving sounding out letters and blending them to make words are introduced alongside teaching of the common vowel sounds and consonants. For example, at the simplest level, adding the /a/ sound to the sound /m/ makes *am*; adding /a/ to /t/ produces *at*; adding /o/ to /n/ makes *on*; and adding /u/ to /p/ makes *up*, etc. Later, when CVC words (e.g. *rub, sat*) are being introduced for sounding and blending, particular attention should be paid to the middle vowel. Children with learning difficulties often pay inadequate attention to vowels when trying to identify words, instead guessing too quickly from the initial letter. As well as attending to and reading these units in print, children should also learn to write them unaided when the teacher dictates the sounds.

As simple as this basic work may appear, for many students with learning problems it is often the first real link they make between spoken and written language. It is vital that children who have not recognized the connection between letters and sounds be given this direction early. The only prerequisite skills required are good phonemic awareness and adequate visual perception so that the differences between letters can be perceived easily.

Selecting early text materials

Opinions differ on whether children at this stage should use graded reading books that contain a high proportion of 'regular' words (i.e. simple words that can be decoded easily by sounding and blending their letters). During the 1980s and 1990s such books were utterly shunned by whole-language practitioners because they often presented rather stilted and unnatural language patterns – for example, 'Pat has a bat', 'A dog and a frog sit on a log.' Instead, children were exposed from the start to 'real' books, with no attempt to control vocabulary or sentence length. Times have changed and many publishers have returned now to producing some graded books and programmes that help children build their confidence and automaticity by applying phonic skills successfully. With this confidence they are soon ready to read books that are not controlled for vocabulary.

Moving beyond simple phonics

Obviously, to become a skilled and automatic decoder a child must soon learn far more than single letter-to-sound relationships. It is important that he or she begins to recognize and use *groups of letters* that represent a sound unit. Simple word-building activities will be extended first to the teaching of digraphs (two letters representing only one speech sound, as in sh, ch, th, wh, ph) and blends (two or three consonants forming a functional unit in which each letter contributes a sound, such as br, cl, sw, st, str, scr).

Later, for the highest level of proficiency in recognizing and spelling unfamiliar words, children need experience in working with longer and more complex letter-strings (orthographic units) such as -eed, -ide, -ite, -ight, -ound, -ate, -own, -ous, -ough, -tion. As students become proficient in identifying larger units represented by clusters of letters, they can decode and spell many more words. When children equate these letter groups with pronounceable units such as syllables in spoken words, many inconsistencies in English spelling patterns are removed. The aim of word study activities at this level is to help students recognize orthographic units and to seek out these pronounceable parts of words. The criticism is sometimes made that phonic knowledge is of little value (or even a hindrance) because of the irregularity of English spelling. This is true only if children's phonic knowledge is limited to *single* letter-to-sound correspondences.

It is essential to point out at this stage that all word-building activities are used as a supplement to reading and writing for real purposes, not as a replacement for authentic literacy experiences. For example, words used to generate lists containing important orthographic units for young children to learn can be taken from words encountered in shared-book approach, guided reading activities (described later) and from their daily writing.

It must be emphasized here that *no teacher ever uses a phonic approach exclusively*; to do so would be to teach early reading and writing in the most unnatural and boring way. Valid criticisms have been made of some forms of remedial teaching of reading that, in the past, have erred in this direction and involve nothing but repetitive drilling of isolated skills.

Building sight vocabulary

Alongside explicit instruction in phonics, children also need to acquire as rapidly as possible a mental bank of words they know automatically by sight. Much of a child's learning in this area arises naturally from their daily reading and writing experiences. The more frequently a child reads a word, the more likely it is that the word will be retained in long-term memory. During early reading experience the more often a word is decoded from its letters, the more rapidly it becomes known instantly by sight, without the need for further decoding. Immediate recognition of commonly occurring words contributes very significantly to fluent reading and easy comprehension of text.

Teachers often remark that children with learning difficulties can recognize a word on Monday but appear to have forgotten it completely by Tuesday. These students need to practise recognition of key words more frequently and systematically in order to build their 'sight vocabulary' (McDougall *et al.* 2009). The use of flashcards can be of great value for this purpose. Playing games or participating in other activities involving the reading of important words on flashcards can provide the repetition necessary for children to store these words in long-term memory. Among the many other available resources, computer software has also proved to be effective in increasing children's word recognition skills (Karemaker *et al.* 2010).

Many writers have produced lists of words, arranged in frequency of occurrence beginning with the most commonly used words. The list below contains the first sixty most commonly occurring words derived from various lists.

a	I	in	is	it	of	the	to	on	and	he	she
was	are	had	him	his	her	am	but	we	not	yes	no
all	said	my	they	with	you	for	big	if	so	did	get
boy	look	at	an	come	do	got	girl	go	us	from	little
when	as	that	by	have	this	but	which	or	were	would	what

Some words that occur very frequently are often confused and misread by beginning readers and students with reading difficulties. Basic sight words often confused include:

were	where	when	went	with	want	which	what
who	how						
here	there	their	they	them	then	than	

Comprehension

Reading comprehension is not something that comes *after* learning the mechanics of reading. Reading for meaning must be the focus of any language and literacy programme from the very beginning. When teachers read stories to children, they discuss the material with the children. They encourage them to think about and evaluate ideas in the story, clarify meaning, explain details, look for cause and effect, interpret, make predictions of what may happen next, and summarize main points.

Reading comprehension has been defined as an active thinking process through which a reader intentionally constructs meaning and deepens understanding from text (Neufeld 2006). Children who comprehend effectively draw upon prior knowledge and use many cognitive processes as they read. For example, they may visualize images associated with narrative material, they may pose questions to themselves, they may reflect upon the relevance of what they are reading, they may challenge the accuracy of stated facts, and (most importantly) they monitor their own level of understanding.

It is often observed that in many primary school classes comprehension activities linked to the reading of text rarely demand responses beyond the recall of factual information as stated directly on the page. A curriculum that sets out to develop children's comprehension should include other more challenging questions and activities that demand reflection, interpretation, prediction and critical thinking. The example below illustrates how questions can be designed to evoke different levels of thinking.

Following the reading of a short story about the crash of a passenger aircraft these questions might be posed:

- How many passengers escaped the crash? (factual)
- Did failure of cabin pressure lead to the crash? (interpretation)
- From the way he behaved before the crash, what kind of man do you think the pilot was; and could his judgement be trusted? (inferential, critical)
- A newspaper report later gave information obtained from eyewitness accounts of the crash. Is this information likely to be entirely accurate and trustworthy? Why? (critical)

Difficulties with comprehension

Some students can be reasonably accurate and fluent in their reading performance at word level but still have problems in comprehending. They may be weak at inferring meaning beyond the words on the page, and they tend not to read critically or attend to detail. In order to improve students' comprehension, it is important to consider the possible underlying difficulties.

Sometimes comprehension problems stem from a student's limited vocabulary knowledge or lack of fluency. A student may be able to read a word correctly on the page but not know its meaning (Kroeger *et al.* 2009). If a student has difficulty understanding what is read, it is worth considering whether there is a serious mismatch between the student's own listening vocabulary and the words used in the book. In this situation there is a need to devote more time to word study and to vocabulary. There is also a need sometimes to pre-teach difficult vocabulary before the text is read.

Obviously the readability level of the text is a major factor influencing whether or not material can be read easily with understanding. Difficult text – in terms of concepts, vocabulary, sentence length and complexity – is not easy for any reader to process and can cause frustration and loss of motivation. Difficult text leads to slow reading and a high error rate. Matching the readability level of books to students' current reading ability level can do much to increase comprehension and confidence.

There appears to be an optimum rate of fluency in reading that allows for accurate processing of information. Automaticity in reading, based on smooth and effortless word identification and contextual cueing, allows the reader to use all available cognitive capacity to focus on meaning. Children who read very slowly (or much too fast) often have great difficulty comprehending. Slow word-by-word reading makes it difficult for the reader to retain information in working memory long enough for meaning to be maintained. Slow reading also tends to restrict cognitive capacity to the low-level processing of letters and words, rather than allowing full attention to higher-order ideas and concepts within the text. Fast reading may result in important detail being overlooked. Sometimes modifying rate of reading needs to be a specific focus in children's intervention programmes (McDougall *et al.* 2009).

Some children have difficulty recalling information after reading. Recall is dependent partly upon such factors as vividness and relevance of the information in the text; but it is also dependent upon a student giving focused attention to the reading task and knowing that it is important to remember details. Recall is best when readers connect passage content to their own previous knowledge and experience, and when they discuss or rehearse key points from the text. These factors may provide clues to help identify why a particular child is having problems in remembering what he or she has read.

Improving comprehension

The reading comprehension skills of all children can be increased when teachers spend time demonstrating effective strategies for processing and reflecting upon text (Coyne *et al.* 2009). The explicit teaching of comprehension strategies

requires direct explanation, modelling, thinking aloud and abundant guided practice. Strategies such as self-questioning, self-monitoring, rehearsing information,
constructing story maps or graphic organizers, and creating mnemonics to assist
recall have all proved valuable. Students with reading difficulties benefit greatly
from strategy training, and tend to make significant gains in reading comprehension. However, they usually take very much longer than other students to master reading comprehension strategies, so training and practice must be continued
longer than many teachers expect.

Comprehension strategies must encompass:

- previewing the material before it is read to gain an overview;
- locating the main idea in a paragraph;
- generating questions about the material by thinking aloud;
- predicting what will happen, or suggesting possible causes-and-effects;
- summarizing or paraphrasing the main content.

A successful programme for the development of comprehension should include at
least these components:

- large amounts of time devoted to reading;
- teacher-directed instruction in comprehension strategies;
- using text as one source from which to obtain new information;
- frequent occasions when students can talk with the teacher and with one
  another about their response to a particular text.

One example of a simple reading comprehension strategy is *PQRS*, where each
letter in the mnemonic signifies a step in the strategy. The four steps are:

1. **P** = *Preview*. First scan the chapter or paragraph, attending to headings,
   subheadings, diagrams and illustrations. Gain a very general impression of
   what the text is likely to be about. Ask yourself, 'What do I know already
   about this topic?'
2. **Q** = *Question*. Next generate some questions in your mind: 'What do I
   expect to find out from reading this material? Will I need to read the text very
   carefully or can I skip this part?'
3. **R** = *Read*. Then read the passage or chapter carefully for information. Read it
   again if necessary. 'Do I understand what I am reading? What does this word
   mean? Do I need to read this section again? Are my questions answered?
   What else did I learn?'
4. **S** = *Summarize*. Finally, identify the main ideas, and state briefly the key
   points in the text in your own words.

The teacher models the application of the PQRS strategy several times using different texts, demonstrating how to focus on important points in the chapter or

article, how to check one's own understanding, how to back-track or scan ahead to gain contextual cues, and how to select the key points to summarize. This modelling helps students appreciate the value of having a plan of action for gaining meaning from text, and the value of self-questioning and self-monitoring while reading. The students are helped to practise and apply the same approach with corrective feedback from the teacher. To aid generalization, it is important to use different types of reading material used for different purposes and to remind students frequently to apply the strategy when reading texts in different areas of the curriculum.

Reading and study-skill strategies are best taught through dialogue between teacher and students working together to extract meaning from a text. Dialogue allows students and teachers to share their thoughts about the process of learning and to learn from the successful strategies used by others. Dialogue also serves a diagnostic purpose by allowing a teacher to appraise the students' existing strategies used for comprehending and summarizing texts.

Peers can facilitate each other's learning of reading strategies in small groups. An approach known as *reciprocal teaching* has proved extremely useful in a group situation to facilitate dialogue and to teach specific cognitive strategies (Alfassi *et al.* 2009; Rosenshine and Meister 1994). In this approach, teachers and students work together, sharing and elaborating ideas, generating questions that may be answered from a specific text, predicting answers, checking for meaning and finally collaborating on a summary. The teacher's role initially is to demonstrate effective ways of processing the text, to ask relevant questions and to instruct the students in strategic reading; the long-term aim is to have students master these strategies for their own independent use across a variety of contexts.

The following general principles may also help to facilitate the development of comprehension skill for all students, including those with learning difficulties.

- Ensure that the reading material presented is interesting to the students and at an appropriate readability level.
- Always make sure students are aware of the purpose in reading a particular text.
- Apply comprehension strategy training to real texts; do not rely on contrived comprehension exercises for strategy training.
- Prepare students for entry into a new text. Ask: What might we find in this chapter? What do the illustrations tell us? What does this word mean? Let's read the subheadings before we begin.
- Read comprehension questions *before* the story or passage is read so that students enter the material knowing what to look for in terms of relevant information.
- After reading the text, encourage students to set comprehension questions for each other; then use these questions to discuss what is meant by factual level information, critical reading, inferring, predicting. This type of activity lends itself to the reciprocal teaching format described above.

- Devote time regularly to discussing how a particular sample of text can be summarized. Making a summary is an excellent way of ensuring that students have identified main ideas.
- Make frequent use of advance organizers such as a list of key points to look for. Use graphic organizers or story maps to summarize relationships among key points after reading the text. These tactics have proved very helpful for students with learning difficulties.
- Use newspapers, magazine articles and online documents sometimes as the basis for classroom discussion and comprehension activities.
- In general, aim to *teach* comprehension skills and strategies, rather than simply *testing* comprehension.

Teaching approaches

Two teaching approaches that can be used effectively alongside and after phonics instruction to develop children's language comprehension, vocabulary, word recognition and reading with understanding are *shared book approach* and *guided reading*.

Shared-book approach

Shared-book approach is highly appropriate for young children in the early stages of learning to read, but the basic principles can also be applied to older children with learning difficulties if age-appropriate books are used. As a beginning-reading method, shared-book approach has proved equal or superior to other methods and produces very positive attitudes towards reading, even with slower children (Allington 2005). The activities involved in shared-book sessions provide opportunities for thinking, discussion, reflection and writing.

Shared-book approach aims to develop:

- children's enjoyment and interest in books and stories;
- thinking and comprehending
- concepts about books and print;
- awareness of English language patterns (syntax);
- word-recognition skills;
- phonic skills.

In a typical shared-book session children encounter stories, poems, jingles and rhymes read to them by the teacher using a large-size book with enlarged print and colourful pictures. Sitting in a group close to the teacher, all children can see the 'big book' easily. They can see the pictures and words, and can follow the left-to-right direction of print as the teacher reads aloud. The book should have the same visual impact from several feet away as a normal book would have in the hands of a child.

The children's attention is gained and maintained by the teacher's enthusiastic presentation of the story and discussion of the pictures. Familiarity with the language patterns in the story is developed and reinforced in a natural way. Stories that children may already know and love are useful in the early stages because they present an opportunity for the children to join in even if they cannot read the words. The first time the story is read, the teacher does not interrupt the reading with questions or teaching points. The main aim is to understand and enjoy the story.

The basic steps for implementing shared book approach include:

- *Before reading:*
  - read together the story title;
  - refer to the cover picture or other pictorial material;
  - stimulate some brief discussion about the topic and title;
  - praise children's ideas.

- *During reading the teacher:*
  - reads the story aloud;
  - maps the direction of print with finger or pointer;
  - thinks aloud sometimes: 'I wonder if she is going to . . .'
  - pauses sometimes at predictable words to allow children to guess;
  - sometimes asks children, 'What do you think will happen next?'

- *After first reading:*
  - children and teacher discuss the story;
  - recall main information.

- *Second reading of the story the teacher:*
  - aims to reinforce some word-recognition skills;
  - covers certain words to encourage prediction from context;
  - increases children's phonic knowledge by asking them to sound out certain words;
  - encourages writing (spelling) of a few of the words.

- *Follow up:*
  - writing and drawing activities;
  - word families;
  - individual and partner reading of small books (same story);
  - children make up some questions about the story.

Shared-book approach, when implemented efficiently, embodies all the basic principles of effective teaching, particularly the elements of motivation, demonstration by the teacher, student participation, feedback and successful practice. It also encourages cooperative learning and sharing of ideas between children and adults in a small group situation. The method can serve a valuable compensatory role for children with special needs who enter school lacking rich language and literacy experiences from the preschool years. The discussion of each story should not simply focus on low-level questions of fact and information, but rather should encourage children to make personal connections, think, feel, predict and extend ideas. The study of the text should also facilitate vocabulary growth.

Mueller and Hurtig (2010) provide advice on how to conduct shared reading with deaf and hard-of-hearing students, using sign language and technology. Liboiron and Soto (2006) describe the application of shared-book activities using alternative and augmentative communication with SEN students.

Guided reading

In the literature on reading methodology, 'guided reading' is most often presented as an approach for use with children after the third school year. Most of the suggestions for providing guidance are, however, merely extensions of what should have been occurring from an early stage during shared-book approach. It is an excellent way to develop a strategic, reflective and critical approach in children who are now beyond the beginner stage.

Guided reading is an approach in which the teacher supports each child's acquisition of effective reading strategies for unlocking text at increasingly challenging levels. For this reason guided reading is considered an essential part of any balanced approach to literacy teaching. It addresses the need to help students become efficient in comprehending various genres of text. The guidance provided for the students may focus at times on sub-skills such as word identification and decoding, but its main emphasis is the development of a strategic approach to comprehension.

The guided reading sessions are usually conducted by the teacher, but with heavy emphasis placed on students' active participation through discussion, cooperative learning and sharing of ideas. As with shared-book experience, there are three main stages at which guidance from the teacher is provided: *before* reading the text, *during* the reading, and *after* reading the chosen text.

• *Before reading*
Guidance before reading prepares the readers to enter the text with some clear purpose in mind. At this stage the teacher may, for example, focus children's attention on their prior knowledge related to the topic, encourage them to generate questions, raise issues, or make predictions about information that may be presented in the text, remind them of effective ways of reading the material, alert them to look out for certain points, and pre-teach some difficult vocabulary to be encountered later in the text.
• *During reading*
The guidance during reading may encourage the students to generate questions, look for cause–effect relationships, compare and contrast information, react critically, check for understanding and highlight main ideas.
• *After reading the text*
The guidance provided by the teacher may help children summarize and retell, check for understanding and recall, and encourage critical reflection and evaluation.

The processes involved in guided reading sessions, while primarily serving a teaching function, also allow the teacher to observe and assess the students' comprehension strategies. This is a very important diagnostic function, enabling a teacher to adapt reading guidance and questioning to match students' specific needs.

Reading aloud

Although almost all the reading that children will do eventually is carried out silently, there is great value in having children who are still working their way towards proficiency read aloud on a fairly regular basis. The book should be at a suitable readability level to ensure success. Reading aloud serves a number of purposes. First, it can give the child a feeling of competence and can help in developing expression and fluency. Second, it can give a clear indication to the teacher or tutor the extent to which the child has developed a sight vocabulary, is applying decoding skills when encountering unfamiliar words, is making use of contextual cues, and is self-correcting when necessary. Third, reading ability can be further enhanced during the reading as the teacher provides appropriate scaffolding, feedback and support (Pentimonti and Justice 2010).

When a child is being tutored individually, the child and adult should take turns in reading each paragraph or a page. This 'reading together' enables the adult to model good phrasing and expression and takes some of the pressure off the child. The momentum of the reading is maintained and more of the story is read during the session. Reading aloud during a tutoring session should not go on for too long or the child will become fatigued and error rate will rise.

Sustained Silent Reading

Sustained Silent Reading (SSR) is a specific period of classroom time set aside each day for students and teacher to read material of their personal choice. Often the first fifteen minutes of the afternoon session are devoted to SSR across the whole school. When SSR is implemented efficiently, all students engage in much more reading than previously. In doing so they increase their ability to concentrate on reading tasks and develop greater interest in books. In some cases the students are seen to become more discriminating readers, and the range and quality of what they choose to read improves.

If SSR is implemented inefficiently, it can result in some students wasting time. A problem emerges when students with reading difficulties select books that are too difficult for them to read independently. Teachers need to guide the choice of books to ensure that all students can read the material successfully during these periods.

The following chapter deals in more detail with strategies and specific programmes designed to help students overcome their reading difficulties. The approaches described can be regarded as appropriate for use in Tier 2 and Tier 3 teaching within the Response to Intervention model.

Online resources

- A commentary on the validity of the *Simple View of Reading* can be found at: www.ite.org.uk/ite_readings/simple_view_reading.pdf (accessed 28 March 2010).
- Additional information on implementing Shared Book Approach can be located at: www.hubbardscupboard.org/shared_reading.html (accessed 28 March 2010).
- Examples of activities for Guided Reading are provided at: www.tes.co.uk/article.aspx?storycode=354516 (accessed 28 March 2010).
- A fund of information on the phonic approach for early reading can be found on the National Literacy Trust website at: www.literacytrust.org.uk/reading_connects/resources/1035_phonics-methods_of_teaching (accessed 28 March 2010).
- Lauritzen, C. (2009) *Word Sorting: Why and How.* Paper presented at the Oregon Reading Association Conference, 06 February 2009. Available online at: www.eou.edu/ed/documents/LauritzenORA2009.doc (accessed 28 March 2010).

Further reading

Berne, J. and Degener, S.C. (2010) *Responsive Guided Reading in Grades K-5*, New York: Guilford Press.

Cohen, V.L. and Cowen, J.E. (2011) *Literacy for Children in an Information Age: Teaching Reading, Writing and Thinking*, Belmont, CA: Wadsworth Cengage.

Fox, B.J. (2010) *Phonics and Structural Analysis for the Teacher of Reading* (10th edn), Boston, MA: Allyn and Bacon.

Hipsky, S. (2011) *Differentiated Literacy and Language Arts Strategies for the Elementary School,* Boston: Pearson-Allyn and Bacon.

O'Connor, R.E. (2007) *Teaching Word Recognition: Effective Strategies for Students with Learning Difficulties*, New York: Guilford Press.

Podhajski, B., Varricchio, M., Mather, N. and Sammons, M.A. (2010) *Mastering the Alphabetic Principle*, Baltimore: Brookes.

Saunders-Smith, G. (2009) *The Ultimate Guided Reading How-to Book* (2nd edn), Thousand Oaks, CA: Corwin Press.

Smartt, S.M. and Glaser, D.R. (2010) *Next STEPS in Literacy Instruction*, Baltimore: Brookes.

Chapter 10

Intervention for reading difficulties

Under the Response to Intervention model (see Chapter 1) children who appear to be struggling with reading during the first year of school, even though they are receiving high-quality differentiated instruction, are soon given regular additional intensive tuition in small groups of up to five students. These groups are often referred to as 'booster classes'. The supplementary methods of instruction used at this Tier 2 level are research-based and of proven efficacy. The students' progress is closely monitored and when a child begins to read at or above the standard expected for his or her age, the additional support is phased out. Those who do not respond well are provided with Tier 3 intensive individual instruction.

General principles for reading intervention

- Struggling readers need to be identified as early as possible and given additional teaching in small groups.
- Daily instruction for approximately 30 minutes is recommended because it achieves very much more than twice-weekly intervention.
- Children experiencing reading difficulties must spend considerably more active learning time in developing decoding skills, word recognition, comprehension and fluency.
- Frequent practice at a high rate of success is essential to build skills to a high level of automaticity and to strengthen children's confidence to learn.
- Texts used with struggling readers must be carefully selected to ensure a very high success rate. Books with repetitive and predictable vocabulary and sentence patterns can be particularly helpful in the early stages.
- Children should be explicitly taught the knowledge, skills and strategies they seem to lack for identifying words and extracting meaning from text.
- Writing should feature in each session because this helps to strengthen concepts about print and spelling. A great deal of phonic knowledge, as well as word analysis and blending skills, can be developed by helping children work out the sounds they need when spelling the words they want to use.

- Children must perceive genuine and realistic reasons for engaging in reading and writing activities. There is a danger that struggling readers may simply receive a remedial programme comprising routine skill-building exercises.
- Multisensory and multimedia approaches often help children with learning disabilities attend to and remember letter-to-sound correspondences and sight words.
- Early intervention must also focus on the correction of any negative behaviours the children may display that impair their progress, such as disruptive behaviour, poor attention to task, or task avoidance.
- Maximum progress occurs when parents or others provide additional support and practice outside school hours. For this reason, children should also be provided with appropriate books they can read independently at home.
- Withdrawing students for tuition in small groups or individually can achieve a great deal, but it is also essential that the regular classroom programme also be adjusted (that is, differentiated in terms of reading materials, skills instruction and assignments) to allow weaker readers a greater measure of success in that setting. Failure to adapt the regular class programme frequently results in loss of achievement gains when the students no longer receive extra assistance.

Teaching procedures at Tier 2 and Tier 3 draw on what is already known about effective instruction that results in optimum learning. In particular, the following components are required:

- creation of a supportive learning environment;
- presentation of learning tasks in easy steps;
- resource materials provided at an appropriate level of difficulty;
- direct teaching, with clear modelling and demonstration of skills and strategies by the teacher or tutor;
- provision of much guided practice with feedback;
- efficient use of available instructional time;
- close monitoring of each child's progress, and re-teaching where necessary;
- independent practice and application;
- frequent revision of previously taught knowledge and skills.

Using tutors

Given the heavy workload and crowded timetable that most teachers face each day, it is becoming increasingly common in schools to find that the additional support needed by some children at Tier 2 is provided by other personnel, working under direction from the teacher. Such personnel include volunteer helpers, parents and paraprofessionals (e.g. classroom aides). These tutors must always implement learning activities that have been designed or selected by the teacher, and must follow the teacher's precise advice. It is essential that unqualified tutors also be provided with a great deal of guidance on how to function in their role of tutor-supporter (Howard 2009). In particular, they usually need help in breaking a learning task down into easier steps, giving positive corrective feedback, listening more and talking less, praising and encouraging the tutee, and being supportive rather than overly critical or 'didactic'.

The tutoring approach known as 'Pause, Prompt, Praise' (PPP) should be taught to all tutors. In this approach, when a child encounters an unfamiliar word the tutor, instead of stepping in immediately and supplying the word, waits for about 5 seconds to allow time for the child to recognize or decode it. If the child is not successful, the tutor provides a prompt, perhaps suggesting that the child attend to the initial letter, sound out the letters, or read to the end of the sentence and think of the meaning of the passage. When the child succeeds in identifying the word, he or she is praised very briefly. If the child cannot read the word after prompting, the tutor quickly supplies the word. The child is also praised for self-correcting while reading.

Another teaching strategy that should be taught to all tutors is *constant time delay* (Browder *et al*. 2009; Miller 2009). This strategy is useful for teaching and consolidating basic sight vocabulary, letter or numeral recognition, number facts and naming shapes, but can also be used in most situations where a student is asked a question. An example of time delay is when a tutor displays a word on a card and asks the child to 'Please say this word', then waits for up to 5 seconds to allow the child to think and respond. If the response is correct, the teaching sequence moves on. If incorrect, the teacher provides the correct answer, and asks the question again. The child then responds with the correct answer.

Within the classroom context support can also be provided by peer tutors (other students). The effectiveness of peer tutoring for academic improvement is well documented (e.g. Heron *et al*. 2006). The use of a partner or peer tutor has beneficial effects for students with learning difficulties by increasing time-on-task, facilitating practice with feedback and improving reading performance.

Specific programmes for intervention

In recent years, several specific intervention programmes have emerged. These programmes include *Reading Recovery, Success for All, QuickSmart, MULTILIT* and *Reading Rescue.*

Reading Recovery

Reading Recovery is an early intervention programme first developed in New Zealand and now used in many other parts of the world. In the UK, the 'Every Child a Reader Project' (2005–08) utilized *Reading Recovery* as the main intervention.

Children identified as having reading difficulties after one year in school are placed in the programme to receive intensive daily tuition tailored to their needs by a teacher specifically trained in *Reading Recovery*. The children receive this individual support for approximately fifteen to twenty weeks.

A typical *Reading Recovery* lesson includes seven activities:

- re-reading of familiar books;
- independent reading of a new book introduced the previous day;
- letter-identification activities, using plastic letters in the early stages;
- writing of a dictated or prepared story;
- sentence building and reconstruction from the story;
- introduction of a new book;
- guided reading of the new book.

The texts selected are designed to give the child a high success rate. Frequent re-reading of the familiar stories boosts confidence and fluency. Optimum use is made of the available time and students are kept fully on-task. Teachers keep 'running records' of children's oral reading performance and use these to target accurately the knowledge or strategies a child still needs to learn. It is probable that volunteer helpers would improve the quality and impact of their assistance to individual children if they utilized teaching strategies similar to those in *Reading Recovery,* under the teacher's direction.

Evidence has accumulated to indicate that *Reading Recovery*, when correctly implemented, can be effective in raising young children's reading achievement and confidence (e.g. Lee 2009; US Department of Education 2008). It is claimed that the programme is highly successful with low-performing children in Year 1, and that at least 80 per cent of children who undergo the full series of lessons can then read at the class average level or better. Evidence also suggests that children who participate in *Reading Recovery* are less likely to be referred later for remedial support. It must be noted, however, that data from the Ministry of Education in New Zealand, where 14 per cent of six-year-old children enter the programme, indicate that 9 per cent of children still do not make adequate progress and have to be referred for longer and more intensive specialist support (Lee 2009). Children's responses to *Reading Recovery* vary a great deal (Scull and Lo Bianco 2008). Reynolds *et al.* (2007) suggest that the approach fails to meet the needs of the lowest-achieving children. It is possible that these children have a genuine learning disability or some other disorder that causes a problem in learning.

Reading Recovery is not without its critics (e.g. Reynolds *et al.* 2009). For example, it is felt by some that far too little attention is devoted to explicit instruction in phonics and decoding for children with major weaknesses in this area. Other observers question the success rate of those who complete all sessions, suggesting that gains made during the programme are not always maintained later. It has also been noted that skills and motivation acquired in the *Reading Recovery* lessons do not necessarily spill over into better classroom performance. This is possibly because the reading materials provided in the regular setting are not so carefully matched to the child's ability level and the child receives much less individual support. Other difficulties associated with *Reading Recovery* include the need to organize time in the school day for some children to be taught individually; and the need to provide appropriately trained personnel to give the daily tuition. Criticisms also relate to the labour-intensive nature of the intervention, and cost effectiveness remains an unresolved issue. However, Iverson *et al.* (2005) provided evidence to show that children can be taught in pairs without any detrimental effect on their progress. Teaching children in pairs needs a little more time, but by increasing instructional time by about a quarter, *Reading Recovery* teachers can double the number of students served without compromising the outcome.

Success for All

Success for All is a whole-school programme to prevent reading failure, designed in the US by Robert Slavin and his associates (Slavin *et al.* 2009). The programme spans the school years from Kindergarten to Grade 8 and also provides training and follow-up support for tutors. *Success for All* is widely used in the US and has also been adopted and adapted for use in several other countries. Although instruction in blending and phonics were included in the programme from the start, in recent years the amount of attention given to synthetic phonics has been increased.

   Success for All involves intensive one-to-one teaching using teachers or trained paraprofessionals to help improve the literacy learning rate for at-risk and socially disadvantaged children. These reading and language lessons operate daily for 90 minutes, thus providing for intensive instruction and practice. One unique feature of *Success for All* is that junior classes throughout the school usually group for reading at the same time, with children going to different classrooms based on their ability level. This arrangement necessitates block timetabling which some schools find difficult to implement.

   Chan and Dally (2000: 226) describe the intervention thus:

> The tutoring process in *Success for All* is similar to the *Reading Recovery* program in that its first emphasis is on reading meaningful texts. Initial reading experiences are followed by phonics instruction which provides systematic strategies for cracking the reading code. Emphasis is also given to strategies to assist and monitor comprehension, such as teaching students to stop at the end of a page and ask, 'Did I understand what I just read?'

In an attempt to overcome the lack of generalization and transfer of skills sometimes found with *Reading Recovery*, the *Success for All* teacher also participates in the mainstream reading programme and assists with reading lessons in the regular classroom. This helps ensure that one-to-one tutoring is closely linked to the mainstream curriculum, not divorced from it.

   Research evidence in general has supported *Success for All* as an effective intervention model (IES 2009c), but some observers question its longer-term benefits.

A few students fail to maintain their standard after leaving the programme; and as with *Reading Recovery*, students with genuine learning disabilities appear to require even more intensive instruction than *Success for All* supplies.

QuickSmart

QuickSmart is an intervention programme designed and implemented in Australia. It targets middle years students (ages 10 to 13 years) who exhibit ongoing difficulties in acquiring functional literacy or numeracy (Graham *et al.* 2007). The total programme is extremely comprehensive and includes preparation sessions for school principals, teachers and instructors, professional follow-up, resource materials for teachers and students, a computer-based assessment and monitoring component, and the use of data from formal standardized measures of attainment for objective evaluation of students' progress. Over the period 2001 to 2010 the programme has undergone regular evaluation and revision in both the numeracy and the literacy strands. Results from several evaluation studies indicate that *QuickSmart* students are able to narrow the gap between their performance standard and that of their higher-achieving peers (NCSiMERRA 2009).

The lesson format for *QuickSmart* is designed to ensure maximum engagement in learning and a high success rate for students during each 30-minute session. Students are taught in pairs and the programme is normally implemented three times a week for thirty weeks. *QuickSmart* literacy strand aims to increase fluency (automaticity) in basic skills such as word recognition, vocabulary knowledge and sentence reading that underpin proficient performance in reading with understanding. Similarly, the numeracy strand increases speed in recall of number facts, simple calculations and problem solving. The guiding principle is that building fluency and confidence in the most basic skills enables students to devote much more cognitive effort to the higher-order processes involved in reading for meaning and in solving mathematical problems.

QuickSmart learning and teaching strategies are drawn from research evidence identifying effective methods for students with learning difficulties. These include explicit strategy instruction, modelling, discussion, questioning, feedback, guided and independent practice, and frequent reviews. Each lesson involves brief revision of work covered in the previous session, a number of guided practice activities featuring overt self-talk, discussion and practice of memory and retrieval strategies, and games and worksheet activities followed by timed and independent practice activities. Strategy instruction and concept development are seen as key components of each lesson.

The professional development component of *QuickSmart* focuses on training teachers and tutors to provide effective instruction to maximize students' engagement in learning activities during the available time, embodies abundant guided and independent practice for developing fluency and confidence, and gives positive feedback for success.

MULTILIT

The name *MULTILIT* stands for 'Making up Lost Time in Literacy' (Ellis *et al.* 2007). This comprehensive approach to teaching low-progress readers aged 7 or above addresses five key areas necessary for effective reading instruction – namely, phonemic awareness, phonic decoding, fluency, vocabulary and comprehension. It has three strands covering *word attack* (phonics), *sight words* and *reinforced reading* (reading of meaningful text). The teaching approach within *MULTILIT* draws on evidence from research into the most powerful strategies to help readers who are significantly behind their peers. The student is given a placement test at the beginning of intervention to ensure that he or she is placed at the correct level within the programme. It is claimed that a child undertaking *MULTILIT* can make fifteen months progress in word recognition in two terms of instruction.

As well as providing programme and materials development, *MULTILIT* also incorporates a strong component of professional training for teachers and tutors. The designers conduct ongoing research into the overall effectiveness of the approach.

The programme is tutor or teacher led and should be delivered at least three to four times a week. The tutor and student work through each of several levels of instruction for tackling unfamiliar words, progressing to the next level once the student has mastered the current level. Sight vocabulary is targeted at the same time, with particular reference to a list of 200 key words. Rapid automatic recognition of sight words helps to develop reading fluency. The other component in the programme is termed 'reinforced reading'. During this part of each session the student is able to transfer and generalize knowledge and skills by reading books chosen carefully to be at an instructional level.

The designers of *MULTILIT* suggest that *Reading Recovery* fails to provide the least able students with sufficient explicit training in phonemic awareness and decoding. To address this need they have also devised *MINILIT* (Meeting Individual Needs in Literacy) (Reynolds *et al.* 2007). This involves a fifteen-week tutoring programme with groups of three to six students working for one hour daily with a tutor. Each session involves time spent on phonemic awareness, sight vocabulary, word-attack skills, text reading and story time. The intervention paves the way for smooth entry into the classroom reading programme, or into *MULTILIT*.

Reading Rescue

This intervention provides intensive training for teachers and paraprofessionals in methods suitable for individual tutoring of children with literacy difficulties in Year 1 and Year 2. The programme was developed by the University of Florida and the Literacy Trust (US). A study by Ehri *et al.* (2007) suggests that adults who have undertaken the training become as effective as reading specialists in improving children's word reading skills and comprehension. See online resources at the end of this chapter for details.

Other intervention and support initiatives

Under the provisions made in the National Literacy Strategy (now part of the National Strategy: Primary) in the UK, a number of intervention measures were introduced in schools from Year 1 to Year 6. These include Early Literacy Support (ELS), with an emphasis on building phonic skills for Year 1 struggling readers, Additional Literacy Support (ALS) with a focus on skills at word level, sentence processing level, and guided reading for children in Years 3 and 4, Further Literacy Support (Year 5), and Booster Classes in Year 6 to encourage fully independent reading. Several of these interventions have undergone objective evaluation, and most are described fully on the National Literacy Trust website under 'Programmes to support pupils who are falling behind' (see online resources).

In Australia, COAG (Council of Australian Governments) initiated a project in 2009 called *Smarter Schools: Literacy and Numeracy National Partnership* to fund a range of initiatives involving evidence-based methods for improving students' achievement levels in basic skills. For details refer to online resources. Another initiative in Australia was called *An Even Start: National Tuition Program*, and operated in the period 2008–09. Parents received $700 credit to pay for individual tuition for their primary-age child. By June 2009, 87,057 children had been tutored. This programme differs from the project of the same name in the US. The US version targets low-income families to improve parents' own educational level as well as the child's. The main focus is on literacy. For details of these initiatives see online resources.

Supplementary tutoring strategies and activities

In the early stages of intervention it is helpful to incorporate materials and activities that will hold a child's attention effectively and provide additional opportunities for practising important skills. These activities should always be linked with the main theme of the lesson or topic and not simply be provided as unrelated time-fillers or 'busy work'.

Games and apparatus

Games and word-building equipment can be used as adjuncts to any early literacy programme. For example, games and activities provide enjoyable ways of discovering and reinforcing letter-sound relationships and word recognition (McDougall *et al.* 2009). Games provide an opportunity for learners to practise and over-learn essential material that might otherwise become boring and dull. Such repetition is essential for children who learn at a slow rate or who are poorly motivated. Concrete and visual materials such as flashcards, plastic letters and magnet boards can be very effective in holding a student's attention and ensuring active involvement in the lesson. The use of games and equipment may also be seen as non-threatening, thus serving a therapeutic purpose within a group or individual teaching situation.

There can be little doubt that well-structured games and apparatus perform a very important teaching function. Games and apparatus should contribute to the objectives for the lesson, not detract from them. A game or apparatus must have a clearly defined purpose and be matched to genuine learning needs in the children who are to use it.

Multisensory approaches

For students with severe learning difficulties who cannot easily remember letters or words, it is helpful to use methods that engage learners more actively with material to be studied and remembered. The abbreviation VAKT is often used to indicate that multisensory methods are visual, auditory, kinaesthetic and tactile. The typical VAKT approach involves the learner in finger-tracing over a letter or word, or tracing it in the air while at the same time saying the word, hearing the word and seeing the visual stimulus.

The best-known multisensory method is the Fernald VAK Approach, which involves the following steps. First, the learner selects a particular word that he or she wants to learn, and the teacher writes the word in blackboard-size cursive writing on a card. The child then finger-traces over the word, saying each syllable as it is traced. This is repeated until the learner feels capable of writing the word from memory. As new words are mastered, they are filed away in a card index for later revision. As soon as the learner knows a few words, these are used for constructing simple sentences.

It can be argued that multisensory approaches using several channels of input help a child to integrate, at a neurological level, what is seen with what is heard, whether it be a letter or a word. On the other hand, VAKT approaches may succeed where other methods have failed because they cause the learner to focus attention more intently on the learning task. Whatever the reason for its effectiveness, this teaching approach involving vision, hearing, articulation and movement usually does result in improved assimilation and retention. It is obviously easier to apply VAKT approach with young children (or children with intellectual disability), but in a private one-to-one tutoring situation it is still a viable proposition with older students.

Language-Experience Approach

The Language-Experience Approach (LEA) has been used very effectively in mainstream literacy programmes and as an individualized approach within remedial or intervention contexts. It forges a clear connection between speech and print. From the student's point of view, the principle underpinning the method is summed up as:

What I know about, I can talk about.
What I say can be written down by someone.
I can read what has been written.

The Language-Experience Approach uses the child's own thoughts and language to produce carefully controlled amounts of personalized reading material. In some ways, it can be described as a form of 'dictated-story' approach, with young children (or older children with literacy problems) being helped to write material that is personally meaningful and relevant to them. With assistance and practice they can read what they have written and can begin to store some of the words and spelling patterns in long-term memory. Reading their own material several times also contributes to confidence and fluency (Bixler 2009). From the daily writing, and from activities conducted in parallel with the writing, the children can also be taught important phonic knowledge and skills (Sheakoski 2008).

The Language-Experience Approach combines two major advantages that are of great benefit to struggling readers. First, the approach uses the child's own interests to generate topics and material for reading and writing in the child's own language-experience book. This tends to be more intrinsically motivating for the child than attempting to read difficult material in published texts. Second, the teacher is able to work within the child's current level of oral language competence in terms of vocabulary and sentence length. This is of great help for children who are well below average in general language ability, due perhaps to restricted preschool language experience, hearing impairment, intellectual disability, or a language disorder. The basic principles of the Language-Experience Approach can also be used within intervention programmes for non-literate adults or those learning English as a second language.

When implementing this approach, the child and tutor talk together about the chosen topic. A simple statement, using the child's own words, is then written by the teacher on the first page in the child's language-experience book – for example, 'My new bike' or 'I go to school by bus.' They read the statement together at least twice. The child may then draw or cut out a picture to accompany the statement. The teacher then writes out the child's statement again on a small strip of card (or the child copies it with assistance) and the strip is cut into separate word cards. The child engages in an activity to rebuild the sentence, using the word cards in the correct left-to-right sequence. He or she reads the statement again. The cards can then be presented in random order to practise word recognition and to identify initial sounds.

In each new lesson, a topic is selected related to the child's personal interests and the procedure described above is repeated. Teacher and child talk together about the topic, and from the discussion they agree upon one brief statement that can be written in the book. The teacher writes the agreed statement for the child who then copies it carefully under the teacher's version. Older children can be encouraged also to type or word process the same sentence on a sheet of paper and then paste that version into the book. The sentence is then written again on a strip of card and cut into separate word cards for sentence building.

Each day the child revises the sentence from the previous lesson and engages in word recognition using the separate word cards. The teacher's control over what is written each day ensures that not too much new vocabulary is added. If too much material is written, the overload will result in failure to learn.

Important sight words will occur naturally during the daily writings. When the child can recognize these easily, they can be highlighted on a vocabulary list in the front cover of the child's book. If certain common words seem to present particular problems for the child, additional activities such as flashcard quiz or Word Lotto can be introduced to practise and overlearn these words.

Gradually the amount written each day can be increased and the child will need less and less direct help in constructing sentences. The use of Language-Experience Approach in this way is highly structured and is based on mastery learning principles at each step. The approach may sound slow and tedious but it does result in progress in even the most resistant cases of reading failure. The growth in word recognition skills is cumulative.

Although opportunities are taken to teach and apply phonic decoding skills during the daily language-experience recordings and activities, it is also necessary to set aside additional time in the early stages to teach the child all basic letter-sound correspondences and to practise sounding and blending. LEA used alone is not sufficient to ensure complete mastery of essential decoding skills.

Once a child has made a positive start using the Language-Experience Approach and learning the alphabetic code, he or she can be introduced to a graded reading book. It is wise to prepare the way for this transition by including in the child's language-experience material some of the vocabulary that will be met in the first reader.

The activity of 'sentence building' is also an essential component in this approach. At any age level a learner who is beginning to read should be given the opportunity to construct and reconstruct sentences from word cards. This sentence-building procedure is valuable as a teaching technique and for informal assessment. The child's ability to construct, reconstruct and transform sentences reveals much about his or her language competence, sequencing ability and memory for words. Sentence building is particularly helpful to students with impaired hearing and those with language disorders.

Cloze procedure

Cloze procedure is a simple technique designed to help a reader become more skilled in using context to support recognition of unfamiliar words. The procedure merely requires that certain words in a sentence or paragraph be deleted and the reader asked to read the paragraph and supply possible words that might fill the gaps.

It was Monday morning and Leanne should have been going to sch____. She was still in ____. She was hot, and her throat was ____.
'I think I must take you to the d____,' said her ____. 'No school for you t____y.'

Variations on the cloze technique involve leaving the initial letter of the deleted word to provide an additional clue; or at the other extreme, deleting several consecutive words, thus requiring the student to provide a phrase that might be appropriate. The use of the cloze procedure can be integrated easily into the shared-book experience and guided reading activities described in Chapter 9.

Cloze activities can be used with individuals or with a small group of students. The prepared paragraphs are duplicated on sheets for the children or displayed on an overhead projector. In a group, the children discuss the best alternatives for the missing words and then present these to the teacher. Reading, vocabulary and comprehension are all being developed by a closer attention to logical sentence structure and meaning.

Repeated Reading and the Impress Method

Repeated Reading is a procedure designed to increase fluency, accuracy, expression and confidence in children who are already under way with reading (Bixler 2009; Staudt 2009). The procedure can be particularly useful with secondary school students with reading difficulties. Repeated Reading simply requires readers to practise reading a short passage aloud until their accuracy rate is above 95 per cent and the material can be read aloud fluently. The teacher first models the reading while the student follows in the text and then spends a few minutes making sure that the student fully understands the material. The student practises reading the same material aloud, with corrective feedback from the teacher if necessary. The student continues to practise reading the text until nearly perfect, and finally records the reading on audiotape. When the recording is played back, the student hears a fluent performance, equal in standard to the reading of even the most competent student in class. This provides an important boost to the student's confidence. Greater fluency also leads to improved comprehension because the reader is expending less mental effort on identifying each word (O'Connor 2007). Oral reading fluency (ORF) is a useful aspect of reading performance that can be measured reasonably accurately and can be used as one indicator of improvement over time.

The Impress Method is a variation of Repeated Reading using a unison reading procedure in which the student and tutor read aloud together at a natural rate (Flood et al. 2005). It may be necessary to repeat the same sentence or paragraph several times until the student becomes fluent at reading the material with low error rate. The Impress Method is particularly useful when a child has developed a few word-recognition skills but is lacking in fluency and expression. It is recommended that sessions should last no more than 5 to 10 minutes but provided on a very regular basis for several months.

The Impress Method is very appropriate for use in peer tutoring, where one child who is a better reader provides assistance for a less able friend. In such cases the peer tutor usually needs to be shown how to act effectively as a model reader, and how to be supportive and encouraging to the tutee, as suggested above.

ICT and reading

The main benefit of computer-assisted learning is that the technology makes use of well-established principles of instruction such as clear presentations, modelling in easy steps, active participation and practice to mastery level. Computers are infinitely patient, allow for self-pacing by the student and provide immediate feedback. Students are active throughout the learning session and have high levels of motivation. Many programs provide scaffolding and feedback to the learner while at the same time ensuring practice with high success rate. Whether used by one student alone, or by two students working together, the computer is an excellent tool for learning in the regular classroom (Lan *et al.* 2009; Pletka 2007).

Information and communication technology has created many new and interesting ways for children to engage in literacy activities for authentic purposes (Hamilton 2009; Ingram 2010). For example, a study by Cooney and Hay (2005) found that a structured use of the Internet as a medium for applying and practising reading skills was very effective in middle school, with improvements in reading achievement, engagement rates and attitude. Studies have indicated that children with reading difficulties can gain much from using text-to-speech (TTS) software, with its combined visual and auditory presentation. Gibson (2009) has reported that a computer program, *Read Naturally*, was effective in increasing oral reading fluency and comprehension standard in First Grade children. This study also provided added support for the value of repeated reading.

At the most basic level of computer-assisted learning (CAL), computer programs exist that will help students improve letter recognition, alphabet knowledge, word recognition, decoding, sentence-completion, cloze and spelling skills (Chambers *et al.* 2008; Karemaker *et al.* 2010). Spelling and word study may be presented through age-appropriate programs in which a target word is displayed on the screen and the student is required to copy (retype) the word. The word is then embedded in a sentence for the student to read and again copy. Gradually the cues are removed until the student is reading, writing and using the word correctly in context with a high degree of automaticity.

At higher levels, programs may focus more on comprehension, application, and 'reading to learn' rather than 'learning to read'; but students with reading problems are often limited in their ability to use ICT to research information for classroom projects. Close monitoring by the teacher, and judicious use of peer tutoring, can help to reduce this problem and at the same time help the student acquire computer skills.

In the home situation, the computer can also aid literacy development because children can work alone or with a parent on early reading and writing skills (Ingram 2010). Parents who are computer literate can also help their children search for, read and interpret information from Internet for homework or personal interest.

Online resources

- Information on *Every Child a Reader Project* (UK) and *Reading Recovery* can be found online at the National Literacy Trust website: www.literacytrust. org.uk/reading_connects/resources/1091_every_child_a_reader_and_ reading_recovery (accessed 29 March 2010).

- Research data on the effectiveness of *Reading Recovery* can be located at the Reading Recovery Council of North America website at: www.readingrecovery.org/research/effectiveness/index.asp (accessed 29 March 2010).

- Details of *MULTILIT*, including research data, can be found at: www.multilit. com/Home/tabid/1354/Default.aspx (accessed 29 March 2010).

- Teachers can obtain information on *Success for All* from: www.successforall. org.uk. Or from the Success for All Foundation website at: www.successforall.net/elementary/sfa.htm (both accessed 29 March 2010).

- Details of *QuickSmart* literacy and numeracy intervention can be found online at: www.une.edu.au/simerr/quicksmart/pages/index.php (accessed 29 March 2010).

- A useful summary of intervention methods and resources is available on the National Literacy Trust website: www.literacytrust.org.uk/Database/ resources2.html#intervention (accessed 29 March 2010).

- Details of the professional training programme titled *Reading Rescue* can be found at www.literacytrust.org/home (accessed 29 March 2010).

- Details of the Australian Project *An Even Start* can be located at: www. anevenstart.deewr.gov.au/ (accessed 29 March 2010).

- The programme *Even Start* in the US is described fully at: www2.ed.gov/ programs/evenstartformula/index.html (accessed 29 March 2010).

- *Smarter Schools: Literacy and Numeracy National Partnership* is described at: www.coag.gov.au/coag_meeting_outcomes/2008-11-29/docs/20081129_ literacy_numeracy_factsheet.rtf (accessed 29 March 2010).

- The Language-Experience Approach is clearly described at the Literacy Connections website: www.literacyconnections.com/InTheirOwnWords.php (accessed 29 March 2010).

- General information on computer-assisted reading, together with some examples of formats, can be located at the American Institutes for Research website at: www.k8accesscenter.org/training_resources/computeraided_reading.asp (accessed 29 March 2010).

- For information on using computers for literacy purposes with vision-impaired students, see University at Buffalo Website, Assistive Technology Training Online Project (ATTO): http://atto.buffalo.edu/registered/ATBasics/ Populations/LowVision/reading.php (accessed 29 March 2010).

Further reading

Alber-Morgan, S. (2010) *Using RTI to Teach Literacy to Diverse Learners K-8*, Thousand Oaks, CA: Corwin Press.

Glover T.A. and Vaughn, S. (eds) (2010) *The Promise of Response to Intervention.* New York: Guilford.

McCormick, S. and Zutell, J. (2011) *Instructing Students who have Literacy Problems* (6th edn), Boston: Pearson-Allyn and Bacon.

McEwan-Adkins, E.K. (2010) *40 Reading Intervention Strategies for K-6 Students: Research-based Support for RTI,* Bloomington, IN: Solution Tree Press.

Rasinski, T.V., Padak, N.D. and Fawcett, G. (2010) *Teaching Children Who Find Reading Difficult* (4th edn), Boston, MA: Allyn and Bacon.

Richards, C. and Leafstedt, J. (2010) *Early Reading Intervention: Strategies and Methods for Struggling Readers*, Boston: Allyn and Bacon.

Scanlon. D.M., Anderson, K.L. and Sweeney, J.M. (2010) *Early Intervention for Reading Difficulties,* New York: Guilford Press.

Schirmer, B.R. (2010) *Teaching the Struggling Reader*, Boston: Pearson-Allyn and Bacon.

Chapter 11

Difficulties with writing

Writing is one of the most complex skills that students must learn and it is not surprising that some have great difficulty in achieving proficiency (Svensson 2010). While reading and writing are separate processes, and in some respects draw upon different areas of knowledge and skill, there is also some overlap between reading and writing. For example, automaticity in recognition of sight words is fairly closely linked with automaticity in writing those common words correctly; knowledge of phonics helps both reading and spelling; familiarity with grammar and sentence structure is important in writing and is also one of the cueing systems used in fluent reading.

In the same way that a 'simple view of reading' has been proposed (see Chapter 9), so too a 'simple view of writing' has emerged (Beringer *et al.* 2002; Westwood 2009b). This simple view suggests that the active creation of written text involves just two areas of skill: (i) lower-order transcription skills such as handwriting (or keyboarding) and spelling; and (ii) the self-regulated thinking, planning and creating that are involved in generating, sequencing and expressing ideas. The more automatic the lower-order skills become, the greater will be the cognitive capacity available to the writer for thinking, composing and revising (Medwell *et al.* 2009).

Areas of difficulty

Many of the most basic problems that students with learning difficulties experience occur first in the lower-order skills of handwriting and spelling. To illustrate this point, a study in the UK found that at age 11 to 12 years at least 33 per cent of children could not meet the age-appropriate standard for spelling, and 95 per cent could not meet the standard for speed of writing (25 words per minute). Boys' results in the study were well below those of the girls (Montgomery 2008).

Moving beyond lower-order skills, the higher-order demands of written expression are even more difficult for some children to acquire. Written expression involves much more than adding or combining discrete skills in a linear sequence. Competence in expression draws heavily upon an individual's background knowledge, vocabulary, life experience, imagination, and sense of audience, as well as possession of effective strategies for planning, encoding, reviewing and revising written language.

According to Chalk *et al.* (2005), students with learning difficulties often lack a basic knowledge of how best to approach the writing process. They often display the following weaknesses:

- limited ability in planning, executing and revising written work;
- difficulties in formulating goals and generating ideas;
- inability to organize an appropriate structure for a composition;
- a tendency to spend no time in thinking before writing;
- slowness and inefficiency in executing the mechanical aspects of writing;
- limited output of written work in the available time.

In addition, weak writers often use either very simple sentence structures, or tend to produce long and rambling sentences with repetitive use of conjunctions. They favour simple words with known spellings over more interesting and expressive words – but still make many spelling errors. Above all else, they do not enjoy writing and would prefer to avoid it.

It seems that boys often have more difficulty than girls in achieving a satisfactory standard in written work – as in most other aspects of literacy (Montgomery 2008; Watson *et al.* 2010). However, an intervention project in the UK found that boys could improve their skills significantly if writing activities are linked more closely with visual stimuli, real experiences and ICT. They appear to work best when writing sessions are carefully structured, with adequate discussion, preparation and modelling by the teacher so that they have a clear understanding of the demands of the task. Among positive outcomes from this project was the observation that both quantity and quality of writing improved, and the boys' willingness to write increased (UKLA/PNS 2004).

Losing confidence and motivation

A student who has problems writing will experience no satisfaction in pursuing the task and will try to avoid writing whenever possible. Avoidance reduces the opportunities for practice, and lack of practice results in no improvement. The student loses confidence and self-esteem in relation to writing, as well as developing an even more negative attitude. The problem for the teacher is to motivate these students to write and to provide them with enough support to ensure increased success. It is clear that they need to be taught effective strategies for approaching writing tasks.

It is fortunate that contemporary approaches to the teaching of writing have done much to alleviate the anxiety and frustration that many of the lower-ability students experienced in years gone by whenever 'composition' appeared on the timetable. To them it meant a silent period of sustained writing, with little or no opportunity to discuss work with others or ask for assistance. Great importance was placed on accuracy and neatness at the first attempt, and many children felt extremely inhibited. Even when the teacher was not a severe judge of the product, the children themselves sometimes carried out self-assessment and decided that they could not write because their product was not perfect. An attitude quickly developed in the child, 'I can't write' or 'I hate writing', and a failure cycle was established. It is therefore important to consider approaches to teaching that may prevent loss of confidence and motivation, and instead make students feel successful as writers.

Teaching approaches

There are two main approaches to teaching writing – the traditional *skills-based approach* with a focus on instruction in basic skills of writing, and the *process approach* with a focus on how best to generate ideas and express them clearly through a process of drafting and revising.

Skills-based approach to writing

The skills-based or traditional approach usually involves fairly tight control imposed by the teacher. Writing skills are developed mainly through structured exercises, practice materials and set topics. When more extensive writing is required, the teacher usually selects a common essay topic about which all students will be expected to write. The audience for the writing is thus the teacher. Often a teacher simply sets a writing topic but provides no instruction in how best to attempt the task. Without this guidance the writing activity becomes more of an *assessment* procedure rather than a learning experience.

This traditional skills-based approach is believed to be less motivating for students than having them working on topics and genres they have chosen for themselves. There is also some doubt that skills taught in routine exercises ever transfer to children's free writing, and it is argued that these component skills of writing and editing should be taught in an integrated way as part of the feedback given to children as they write on their own chosen topics. Tompkins (2007) reminds teachers that rather than teaching isolated skills in the hope of improving writing they should scaffold and support students' own developing strategies as they write for authentic purposes of communication. Unfortunately, the evidence suggests that teachers often devote more time to the mechanics of transcription than they do to the teaching of strategies necessary for thoughtful drafting and revising (Graham and Harris 2005).

Process approach to writing

In the 1980s, there was a significant shift of emphasis away from routine skills-based instruction to an exploration of the processes involved in composing, editing and revising written work (Graves 1983). In recent years, the approach has become very popular in primary and secondary schools around the world. Variants of the process approach are described later, and include writing workshop, shared writing and guided writing.

Process approach helps young children understand that a first attempt at writing rarely constitutes a finished product. Writing usually has to pass through a number of separate stages, from the initial hazy formulation of ideas to the first written draft, through subsequent revisions and editing to a final product (although not *all* writing should be forced to pass through all stages). Teachers themselves should model this writing process in the classroom and demonstrate the planning, composing, editing and publishing stages in action.

In the process approach, children confer with the teacher and with peers to obtain opinions and feedback on their written work as it progresses. Although process writing is very much a child-centred approach, it still provides abundant opportunities for a teacher to give as much individualized direct instruction as necessary to advance children's writing abilities. Students' responses are deliberately shaped and refined through a natural process of feedback and reinforcement. In addition, children are taught specific aspects of drafting, editing, grammar and style through the provision of appropriate 'mini lessons' from time to time.

Since the process approach depends so much upon student-writers having someone with whom to confer, it is important to consider possible sources of assistance in the classroom beyond the teacher and classmates. Teacher aides, older students, college and university students on teaching practice and parent volunteers can all provide help within the classroom programme. In all cases, these helpers must understand their role and they require some informal training by the teacher if they are to adopt an approach that is supportive rather than critical or didactic.

Writing workshop

Writing workshop (or writers' workshop) is a whole-class session where all children are engaged in various forms of coordinated writing activity and are supported in their endeavours by classmates and teacher (Conroy *et al.* 2009). Children in writing workshop are helped to go through the complete prewriting, drafting, revising and publishing cycle, and their products become part of the reading material available in the classroom.

The motivation for writing workshop comes mainly through the freedom of choice that children are offered in terms of topics and genre. Choice of topic on which to write is usually made by the writer rather than the teacher. It is believed that selecting a personal topic reduces the problem of generating new ideas that are necessary for a teacher-chosen topic. A familiar topic reduces cognitive load in the initial planning and drafting stages.

Typically, a writing workshop session begins with teacher presentation or sharing time (5–10 minutes), followed by a mini-lesson on some aspect of writing (for example, the use of adjectives) (10 minutes). Students then work independently on their own writing or work in small groups with the teacher (30–40 minutes).

During this time word processing and access to other forms of information tech-nology may be appropriate and beneficial. Finally, children share their writings with their peers.

The teaching of specific skills takes place in three ways:

- near the beginning of the lesson in the form of a mini-lesson;
- in discussion with individual children throughout the lesson;
- through whole-class sharing time at the end of the lesson.

During the session the teacher should confer with almost every student about his or her writing. This conference with the student involves far more than dispensation of general praise and encouragement. The conference between teacher and indi-vidual students should represent the 'scaffolding' principle whereby the teacher supplies the necessary support and specific guidance to help students gain increas-ing control over their own writing strategies. Differences in abilities among the students will determine the amount of time the teacher spends with individuals.

Shared writing

Comments, advice and feedback in writing workshops come not only from teacher but also from peers. A friend or partner can be used as a sounding board for ideas and can read, discuss and make suggestions for written drafts. Group sharing and peer editing are essential elements in the sessions. The underlying principle is 'writers working together', cooperating and providing feedback to one another.

By middle primary school, most children are capable of evaluating the quality of their own writing, but they still need guidance from the teacher and peers on how best to revise and improve their work. Peer critiquing of this type is often written about as if it is a simple strategy to employ in the classroom; but in real-ity it needs to be done with great sensitivity. Children with learning difficulties or with low social status within the class may not cope well with negative and critical feedback from their peers because it may seem to draw public attention to their weaknesses. Teachers must spend time modelling the positive aspect of helpful critiquing before expecting students to implement it – how to give descrip-tive praise, how to highlight good points, how to detect what is not clear, how to help with the generation of new ideas and how to assist with polishing the final product.

Guided writing

Guided writing is also an element within the process approach. Guided writing involves demonstrations by the teacher of specific writing strategies, styles or genres, followed by guided and independent application of the same techniques by the students. Using a whiteboard, a teacher might begin by demonstrating, for example, how to generate ideas for a new topic, how to create and structure an opening paragraph and how to develop the remaining ideas in logical sequence. Later, students take it in turns to present their own material to the group, receiving constructive feedback from peers.

The students can be given guidelines or checklists to help them evaluate and revise their written work. For example, the checklist might contain the following questions.

- Did you begin with an interesting sentence?
- Are your ideas easy to understand?
- Are your ideas presented in the best sequence?
- Did you give examples to help readers understand your points?
- Is your material interesting? Can you make it more interesting?
- Have you used paragraphs?
- Have you checked spelling and punctuation?

The guided approach is thought to be more effective in fostering students' writing skills than either the traditional teacher-direct method or unstructured use of process method.

Strategy training

The weaknesses in writing described earlier indicate that students need to be taught effective plans of action for approaching writing tasks. In the same way that strategy training can improve reading comprehension, it can also be effective in improving writing, particularly the aspects of planning, drafting, revising and self-correcting (Baker *et al.* 2009; Joseph and Konrad 2009). Students begin to exhibit more sophisticated writing once they develop effective strategies for planning and revising text, and as they learn to self-regulate.

An appropriate starting point for strategy training is for the teacher to demonstrate, step by step, an effective plan for tackling a particular writing topic. The teacher uses 'thinking aloud' to reveal the way he or she goes about planning, generating ideas, drafting, revising and editing the piece of writing. This can be demonstrated on the whiteboard, overhead projector, or computer screen. The students then apply the steps within the strategy to a similar topic, and receive support and feedback from the teacher.

During strategy training students are typically taught to use self-questioning or self-instruction to assist with the process of planning, writing, evaluating and improving a written assignment. Questions similar to those listed above under 'Guided writing' can be used as prompts within the strategy. Emphasis is placed on metacognitive or self-regulating aspects of the writing process (self-checking for clarity in what is written, self-monitoring, self-correction). In the early stages the students may be required to verbalize the steps or questions as they work through the plan of action. Later, as the student becomes more confident in using the strategy independently, overt verbalization is unnecessary.

A simple example of a strategy for writing uses the mnemonic LESSER ('LESSER helps me write MORE'). The strategy guides students to organize their thoughts and to write a longer and more interesting assignment than they would otherwise produce.

L = List your ideas.
E = Examine your list.
S = Select your starting point.
S = Sentence one will tell us about this first idea.
E = Expand on this first idea with another related sentence.
R = Read what you have written. Revise if necessary. Repeat for the next paragraph.

Many low-achieving students have, in the past, written very little during times set aside for writing. This is part of the vicious circle which begins with 'I don't like writing so I don't write much, so I don't get much practice, so I don't improve . . .'. Use of strategies such as LESSER can help reduce this problem.

It is always necessary to maximize the possibility that a strategy will generalize beyond the training sessions into students' everyday writing. This may be achieved by:

• continuing with instruction and practice until students have thoroughly mastered the strategy;
• helping students understand how the strategy works, and how it helps them to produce better results;
• leading students to consider when and where a particular strategy can be used;
• discussing how to modify a strategy for different situations;
• teaching students to use self-statements as a means to reinforce strategy use and to cope with any difficulties.

Intervention for individuals and groups

Students who exhibit difficulties in written expression fall into one of two groups. The groups are not mutually exclusive and there is overlap in terms of instructional needs. The first group comprises those students of any age level who have learning difficulties or who have a learning disability. For these students, the teacher needs to structure every writing task carefully and provide appropriate support to ensure the students' successful participation (Polloway *et al.* 2008).

The second group comprises those students of any age who can write but do not like to do so – the reluctant and unmotivated students. These students appear not to see the relevance of writing, or have not experienced the excitement of written communication and get no satisfaction from it. Some of these students may have encountered negative or unrewarding experiences during the early stages of becoming writers. They may have acquired what has been termed 'writing apprehension' which now causes them to avoid the task whenever possible. Their problem is one of poor motivation leading to habitually low levels of practice and productivity. Here the teacher must try to regain lost interest and build confidence.

Ideally, a student receiving extra assistance will choose his or her own topics for writing; if not, it is essential to give the student an appropriately stimulating subject. The topic must be interesting and relevant, and the student must see a purpose in transferring ideas to paper. Regardless of whether the activity involves writing a letter or email to a friend or composing a science-fiction fantasy story, the student should perceive the task as enjoyable and worthwhile.

The first important step in improving a student's writing skills is to allocate sufficient time for writing within the school day. To some extent the introduction of 'literacy hour' in many schools has addressed this issue. If writing occurs daily, there is much greater likelihood that writing skills, motivation and confidence will all improve.

In general, students with difficulties need help in two basic stages of the writing process: (i) planning to write, and (ii) revising or polishing the final product. The teaching of each of these stages should embody basic principles of effective instruction – namely, modelling by the teacher, guided practice with feedback and independent practice and application.

Paving the way to success

A classroom atmosphere that encourages students to experiment with their writing without fear of criticism or ridicule is a very necessary condition for the least able students. In many cases, particularly with the upper primary or secondary student with a history of bad experiences in writing, simply creating the atmosphere is not enough. Much more than the ordinary amount of guidance and encouragement from the teacher will also be needed. Students with writing difficulties benefit from being given a framework they can use whenever they write (see 'Strategy training' and 'Guided writing' above). They need specific guidance in how to begin their writing, how to continue, and how to complete the task. In this context, they can be taught a set of questions to ask themselves which will facilitate the generation of ideas and will assist with the organization and presentation of the material across different writing genres.

Students with difficulties need to be helped *daily*. With low-achieving students or those lacking in confidence, the teacher must structure each writing assignment very carefully – for example, by talking through the topic first, then writing down key vocabulary and a few possible sentence beginnings on the whiteboard for the student to use. During discussion and feedback stages, the teacher should not over correct, but rather encourage the student to talk and think. The main aim is to help the student generate ideas and sort these into a logical sequence.

In the early stages, it is important not to place undue stress upon accuracy in spelling since this can stifle the student's attempts at communicating ideas freely. Invented spelling gives students the freedom to write with attention to content and sequence. As the student becomes more confident and productive, the teacher, while still remaining supportive, will make the conferring stage rather less structured. Open-ended questions can still be used to extend the student's thinking and to build upon the writing so far produced.

Small booklets are usually better than exercise books for students who are unskilled and reluctant writers. The opportunity to make a fresh start every week is far better than being faced with the accumulation of evidence of past failures which accrue in a thick exercise book. For students of all ages, a loose-leaf folder may be a useful replacement for the traditional exercise book.

Paired writing

In the same way that working with a partner can improve reading skills, having a partner for writing is also beneficial. Paired writing can be used with cross-age tutoring, peer tutoring, parent–child tutorial groupings and in adult literacy classes. The pairing comprises a helper and a writer. The helper's role is to stimulate ideas from the writer that the helper notes down on a pad. When sufficient ideas have been suggested, the helper and writer review the notes on the pad and discuss the best sequence for presenting these. A story planner format could be used (see below). The writer then begins first draft writing, based mainly on the notes. In the case of students with severe learning difficulties, the helper may act as scribe as the 'writer' dictates. The helper then reads aloud the draft that has been written. The writer then reads the draft. Working together, the pair will edit the draft for clarity, meaning, sequence, spelling and punctuation, with the writer taking the lead if possible. The writer then revises the material by writing or word processing a 'final copy'. Helper and writer discuss and evaluate the finished product.

Suggestions for reluctant writers

The following sections describe various activities and teaching strategies that can be used with struggling writers.

The skeleton story

Getting started is the first obstacle faced by many students who find writing difficult. To address this problem some teachers use 'writing frames' in the form of templates and rubrics designed to scaffold and make simple the task of composing (Hampton *et al.* 2009). One version is to provide some stem sentences that must be completed using the student's own ideas and words. Example:

Something woke me in the middle of the night.
I heard..

> I climbed out of the bed quietly and................
> To my surprise I saw..................................
> At first I...
> I was lucky because...................................
> In the end ....

With groups of low-achieving students it is useful, through collaborative effort first, to complete one version of the skeleton story on the blackboard. This completed story is read to the group. Each student is then given a sheet with the same sentence beginnings, but he or she must write a different story from the one on the blackboard. The stories are later shared in the group. Students of limited ability find it very much easier to complete a story when the demands for writing are reduced in this way, and when a structure has been provided.

Patterned writing

For students with limited writing ability, a familiar story with repetitive and predictable sentence patterns can be used as a stimulus for writing a new variation on the same theme. The plot remains basically the same but the characters and the details are changed. For example, the children write a new story involving a 'Big Grey Elephant' instead of a 'Little Red Hen'; and the Big Grey Elephant tries to get other animals to help him move a log from the path: 'Who will help me move the log?' 'Not I', said the rat. 'Not I', said the monkey, 'Not I', said the snake' and so forth.

Sentence combining

Activities involving the reconstruction of several simple sentences into longer and more interesting sentences have proved valuable for weaker writers. The activities provide an opportunity for writers to construct more interesting and varied sentences within their stories or reports. For example:

> The giant was hungry.
> The giant ate the meat pie.
> The meat pie was huge.
> = The hungry giant ate the huge meat pie.

The main benefit from the experience of sentence combining is that the process can be revisited every time a student is asked to read, edit and improve a piece of writing.

Story planner

A story planner is a form of graphic organizer that provides struggling writers with a starting point for generating ideas for writing. A 'story web' is created by writing the main idea or title in the centre of a sheet of paper, then branching off from the main idea into different categories of information. These ideas and categories might include: the setting for the story, the type of action that takes place, the characters involved, the outcome, etc.

Prompts and cues could be used to stimulate the students' thinking as the web is constructed. Students brainstorm for ideas that might go into the story. In random order, each idea is briefly noted against a spoke in the web. The class then reviews the ideas and decides upon an appropriate starting point for the story. Number '1' is written against that idea. How will the story develop? The children determine the order in which the other ideas will be used, and the appropriate numbers are written against each spoke. Some of the ideas may not be used at all and can be erased. Other ideas may need to be added at this stage, and numbered accordingly. The students now use the bank of ideas recorded on the story planner to start writing their own stories. The brief notes can be elaborated into sentences and the sentences gradually extended into paragraphs.

By preparing the draft ideas and then discussing the best order in which to write them, the students have tackled two of the most difficult problems they face when composing – namely, planning and sequencing.

Expanding an idea

Begin by writing a short, declarative sentence.

We have too many cars coming into our school parking area.

Next, write two or three sentences that add information to, or are connected with, the first sentence. Leave two lines below each new sentence.

We have too many cars coming into our school parking area.

The noise they make often disturbs our lessons.

The cars travel fast and could knock someone down.

What can we do about this problem?

Now write two more sentences in each space.

We have too many cars coming into our school parking area.
The noise they make often disturbs our lessons. The drivers sound their horns and rev the engines. Sometimes I can't even hear the teacher speak. The cars

travel fast and could knock someone down. I saw a girl step out behind one yesterday. She screamed when it reversed suddenly.

What can we do about this problem? Perhaps there should be a sign saying 'NO CARS ALLOWED'. They might build some speed humps or set a speed limit.

Edit the sentences into appropriate paragraphs and combine some short statements into longer, complex sentences. Use of a word processor makes these steps much faster and the process of editing and checking spelling easier. The teacher demonstrates this procedure, incorporating ideas from the class. Students are then given guided practice and further modelling over a series of lessons, each time using a different theme.

Writing a summary

Students with learning difficulties often have problems when required to write a summary of something they have just read. Specific help is needed in this area and one or more of the following procedures can be helpful to such students.

- After the reading, the teacher provides a set of 'true/false' statements based on the text. The statements are presented on the sheet in random order. The student must read each statement and place a tick against those that are true. The student then decides the most logical sequence in which to arrange these true statements. When copied into the student's exercise book these statements provide a brief but accurate summary of the text.
- The teacher provides some sentence 'starters' in a sequence that will provide a framework for the summary. For example: 'The first thing most travellers notice when they arrive at the airport is . . .'; 'When they travel by taxi to the city they notice . . .'. The student completes the unfinished sentences and in doing so writes the summary.
- The teacher provides a summary but with key words or phrases omitted. The words may be presented below the passage in random order, or clues may be given in terms of initial letters of word required. The student completes the passage by supplying the missing words.
- Simple multiple-choice questions can be presented. The questions may deal with the main ideas from the text and with supporting detail. By selecting appropriate responses and writing these down the student creates a brief summary.

All the suggestions above are designed to simplify the task demands for writing, and at the same time motivate the reluctant student to complete the work successfully. In most cases, the use of a word processor will also add interest and an important element of control by the learner.

Word processors

There is now clear research evidence supporting the benefits of using word processors with learning-disabled students (e.g. MacArthur 2009). Undoubtedly, the arrival of word processors in the classroom heralded a new opportunity for students of all levels of ability to enter the realm of writing and composing with more enthusiasm and enjoyment (Moore-Hart 2010). Using a word processor makes the task of writing far less arduous. Word processing seems to be of great benefit to students who do not usually write very much, and to those with the most severe spelling problems. In particular, students with learning difficulties gain confidence in creating, editing, erasing and publishing their own unique material through a medium that holds attention and is infinitely patient.

For students with learning difficulties, word processing de-emphasizes physical aspects such as handwriting and letter formation, and allows more mental effort to be devoted to generating ideas. Students tend to work harder and produce longer essays, of better quality, when using word processors for writing. Polkinghorne (2004: 26) states:

> Computers can change the whole writing process [making] it easier to plan and record ideas. It is much easier to edit, change and work with those ideas and publish and share the final product. Computer access helps alleviate hesitancy caused by poor spelling, lack of grammar skills, poor handwriting, and inability to proofread and edit hand written work easily.

In a tutorial situation, the use of a computer allows the tutor to observe the writing process more directly and gain better insights into the student's existing strategies for composing, editing and proofreading. Targeted support can then be given to the student with greater precision.

Students with learning difficulties need first to develop some basic keyboard skills if the word processing is to be achieved without frustration. It is usually necessary to teach only the most essential skills to enable the student to access the program, type the work and save the material at regular intervals. Even this simple level of operation can give some students a tremendous boost to confidence and can encourage risk-taking in writing and composing. Using a computer regularly can enhance students' written work significantly in terms of organization and control over the writing process.

Online resources

- Hints for improving writing can be found at the *Homework Centre*: www.infoplease.com/homework/writingskills1.html (accessed 28 March 2010).
- *About.com: Learning Disabilities* website also has useful advice on improving writing skills: http://learningdisabilities.about.com/od/instructionalmaterials/ht/3point5paper.htm (accessed 28 March 2010).

- The National Institute of Neurological Disorders and Stroke has information about *dysgraphia* (a specific learning disability affecting writing): www.ninds.nih.gov/disorders/dysgraphia/dysgraphia.htm (accessed 28 March 2010).

Further reading

Carter, J. (2010) *Creating Writers: A Creative Writing Manual for Key Stage 2 and Key Stage 3,* London: Routledge.

Cunningham, P.M. (2010) *What Really Matters in Writing: Research-based Practices across the Elementary Curriculum*, Boston, MA: Allyn and Bacon.

Dudley-Marling, C. and Paugh, P. (2009) *A Classroom Teacher's Guide to Struggling Writers,* Portsmouth, NH: Heinemann.

Graham, J. and Kelly, A. (2010) *Writing under Control* (3rd edn), London: Routledge.

Lenski, S. and Verbruggen, W. (2010) *Writing Instruction and Assessment for Learners K to 8,* New York: Guilford Press.

Moore-Hart, M.A. (2010) *Teaching Writing in Diverse Classrooms K-8*, Boston: Pearson-Allyn and Bacon.

Chapter 12

Difficulties with spelling

For many students with learning difficulties, spelling continues to present a problem long after reading skills have improved. In part, this problem arises in English language because it is impossible to spell every word by a simple translation of sound to letter. But children's difficulties can also result from too little time and attention being devoted to the explicit teaching of spelling skills and strategies. For several decades, instruction in spelling ceased to feature prominently in the primary school curriculum due mainly to the influence of whole-language approach to literacy. However, in recent years, the systematic teaching of spelling has enjoyed something of a renaissance due to a growing awareness that children will not necessarily become adequate spellers if they are left to discover spelling principles for themselves. The current view is that taking a systematic approach to spelling and word study is essential and leads to measurable improvement in students' spelling ability. Current teaching approaches aim to help students become more independent in their spelling, and be capable of detecting and self-correcting errors (Viel-Ruma *et al.* 2007).

Process approach to spelling

The advent of whole-language philosophy saw spelling become fully integrated into children's daily writing activities rather than being treated as a topic in its own right. It was argued that spelling skills are best acquired within a meaningful context, and that students can be helped individually and informally to learn to spell the words they need to use as they write. This integrated approach was deemed to be a 'natural' way of acquiring spelling skill and therefore regarded by whole-language exponents as preferable to any form of direct teaching. This fully-integrated and unsystematic approach to spelling instruction proved inadequate for many children and they failed to become proficient spellers.

Skills-based approach to spelling

In contrast to the whole-language exponents, those who lean towards a more skills-based approach believe that most children require direct teaching of spelling skills and strategies. However, they agree that spelling should not be taught in a decontextualized manner, and that instruction must help children spell words they require for authentic writing purposes. Those who believe in a skills-based approach emphasize that spelling and word study need to be taught explicitly, using principles of modelling, imitation, feedback and practice. Under such instruction, children are directly taught efficient strategies for analysing and remembering unfamiliar words and for generating correct spelling patterns. The aim is to help children become *strategic* spellers. It is clear that even without instruction most children do begin to develop their own unique strategies for spelling difficult words, but some of their strategies are not effective and contribute to ongoing problems. More will be said later about the teaching of spelling strategies.

Developmental stages in spelling acquisition

It is important for teachers to be aware of the normal stages of development through which children pass on their way to becoming proficient spellers (Manning and Underbakke 2005). Students pass through these stages at different rates, and it is unrealistic to expect a student to achieve a level of independence or accuracy in spelling that is beyond his or her current developmental level. The stages have been described in the following way – although the exact name for each stage has differed among the various researchers (e.g. Bissex 1980; Scharer and Zutell 2003):

Stage 1: Prephonetic. At this stage the child 'plays' at writing (often using capital letters) in imitation of the writing of others. There is no connection between these scribbles and speech sounds or real words.

Stage 2: Phonetic. At this stage the child relies mainly upon phonemic aware-ness and some knowledge of letter-to-sound correspondences picked up through incidental learning. The words children invent at this stage are often quite recog-nizable because they are beginning to apply phonic principles when they spell. Many inaccuracies still exist – for example, a phoneme may be equated incor-rectly with a letter *name* rather than the sound, as in 'rsk' (ask), 'yl' (while), 'lfnt' (elephant).

Towards the end of the phonetic stage, approximations move much nearer to regu-lar letter-to-sound correspondences, as in 'sed' (said), 'becos' (because) or 'wotch' (watch). Some children still have difficulty identifying the second or third con-sonant in a letter-string, and may write 'stong' (strong) or 'bow' (blow). Or they may fail to identify correctly a phoneme within the word and may write incorrect letters, as in 'druck' (truck), 'jriv' (drive), 'sboon' (spoon), 'dewis' (juice).

It should be noted that the majority of individuals with poor spelling have reached this phonetic stage but have not progressed beyond it. Their problem is a tendency to be over-dependent on phonic information and therefore to write irregular words as if they have perfect letter-to-sound correspondences. These students now need to be taught to use strategies, such as visual checking of words and spelling by analogy, in order to move to the next stage. Activities involving word analysis are also useful in helping the student to recognize letter patterns within words (orthographic units) (Templeton 2010). The process of building up orthographic images in memory is also facilitated by the study of word families with common letter sequences –for example, *gate, date, late, fate, mate*.

Stage 3: Transitional. At this stage there is clear evidence of a more sophisticated understanding of word structure. The child becomes aware of within-word letter strings and syllable junctures. Common letter sequences such as *str-, pre-, -ough, -ious, -ea-, -ai-, -aw-, -ing* are used much more reliably. The children who gain real mastery over spelling at this stage also begin to use words they know already in order to spell words they have never written before (spelling by analogy).

Stage 4: Independence. At this stage the child has mastery of quite complex grapho-phonic principles, and also uses visual imagery more effectively when writing and checking familiar words. Flexible use is made of a wide range of spelling, proofreading, self-help and self-correcting strategies.

In general, the spellings produced by children provide a useful window into their current phonological knowledge and their thought processes related to encoding written language. Examination of the written work produced by students with difficulties can reveal a great deal about their current skills and specific needs in spelling. Sipe (2008) suggests that observation and assessment should be the starting point for planning instruction. A number of readily available tests for spelling have been reviewed by Kohnen *et al.* (2009).

Spelling by eye, ear, hand and brain

Do we spell by eye, ear, hand or brain? The answer is that we almost certainly use all these resources on the way to becoming proficient spellers. For many years, however, teachers regarded the encoding of words as predominantly a *visual* processing skill. For this reason, if students were fortunate enough to receive any guidance in spelling, the strategies they were taught were mainly concerned with improving visual memory – for example, the 'look-cover-write-check' strategy. Much less importance had been attached to *auditory* processing strategies due to the erroneous belief that sounding out words will lead to too many errors because of the irregularities in English spelling. It was argued that because up to three words in every ten are not written precisely as they sound, with perfect letter-to-sound translation, it is not beneficial to teach children to utilize phonic information when spelling. Counter to this argument is evidence to suggest that learning to read and learning to spell, particularly in the beginning stages, are far more closely related to auditory-processing abilities than we previously believed (Ritchey *et al.* 2010). In the early stages of teaching children to read, the teaching of basic phonics should incorporate teaching of spelling as well as decoding. Knowledge of phonics enhances early spelling because it enables children to relate the sounds they can hear in a spoken word to the letter or letters required to represent that sound in the written form.

Visual perception: spelling by eye

Very proficient spellers appear to make great use of visual information when writing words. It is obvious that visual clues are extremely important when checking for accurate spelling and detecting errors. Strategies that involve deliberate use of visual imagery, such as look-say-cover-write-check, are very effective for the learning of what are termed 'irregular' words – those with unpredictable letter-to-sound correspondences. To this extent we certainly do learn to spell by eye. The effective use of visual perception in learning to spell helps the student build a memory bank of visual images of common letter strings. The knowledge in this store can then be called upon whenever the student attempts to write an unfamiliar word.

Learning to spell by eye does not mean, however, that learners simply acquire the ability to spell by seeing words as they read – just 'looking' at words does not seem to be enough for most learners. It is necessary for them to examine a word very carefully, with every intention of trying to commit its internal configuration to memory. As this behaviour does not come naturally, it is important that any student who lacks this experience be given the necessary instruction and practice. By implication, this means devoting specific time and attention to word study, over and above any help given to individual students as they write (Templeton 2010). It is most unlikely that such an important skill as word analysis could be adequately developed through incidental learning alone.

Auditory perception: spelling by ear

Research has indicated that in the early stages of learning to read and spell it is important that a child can identify sound units within spoken words (phonemic awareness). The basic knowledge upon which successful reading and spelling both develop seems to depend upon the child's awareness that spoken words can be broken down into smaller units and that these units can be represented by letters. In order to spell, young children in the first years of schooling rely on auditory perception to a much greater extent than older children, simply because they have not yet had as much visual exposure to words through daily reading and writing experiences. Building a memory bank of visual images of words and letter strings takes time and experience. The extent to which early attempts at spelling rely upon attention to sounds is evident in children's early attempts at inventing the words they want to use in their writing.

When spelling a word, there is a complementary association between auditory perception and visual perception. The process of writing an unfamiliar word requires the child first to identify the sound units within the word and to match these sound units with appropriate letter clusters stored as visual images in what is termed 'orthographic memory'. Having identified the sound values in the word, and having represented these units on paper by writing the specific letters in sequence, visual perception is used to check that what the student writes on paper also 'looks right' – for example, *brekfirst* should be recognized as an incorrect visual pattern for the word *breakfast*.

Motor memory: spelling by hand

Since the spelling of a word is typically produced by the physical action of writing or keyboarding, it is fair to assume that kinaesthetic memory may also be involved in learning to spell. Indeed, the rapid speed and high degree of automaticity with which a competent speller encodes a very familiar word directly from meaning to its graphic representation supports the view that motor memory is involved. The frequent action of writing may be one of the ways of establishing in orthographic memory the stock of images of words and letter strings. It is clear that poorly executed handwriting and uncertain letter formation inhibit the easy development of spelling habits at an automatic response level.

It is often recommended that we should not think of spelling words letter-by-letter but rather by concentrating upon the *groups of letters* that form common units in many words. This has some implications for the way in which we teach handwriting in the early years of schooling. Some evidence exists to support the notion that it is beneficial to teach young children to join letters together almost from the beginning of their instruction in handwriting, rather than teaching print script first and linked script much later. It is believed that joining the letters together in one smooth action helps children develop an awareness of common letter strings (Cripps 1990).

The brain's contribution to spelling

Obviously the brain plays the central role in generating and checking plausible spelling alternatives. The learning of new words and the analysis of unfamiliar words prior to writing are both brain-based (cognitive) activities. The brain coordinates and integrates various sources of perceptual information to help predict the spelling of a word. Working out the most probable way to spell an unfamiliar word also requires the writer to consider the meaning of the word or the separate *morphemes* (units of meaning) that make up the word, to reduce the word to sound units, to select feasible letter groups to represent these sounds, and to compare and contrast the written word (or part of the word) mentally with a known word.

It is also the brain that makes the decision whether to apply auditory, visual, or some other strategy to encode the word. The ability to recall and apply spelling rules and strategies, or to recognize when a word is an exception to a rule, reflects a cognitive aspect of spelling. Similarly, devising some form of mnemonic to help one recall a particularly difficult word illustrates a cognitive solution to a problem.

Teaching spelling

Adequate time must be devoted to spelling instruction, particularly in the primary school years, to ensure that students' spelling development is optimized. The starting point for enhancing spelling skill development is the arousal of children's genuine interest in words. This requires that teachers and tutors display personal enthusiasm for all forms of word study and application. In the early years, children benefit from guided experience in listening carefully to words, stretching words out and segmenting them into pronounceable sub-units (see Chapter 9).

Effective instruction does not set out to teach students how to spell every individual word they may need in their writing; rather, it should teach students how to think about constructing words by drawing on the multiple linguistic factors that underlie spelling. Students make most progress in spelling when they are explicitly taught strategies for working out how words are constructed, so effective instruction must help students understand the phonological and morphological principles that underpin English spelling. These principles apply equally to teaching students with or without spelling difficulties, but in addition students with difficulties need more individualized attention, systematic error correction, more frequent practice, and sometimes the use of teaching methods that involve multisensory input, such as tracing, writing and keyboarding.

Applying a visual approach

A visual approach to spelling requires students to memorize the overall appearance of words and the correct sequence of letters. Rather than attending to sounds and syllables within the word, the student attempts to store a visual image of the word, or key parts of the word, in long-term memory. Research has suggested that children can be trained to focus more attentively on words and to improve their visual imagery for letter sequences. One of the best-known methods for this is called Look-Cover-Write-Check or Look-*Say*-Cover-Write-Check.

To improve visual processing of words, one of the simplest aids to make and use is the flashcard. These cards are particularly useful for teaching irregular words and for students who need to be weaned away from a predominantly phonetic approach to spelling – for example, students who have reached a developmental plateau at the phonetic stage. Each target word is introduced to the student on a card about 30cm × 10cm. The word is pronounced clearly and attention is drawn to any particular features in the printed word that may be difficult to recall later. The child is encouraged to make a 'mental picture' of the word and examine it. Some teachers say, 'Use your eyes like a camera. Take a picture of the word. Close your eyes and imagine you can still see the word.' With the eyes closed, the child is then told to trace the word in the air. After a few seconds the student writes the word from memory, articulating it clearly as he or she writes. The word is then checked against the flashcard. The rapid writing of the whole word avoids the inefficient letter-by-letter copying habit that some students have developed.

The general look-cover-write-check approach is based on the principle of learning words by giving attention to their visible sequences of letters, rather than using letter-to-sound correspondences. A similar approach is simply called 'Copy-Cover-Compare' (Erion *et al.* 2009). The student is told to cover the correct spelling of the word on the left of the page and to write the word from memory on the right of the page. The student then uncovers the model on the left to check his or her spelling. This strategy has fewer steps than the method described below.

The Look-Say-Cover-Write-Check visual spelling strategy in action involves the following steps:

- look very carefully at the word;
- say the word clearly and try to remember every detail;
- cover the word so that it cannot be seen;
- write the word from memory, pronouncing it quietly as you write;
- check your version of the word with the original – if it is not correct, go back through the steps again until you can produce the word accurately;
- for some students, tracing over the word with a finger may help with assimilation and retention of the letter sequence;
- check for recall a week later.

The Look-Say-Cover-Write-Check approach is far better than any rote learning or recitation procedure for learning to spell. It gives the student an independent system that can be applied to the study of any *irregular* words set for homework or to corrections from free writing. Students can work in pairs, where appropriate, to check that the procedure is being followed correctly by the partner.

The Look-Say-Cover-Write-Check strategy, although regarded as a visual learning method, almost certainly is effective because students are identifying *groups of letters* that represent pronounceable parts of words (orthographic units). From the earlier chapter on reading skills we know that this is precisely the type of information that is also essential for swift and efficient reading.

Several computer programs designed to develop spelling skills are available, and several studies have indicated that these can be quite effective if implemented correctly (e.g. Cekaite 2009; Mayfield *et al.* 2008). Teachers should ensure that the way in which the words are presented on the screen causes the students to attend carefully to the sequence and clusters of letters and requires the student to *type the complete word* from memory each time. Programs that focus too much attention on spelling letter-by-letter, unscrambling jumbled words, or inserting missing letters into spaces are far less effective.

Applying phonic principles

It is unnecessary and inappropriate to use Look-Cover-Write-Check if the target word could be written correctly from its component sounds. The phonemic approach encourages students to attend carefully to sounds and syllables within regular words and to write the letters most likely to represent these sounds. While it is true that some 30 per cent of English words are not phonemically regular, some 70 per cent of words do correspond reasonably well with their letter-to-sound translations, particularly if *groups of letters* are recognized as representing larger sound units (e.g. *-ite, -eed, -ous, pre-, dis-*). The phonic knowledge necessary for effective spelling goes well beyond knowing the sound associated with each single letter. It is necessary to draw on knowledge of *letter groups* that represent pronounceable parts of words. The percentage of words that can be spelled as they sound increases very significantly when students have acquired a working knowledge of common orthographic units.

Spelling from meaning

Children often need to be taught that words related in meaning are frequently related also in spelling pattern. To facilitate the study of words related by meaning, students can be helped to compile word families sharing a common root or base (e.g. *certain, uncertain, certainly, uncertainty, certainty, ascertain*). Dictionary skills can be used to identify such words. This type of activity is valuable because it helps make spelling more predictable by relating it to meaning.

Morphemic approach

An approach that specifically capitalizes on linking spelling with meaning is the morphemic approach. In this approach, children are taught to apply knowledge of sub-units of meaning within a word. The smallest unit of meaning is termed a 'morpheme', and the written equivalent of a morpheme is known as a 'morphograph'. For example, the word *throw* contains only one morpheme, but *throwing* contains two. The word *unhappiness* (un-happ[y]-ness) contains three morphemes. The latter example also illustrates the use of a rule (changing y to i) when combining certain morphemes. When using a morphemic approach, teachers need to teach these rules.

Perhaps the best-known programme using a morphemic approach is *Spelling Through Morphographs* (Dixon and Englemann 2006). The materials are appropriate for students from Year 4 upwards and can be used with adults. In 140 lessons, the students learn all the key morphographs and the basic rules of the spelling system. *Spelling Through Morphographs* has proved particularly valuable for students with learning difficulties.

Spelling rules

Some experts advocate teaching spelling rules to students, but students with learning difficulties find most rules too obscure to be of help when they are faced with a particular word to spell. In many cases, rather than drilling complex rules, it is easier to help students spell the specific words they need for their writing and to teach them strategies to use when learning and checking new words.

Rules may be of some value for older students of well above average intelligence. They can often understand the rule or principle and can apply it appropriately. But even with these students, the rules should be simple and have few exceptions (e.g. 'i' before 'e' except after 'c'– *receive*; words ending with 'e', drop the 'e' when adding an ending that begins with a vowel – *hope, hoping*; words ending in a single vowel, double the consonant before adding an ending that begins with a vowel – *stop, stopped, stopping*).

Activities such as Word Sorts (see below) can be used to help students discover rules and principles for themselves. This process is much more effective than any attempt at rote learning and memorizing a taught rule.

Dictation

Although the regular use of dictation has fallen out of favour in many schools, it is sometimes suggested that dictation develops listening skills and concentration, and at the same time gives students experience of spelling words in context. It is recommended that the material to be dictated should be presented for children to study *before* it is dictated. In this way, there is an opportunity to clarify meaning and to point out any difficult words.

Another approach encourages proofreading and self-correction. An unseen passage at an appropriate level of difficulty is dictated for students to write. They are then given a period of time to check and alter any words that they think are incorrect, perhaps using a different colour pen. The teacher then checks the work and can observe two aspects of the student's performance. First, it is useful to look at the words the child has been able to self-correct (or at least knows to be wrong). Second, the teacher can record words that were in fact wrong but were not noticed by the student. If these are basic words that should be known by the student, activities can be devised that will help the student master them.

Spelling lists

It is known that rote learning of words from a standard all-purpose list does not generally result in any transfer of skill to everyday writing. The limitation of formal lists is that they usually fail to supply a particular word at the time when the student needs to use it for writing or proofreading. In addition, having one common word list for all students in the class ignores the fact that children are at different stages of spelling development and therefore have different learning needs

(Manning and Underbakke 2005). For this reason, teachers remain unsure when and how to use spelling lists, if at all.

There is a place for judicious use of spelling lists if they are tailored to students' needs. From the point of view of the weakest spellers, the most useful list will be one compiled according to personal writing needs and common errors. A copy of this list can be kept in the back of the student's exercise book and used when he or she is writing a rough draft or proofreading a final draft of a piece of work. Other lists might contain words grouped by visual, phonemic or morphemic similarity. The value of lists comprising word families is that they represent yet another way of helping students establish awareness of common orthographic units. This awareness will help a student take a more rational approach to tackling an unfamiliar word – for example, by using analogy to move from the known to the unknown. The decision to use such lists with an individual student or group of students must be made in the light of their specific learning needs.

Another useful list will be of new vocabulary that is introduced during the study of some particular classroom topic. Students may not need to learn all the words on such a list but they can refer to it when writing. 'Word Walls' represent one excellent method of ensuring that the words children need in their daily writing are readily to hand. Words are written in blackboard-size writing on poster sheets on the classroom wall so that children can locate and use them as necessary. Vocabulary is added regularly to the Word Wall as each new topic is studied.

Developing strategic spellers

Students have become truly independent in their spelling when they can look at an unfamiliar word and select the most appropriate strategy for learning that word. For example, they need to be able to look at a word and decide for themselves whether it is phonemically irregular or regular. For an irregular word, they may need to apply the Look-Cover-Write-Check strategy, coupled perhaps with repeated writing of the word. For some irregular words, they may also need to call upon knowledge of the simple principle about doubling letters, or dropping or changing a letter. If the word is phonemically regular, they need to recognize that they can spell it easily from its component sounds. When students can operate at this level of judgement, the shift is from rote learning to an emphasis on studying words rationally.

This level of independence does not come easily to all students. Many individuals need to be taught how to learn new material. Some students, left to their own devices, fail to develop any systematic approach. They may just look at the word. They may recite the spelling alphabetically. They may copy letter-by-letter rather than writing the whole word. They may use no particular strategy at all, believing that learning to spell the word is beyond them. Any serious attempt to help children with spelling difficulties must involve determining *how* they set about learning a word or group of words. Where a student has no systematic approach, it is essential that he or she be taught one.

Cognitive and metacognitive approaches to spelling teach students specific self-regulatory strategies to use when learning new words or checking the accuracy of spelling at the proofreading stage of writing. For example, they are taught to ask themselves:

- How many syllables do I hear in this word?
- Do I have the right number of syllables in what I have written?
- Do I know any other words that sound like this word?
- Does this word look correct? I'll try it again.
- Does this look better?

As with all other examples of strategy training described in this book, the teacher's role is to model effective strategies, to 'think aloud' and to demonstrate ways of going about the task of spelling, checking and self-correcting. Most effective teachers of spelling help children to develop a variety of spelling strategies and also draw their attention to spelling patterns by analogy with other known words.

Remedial strategies

In addition to the general teaching activities described above, several specific approaches have been developed to help struggling spellers. Most of these approaches involve intensive one-to-one instruction.

Simultaneous Oral Spelling

Simultaneous Oral Spelling (SOS) was first developed by Gillingham and Stillman in 1960. It has been applied very successfully for remediation of spelling problems in individual tutorial settings and is appropriate for any age level beyond beginner. The approach involves five steps:

- teacher selects the target word and pronounces it clearly;
- student pronounces the word clearly while looking at it very carefully;
- student says each syllable in the word, or breaks a single-syllable word into onset and rime;
- student *names* the letters in the word twice;
- without reference to the model, the student writes the word while naming each letter.

Note that the *letter name* is used, not its common sound. This makes the method particularly appropriate for older students, who may be embarrassed by 'sounding out' words.

Repeated writing

The practice of having a student correct an error by writing the correct version of the word several times is believed by some teachers to serve no useful purpose.

They consider that it is a mechanical performance that can be carried out without conscious effort on the part of the learner, and that words practised in this way are not remembered later.

It is true that if the student is thinking of other things or is distracted by noise or activity while carrying out the repeated writing, the procedure is of little or no value. However, repeated writing of a target word can be very helpful indeed if (i) the learner has every intention of trying to remedy an error and (ii) if he or she is attending fully to the task. It is one way in which kinaesthetic images of words can be more firmly established. Only a few words (usually *no more than three*) should be practised in any one session.

Old Way/New Way method

Lyndon (1989) identified the psychological construct of 'proactive inhibition' as a possible reason for the failure of many conventional remedial methods to help a student 'unlearn' incorrect responses, such as habitual errors in spelling. Proactive inhibition (or proactive interference) is the term used to describe the situation where previously learned information interferes with one's ability to remember new information or to acquire a new response. What the individual already knows, even erroneous information, is protected from change.

Lyndon's approach, called 'Old Way/New Way', uses the student's error as the starting point for change. A memory of the old way of spelling of the word is used to activate later an awareness of the new (correct) way of spelling the word. The approach has been found to be reasonably effective (Fisher *et al.* 2007).

The following steps and procedures are used in 'Old Way/New Way':

- student writes the word in the usual (incorrect) form;
- teacher and student agree to call this the 'old way' of spelling that word;
- teacher shows student a 'new way' (correct way) of spelling the word;
- attention is drawn to the similarities and differences between the old and the new forms;
- student writes word again in the old way;
- student writes word in the new way, and points out the differences;
- repeat five such writings of old way, new way and statement of differences;
- write the word the new way six times, using different colour pens or in different styles; older students may be asked to write six different sentences using the word in its 'new' form;
- revise the word or words taught after a two-week interval;
- if necessary, repeat this procedure every two weeks until the new response is firmly established.

Word Sorts

Students are provided with word cards containing the words to be studied and compared. The words might be *sock, black, truck, lock, rack, luck, trick, track, block, lick, sack, stick, flock, flick, suck*. The students are asked, 'What is the same about these words?' The response might be that the words all end with /ck/. The words might now be categorized in other ways by sorting the cards into groups (for example, words ending in /ock/; words ending in /ack/). At a more advanced level, Word Sorts can involve words that are grouped according to the meaning–spelling connection, as discussed above – for example, *played, playfully, replay, player, playground, horseplay*.

Word Sorts represent a valuable investigative approach to help children discriminate among orthographic features within and across words. Comparing and contrasting words in this way helps older students (including adults) discover basic spelling rules.

Programming for individual students

When planning an individualized programme in spelling, the following points should be kept in mind:

- analyse some samples of the students' written work and use appropriate spelling tests to discover their existing skill levels and areas of weakness;
- set some clear objectives for teaching and learning – discuss these with the student;
- collect a list of words frequently needed by the students to whom you are giving special help, and use this list for regular review and assessment;
- in secondary schools, obtain vocabulary lists for word study from specific subject areas – for example, *ingredients, temperature, chisel, theory, science, hydrochloric, equation, gymnasium*;
- within each tutorial session, students must work on specific words misspelled in free writing lessons as well as on more general word lists or word families;
- when making a correction to a word, the student should rewrite the whole word, not merely erase the incorrect letters;
- repetition and overlearning are important, so use a range of games, word puzzles and computer tasks to reinforce the spelling of important words;
- games and activities must be closely matched to the objectives of the intervention programme;
- daily attention will be needed for the least able spellers, with weekly revision and regular testing for maintenance;
- requiring students to spell words aloud without writing them down is of very little value for learning, because the visual appearance of the word as it is being written provides important feedback to the speller;
- a neat, careful style of handwriting that can be executed swiftly and easily is an important factor associated with good spelling.

Additional practical advice on activities to improve spelling skills can be found in the books listed below.

Online resources

- A teaching guide *Support for Spelling,* published in 2009 by the Department for Children Schools and Families, is available to download from: http:// nationalstrategies.standards.dcsf.gov.uk/downloader/c9275388873dcd6c647 ff6cf9d1a2841.pdf (accessed 28 March 2010).
- A paper titled *Research-based Tutoring of English Spelling* by Rosevita Warda is available online at: www.learnthat.org/whitepaperenglishspelling. html (accessed 13 August 2010).
- Activities for word study and spelling can be found on the Literacy Connections website at: www.literacyconnections.com/WordsTheirWay.php (accessed 3 April 2010).
- General advice on teaching spelling is available at *Special Connections*: www.specialconnections.ku.edu/cgi-bin/cgiwrap/specconn/main.php?cat= instruction&section=main&subsection=writing/spelling#part3 (accessed 3 April 2010).

Further reading

Benjamin, A. and Crow, J.T. (2010) *Vocabulary at the Centre,* Larchmont, NY: Eye On Education.

Nunes, T. and Bryant, P. (2009) *Children's Reading and Spelling: Beyond the First Steps,* Chichester: Wiley-Blackwell.

Templeton, S., Johnston, F., Bear, D. and Invernizzi, M. (2010) *Vocabulary their Way: Word Study with Middle and Secondary Students,* Boston: Allyn and Bacon.

Wood, C. and Connelly, V. (2009) *Contemporary Perspectives on Reading and Spelling,* London: Routledge.

Chapter 13

Difficulties with basic mathematics

Many children, with and without disabilities or learning problems, find mathematics a difficult subject and failure rates are often quite high in this important subject. In this chapter, some of the possible reasons for this situation are suggested, and appropriate teaching methods to help overcome learning difficulties are described.

Contemporary perspectives on mathematics teaching

As a result of reforms in mathematics education that started in many countries in the late 1980s, schools were encouraged to implement a *constructivist* teaching approach, often referred to as activity-based or problem-based mathematics. Teachers are expected to create learning situations that provide opportunities for children to discover mathematical relationships and develop essential number skills by engaging in problem solving, rather than through traditional drill and practice of arithmetic procedures (National Council of Teachers of Mathematics 2005). A constructivist approach places emphasis on helping students move beyond practising routine calculations to a much deeper understanding of mathematical concepts. It has been said that too often in the past, students have been expected to remember methods, rules and facts without grasping the underpinning concepts or making real sense of mathematics so that they can use it independently (OfSTED 2008).

In theory at least, constructivist approaches appear to have much to offer in learning mathematics; but it must be acknowledged that the exclusive use of a constructivist approach has been seriously questioned (e.g. Latterell 2005; Polloway *et al.* 2008). The notion has been challenged that mathematics can be learned entirely by immersion. Critics suggest that constructivist theory makes unreasonable assumptions concerning children's ability to discover, deduce, conceptualize and remember mathematical relationships for themselves. There is also major concern over the reduced attention given in process methods to developing children's fluency and automaticity in fundamental number skills. Evidence seems to indicate that not all children can make good progress under an approach that requires them to acquire vital skills mainly through incidental learning. Some students make much better progress in mathematics when they are directly taught (Bellert 2009; Farkota 2005; Swain *et al.* 2010). The emerging perspective is that effective teaching and learning in mathematics requires not only student-centred investigative activities but *also* a good measure of teacher-directed explicit instruction and practice (Latterell 2005; Slavin *et al.* 2009). The amount of explicit instruction required varies from student to student and from concept to concept, with direct teaching being of most benefit for students with learning difficulties (Pincott 2004).

Evidence seems to prove that the most effective teachers provide systematic instruction in mathematics in such a way that genuine understanding accompanies mastery of number skills and acquisition of problem-solving strategies. It is also clear that to be an effective teacher of mathematics one has to have deep subject knowledge and a sound understanding of how best to teach new concepts and skills to students (Masters 2009). In countries with high achievement levels in mathematics (e.g. Japan, Korea, Singapore, Hong Kong), teachers have not moved wholeheartedly into student-centred activity methods. Typically the mathematics lessons in these countries reveal that teachers maintain fairly close control over the learning process; but they ensure that all students participate during interactive whole-class lessons involving problem solving and applying new skills. The emphasis is certainly upon constructing meaning, but not through the medium of unstructured activities. Lessons are typically clear, accurate and rich in examples of a particular concept, process or strategy. The teacher takes an active role in imparting relevant information, stimulating students' thinking, clarifying and teaching specific skills.

In countries such as Britain and Australia, where national strategies for enhancing numeracy are in operation, the recommendation is for daily intensive lessons using an interactive whole-class teaching approach. Lessons are conducted at a reasonably fast pace and incorporate a high degree of student participation and practice. The evidence is that the daily lessons have had beneficial impact on the skills and confidence of most students (Kyriacou 2005). However, some authorities have suggested that the fast pace of these lessons can sometimes result in the least capable students being left behind (Frederickson and Cline 2009). It has also been found that many teachers who have been trained in child-centred methods do not find interactive fast-paced teaching easy to implement. Nor are they particularly skilled yet in ensuring that students think more deeply and critically about the mathematics they are learning (OfSTED 2008).

Whole-class teaching and group work

Although there is research support for interactive whole-class teaching in mathematics (e.g. Wilson *et al.* 2006), the use of a direct teaching approach does not mean that teachers should abandon the use of group work and collaborative learning in the classroom. Lessons with well-planned group activities facilitate students' interest, motivation and achievement. Group tasks that involve students in discussion and sharing of ideas appear to help them negotiate a better understanding of key concepts and processes. Such lessons also allow for some degree of differentiation of curriculum content according to students' differing abilities (Taylor-Cox 2008).

Learning difficulties in mathematics

It is suggested that between 5 to 7 per cent of students have significant difficulties learning basic mathematical concepts and skills (Fuchs and Fuchs 2005). A much higher percentage of students are observed to be low achievers in mathematics, displaying a poor attitude towards the subject and having no confidence in their own ability. Some students exhibit anxiety in situations where they are expected to demonstrate competence in applying mathematical skills. While a very small number of these students may have a specific learning disability related to mathematics (*dyscalculia*), most have simply encountered difficulties with mathematics learning at earlier stages (Yu and Murik 2008). Over time, the achievement gap widens between these students and those who are more successful as they progress through the school system (Masters 2009).

Based on information summarized by several writers (e.g. Farkota 2005; Frederickson and Cline 2009; Maccini and Gagnon 2006; Mercer and Pullen 2009), the major factors associated with learning difficulty in mathematics include:

* insufficient or inappropriate instruction;
* students falling behind and becoming discouraged because the pace of the curriculum outstrips their ability to assimilate new concepts and skills;
* little or no differentiation of learning activities and assessment tasks to match students' differing abilities;
* too little structuring of discovery learning or process maths situations, with students failing to abstract or remember anything from them;
* teacher's language when explaining mathematical relationships or when posing questions does not match students' level of comprehension;
* abstract symbols introduced too early in the absence of concrete materials or real-life examples;
* students' reading difficulties contributing significantly to learning difficulties in mathematics;
* students' grasp of simple relationships in numbers to twenty may not be fully developed before larger numbers involving complications of place-value are introduced;
* too little time spent in developing automaticity with number facts, leading later to slowness and inaccuracy in processes and problems;
* too little teaching time devoted to conceptual understanding.

It is important that any student with learning difficulties in mathematics should be identified early and given appropriate support. Several early intervention programmes for children with learning difficulties exist – for example, *Mathematics Recovery* (Wright 2003), *QuickSmart Numeracy* (Bellert 2009) and *Numeracy Recovery* (Dowker 2005). *Mathematics Recovery* involves 30 minutes a day of individualized assessment-based instruction for low-achieving children aged 6 to 7 years. *QuickSmart Numeracy* targets students in the middle school years and is effective in building up fluency and confidence in basic arithmetic and in strategy use. *Numeracy Recovery* targets 6 to 7-year-old children and involves 30 minutes instruction per week over a period of approximately thirty weeks. These programmes give attention to such fundamental skills as counting, numeral recognition, grouping, solving simple addition and subtraction problems, and place value.

The DfES (2005) in the UK produced special materials to help children with learning difficulties in basic number skills. The earlier such interventions are implemented, the more likely it is that young children can develop essential number sense, procedural skills and basic concepts. Intensive intervention, particularly when it incorporates computer-aided practice and application, can definitely enhance the basic number skills of early primary students (Baroody *et al.* 2009; Fuchs *et al.* 2005).

Assisting students who struggle in mathematics

Maccini and Gagnon (2006) identified important components in programmes that are effective for helping weaker students improve in mathematics. Their suggestions apply equally to both primary and secondary school students. The most important components include:

- providing individualized help that is matched to the child's current level of understanding;
- giving additional practice to achieve mastery of basic facts and procedures;
- providing extended time to complete assignments and to work on problems;
- encouraging the use of concrete materials where necessary and helpful;
- reading word-problems aloud to the student to avoid any reading difficulty;
- permitting use of a calculator;
- using cue cards to display the steps to take in carrying out a specific process;
- teaching mnemonics to help recall of procedures;
- facilitating individual support by using a classroom assistant or by adopting peer tutoring.

What should be taught?

In the same way that views have changed in recent years on how best to teach mathematics to students with special needs, views are changing too on *what* should be taught to these students. Traditionally, students with learning problems were usually placed in the lowest-ability group and given a watered-down version of the mainstream curriculum. Sometimes (particularly in special schools and secondary special classes) a 'functional' curriculum would be developed with a title such as 'consumer maths' or, 'real-life maths'. The belief was that students with special needs required an alternative to the mainstream programme with the content significantly reduced in both quantity and complexity, and focused clearly on numeracy skills required in adult life. However, it is argued now that students with special needs, like all other students, are entitled to engage in an interesting, challenging, relevant and inclusive mathematics curriculum. For this reason, coverage of the mathematics course in mainstream schools should be reduced as little as possible for lower-ability students in order to maintain sufficient interest and challenge, and, at the same time, preserve their self-esteem.

In Britain, a new secondary curriculum, *Engaging mathematics for all learners* (QCDA 2009a) aims to make mathematics more interesting and relevant to a diverse range of students. It is suggested that for students at all ability levels, relevant mathematical elements and problems should also be integrated into other school subjects and related to real-life situations. A reality-based approach is more likely to enhance students' motivation and involvement, and also increases the likelihood that mathematical skills will generalize to other situations and uses. However, such an approach does not imply that the most basic skills of numeracy are devalued or left to incidental learning. It is clear that mastery of basic number facts and development of sound 'number sense' must be given high priority in any mathematics programme (Duffy 2009).

A diagnostic approach

There are many reasons why students experience difficulty mastering the facts, concepts and operations in arithmetic and applying these successfully to problem solving. The first steps towards intervention should be to: (i) ascertain what the student can already do in this area of the curriculum; (ii) locate any specific gaps in knowledge which may exist; and (iii) determine precisely what he or she needs to be taught next. Assessment at an appropriate level will help a teacher answer the questions, 'What can the student do independently in mathematics?' and 'What can he or she do if given a little help and guidance (scaffolding)?'

Examining the student's workbooks and conducting some informal testing will determine the level at which he or she is functioning. Children's errors tend to reveal much about their level of knowledge and skill and can thus serve a useful diagnostic function for programming. The nature of a student's errors can help identify gaps in understanding, faulty procedural knowledge, or misconceptions. Appropriate follow-up testing can then be used (Mercer and Pullen 2009). For this purpose teachers can construct their own informal 'mathematical skills inventory' containing items covering key concepts, knowledge and skills presented in earlier years, together with essential material from the current year. Observing a student working through the items can help a teacher discover what the student can and cannot do, and will assist with the ordering of priorities for planning instruction. Curriculum-based assessment of this type is now widely acknowledged as a productive and helpful approach for teachers to use.

There are three levels at which diagnostic work in mathematics can be conducted – concrete, semi-concrete and abstract. At the *concrete level,* the student may be able to solve a problem or complete a process correctly if allowed to manipulate objects (e.g. counters). At the *semi-concrete level,* pictorial representation of objects, together with symbols or tally marks will provide sufficient visual information to ensure success. At the *abstract level,* a student can work successfully with symbols only. During the diagnostic work with a student, the teacher may move up or down within this hierarchy from concrete to abstract in an attempt to discover the level at which the child can succeed with each concept.

Assessment should not be confined to the basic arithmetic processes. The main goal in teaching mathematics to students is the development of problem-solving skills, and therefore assessment of a student's current ability in this domain is important. Close investigation of strategies used by a student when solving a problem can be achieved in a *diagnostic interview.* Using a set of appropriate problems as a focus, discussion between teacher and student can reveal much about the student's flexibility in thinking, underlying knowledge, number skills and level of confidence. Teachers may probe for understanding in the following areas when appraising a student's problem-solving abilities:

- detecting what is called for in a problem;
- identifying relevant information;
- selecting correct procedure;
- estimating an approximate answer;
- computing the answer;
- checking the answer.

It may be helpful to keep the following thoughts in mind when investigating a student's functional level. By referring to any items the student fails to solve in a test or during deskwork, consider:

- *Why* did the student get this item wrong?
- Can he or she carry out the process if allowed to count on fingers, or use a number line or calculator?
- Ask the student to work through an example step by step. Can he or she explain the mathematical process? At what point does the student misunderstand? If a student explains or demonstrates how he or she tackles the problem, the teacher can identify the exact point of confusion and can intervene from there.

The following pages present some teaching points for the most basic levels of number work.

Teaching and learning at the concrete and semi-concrete levels

Teaching at this level addresses the needs of younger students with learning difficulties, students with some degree of intellectual disability, and older students with serious weaknesses in basic mathematics.

Real and structural materials

Alongside real objects, the use of materials such as picture cards, Dienes' Multibase Arithmetic Blocks (MAB), Cuisenaire Rods and Unifix is helpful in the beginning stages of an intervention programme and in remedial teaching contexts. Using structural material provides a bridge between concrete experience and abstract reasoning by taking learners through experiences at the intermediate levels of semi-concrete (not the real object but another object or picture used to represent it) to the semi-abstract (the use of the first stages of symbolic representation, such as tally marks). Using concrete material appears to help children construct deeper mathematical understanding (Baroody *et al.* 2009; Yu and Murik 2008). For example, structural material can be used to illustrate conservation of number, place value, grouping, re-grouping, multiplication and so forth. It can also be used to represent visually the variables contained within word problems.

Structural material is particularly important for students with learning difficulties and learning disabilities as it helps them understand and store *visual representations* of number relationships. It must be recognized, however, that concrete materials have to be used effectively if students are to form necessary connections between the material and the underlying concepts and processes they are designed to illustrate (Moscardini 2009). Problems arise if students simply play with the apparatus or if they come to rely on it too much and do not progress to the next level of processing number relationships mentally.

Counting

Counting is perhaps the most fundamental of all early number skills. Counting can assist with the development of conservation of number because it facilitates comparison of groups. If a child has not acquired accurate counting of real objects, the skill must be taught by direct instruction. The problem is often that very young students (or older students with intellectual disability) fail to make a correct one-to-one correspondence between the spoken number and each object touched in a sequence. If the physical act of counting a set of objects appears difficult for a student with a disability, manual guidance of his or her hands may be needed.

Counting of actual objects will eventually be extended to encompass the 'counting-on' strategy for addition and the 'counting-back' strategy for subtraction, in the absence of real objects. These important strategies will have to be taught directly to certain students.

Recognition of numerals

The cardinal value of number symbols should be related to a wide variety of sets of objects. Teachers can make numeral-to-group matching games (for example, the numeral 11 on a card to be matched with eleven birds, eleven kites, eleven cars, eleven dots, eleven tally marks, etc.). Also of use are teacher-made lotto cards containing a selection of the number symbols being taught or overlearned (one to ten, or one to twenty, or twenty-five to fifty, etc.). When the teacher holds up a card and says the number, the student covers the numeral on the lotto card. At the end of the game, the student must read each number aloud to the teacher as it is uncovered on the card. Later these same lotto cards can be used for basic addition and subtraction facts, the numerals on the cards now representing correct answers to some simple question from the teacher (5 add 4 = ...? The number 1 less than 8 is ... ?).

Activities with number cards can also be devised to help students sort and arrange numerals in correct sequence from one to ten, one to twenty, etc. The early items in the Unifix mathematics apparatus can be helpful at this stage (e.g. inset pattern boards, number indicators, and number line one to twenty).

The writing of numerals should be taught in parallel to the above activities. Correct formation of numerals should be established as thoroughly as correct letter formation in handwriting. This will reduce the incidence of reversals of figures in written recording.

Written recording

There is a danger that some very young students or those with moderate learning difficulties will be expected to deal with symbolic number manipulation and recording too early. Pictorial recording, tally marks and dot patterns are all acceptable forms of representation for the young or developmentally delayed child. Gradually, the writing of number symbols will accompany picture-type recording and then finally replace it, by which time the cardinal values of the numerals are understood. It is important that written recording should evolve naturally from concrete experiences.

Number facts

Functional knowledge in arithmetic involves two major components: mastery of number facts that can easily be retrieved from memory (up to $9 + 9$ and 9×9) and a body of knowledge about computational procedures. Both components are required in typical problem-solving situations. For example, number facts (e.g. $5 + 4 = 9$; $3 \times 6 = 18$) are involved within sub-routines carried out in all computations, and for this reason they need to be recalled with a high degree of automaticity. Many students with learning disabilities have difficulty learning and recalling number facts and tables so require extra attention devoted to this key area. Regular practice and application will help develop automaticity.

Being able to recall number facts easily is important for two main reasons: it makes calculation easier, and it allows time for the deepening of understanding. Knowing number facts is partly a matter of learning through repetition (remembered by constant exposure and practice) and partly a matter of grasping a rule (e.g. that zero added to any number does not change it: $3 + 0 = 3$, $13 + 0 = 13$, etc.; or if $7 + 3 = 10$, then $7 + 4$ must be 'one more than ten', etc.).

Teaching computational skills

Once young students have evolved their own meaningful forms of recording in the early stages, one must move on to the introduction of conventional forms of vertical and horizontal computation. For example, a student should be able to watch as a 'bundle of ten rods and two extra ones' are added to a set already containing a 'bundle of ten rods and three extra ones' and then write the operation as:

$12 + 13 = 25$ or

$$\begin{array}{r} 12 \\ + 13 \\ \hline 25 \end{array}$$

The reverse of this procedure is to show the student a 'number sentence' ($20 - 13 = 7$) and ask him or her to demonstrate what this means using some form of concrete materials. MAB blocks are particularly useful for this purpose. Unifix blocks, being larger in size, are more appropriate for children with poor manipulative skills.

This stage of development is likely to require careful structuring over a long period of time if students with learning difficulties are not to become confused. The careful grading of examples, combined with adequate amounts of concrete practice at each stage, is crucial for long-term mastery.

It has been traditional to teach students verbal self-instructions (cues) for carrying out the steps in a particular calculation. Verbal cueing is only required during the time a child is first mastering a new algorithm. Once mastered, the algorithmic procedure becomes automatic and verbal cueing is phased out. For example, using the decomposition method for the following subtraction problem, the student would be taught to verbalize the steps in some way similar to the wording below.

$5^7 8 \,^1 1$ The child says: 'Start with the units. I can't take 9 from 1 so I must borrow a ten

$-1 \ 3 \ 9$ and write it next to the 1 to make 11. Cross out the 8 tens and write 7 tens.

————   Now I can take 9 from 11 and write 2 in the answer box.

$4 \ 4 \ 2$ In the tens column, 7 take away 3, leaves 4 tens.

In the hundreds column, 5 take away 1 leaves 4. Write 4 in the answer space.

My answer is 442.'

A support teacher, tutor or parent who attempts to help a student in this area of school work should liaise closely with the class teacher in order to find out the precise verbal cues that are used in teaching the four processes so that exactly the same words and directions are used in the remedial programme to avoid confusion.

With the advent of the constructivist approach, the teaching of these verbal cues fell into disrepute. It is felt by some experts that these cues may inhibit the thinking of the more-able students and may prevent them from devising insightful and rapid methods of completing a calculation. It is argued that mindlessly following a memorized set of cues may represent nothing more than rote learning. However, without such verbal cues for working through a calculation, lower-ability students are likely to remain totally confused and utterly frustrated.

It is important that students also be taught other strategies for solving addition and subtraction problems, preferably those which will help develop insight into the structure and composition of the numbers involved. For example, if the student is faced with $47 + 17 = ?$, he or she is encouraged to think of this regrouped as a set of $(40 + 7)$ added to a set of $(10 + 7)$. The tens are quickly combined to make 50, and the two 7s make 14. Finally, 14 combined with 50 produces the result 64. Once children have grasped the principle, fewer errors seem to occur with this method than with the traditional vertical addition. This is almost certainly because the approach is meaningful and does help to develop insight into the structure of numbers. The steps can also be easily demonstrated using MAB blocks or similar concrete materials.

With subtraction the procedure may be illustrated thus:

$(53 - 27 =)$ 53 can be regrouped as $40 + 13$
27 can be regrouped as $20 + 7$
Deal with the tens first: $40 - 20 = 20$
Now the second step: $13 - 7 = 6$
We are left with 26.

Calculators

A calculator provides a means of temporarily bypassing computational weaknesses. There is a valid argument that time spent drilling mechanical arithmetic is largely wasted if students still cannot remember the steps later when working through a calculation. The use of the calculator as a supplement is totally defensible in such cases. The instructional time saved can then be devoted to helping the students think carefully as they select the operation needed to solve particular problems. However, only as a last resort should a teacher decide to abandon completely the teaching of paper and pencil computational skills.

Developing problem-solving skills and strategies

The whole purpose of mathematics education is to acquire information, skills and strategies that enable an individual to solve problems they may encounter during school time, working life, at home and during leisure. Children need therefore to be taught how and when to use computational skills and problem-solving strategies for authentic purposes (Brissiaud and Sander 2010; Montague and Dietz 2009).

From a teacher's point of view, instructing students in problem-solving strategies is more difficult than teaching them basic arithmetic processes, and not all teachers are particularly skilled in teaching these strategies. From the learner's perspective, solving a problem involves much more than simply applying a pre-taught algorithm. Non-routine problems need to be analysed, explored for possible procedures to use, and then the final result checked for feasibility.

Students with learning difficulties commonly display helplessness and confusion when faced with mathematical problems in word form. They may begin by having difficulty reading the words, or with comprehending the exact meaning of specific terms (Yu and Murik 2008). The fact that often they do not really understand what they are being asked to find out compounds their difficulty in selecting a process or processes to use. Their most obvious weakness is a total lack of any effective strategy for approaching a mathematical problem. Their inability and lack of success leads to loss of confidence and undermines self-esteem and motivation. Most students with these difficulties need to be directly taught a range of effective problem-solving and task-approach strategies. The aim is to teach them how to process the information in a problem without a feeling of panic or hopelessness. They need to be able to sift the relevant from the irrelevant information and impose some degree of structure on the problem.

It is generally accepted now that there are recognizable and teachable steps through which an individual needs to pass when solving mathematical problems. These steps can be summarized as:

- interpretation of the problem to be solved;
- identification of processes and steps needed;
- translation of the information into an appropriate algorithm (or algorithms);
- careful calculation;
- checking of the result.

It is also recognized that in addition to cognitive skills involved in the five steps there are also significant metacognitive components. These components include the self-monitoring and self-correcting while working through a problem. For example:

- 'What needs to be worked out in this problem?' (identify the problem)
- 'How will I do this?' (select or create a strategy)

- 'Can I picture this problem in my mind? Can I draw it?' (visualization)
- 'Is this working out OK?' (self-monitoring)
- 'How will I check if my solution is correct?' (reflection, reasoning, evaluation)
- 'I need to correct this error and then try again' (self-correction)

When teaching a problem-solving strategy the teacher needs to:

- model and demonstrate effective use of the strategy for solving routine and non-routine problems;
- 'think aloud' as various aspects of the problem are analysed and possible procedures for solution identified;
- reflect upon the effectiveness of the procedure and the validity of the result obtained.

A problem-solving strategy might, for example, use a particular mnemonic to aid recall of the procedure. For example, in the mnemonic 'RAVE CCC', the word RAVE can be used to identify the first four possible steps to take:

R = Read the problem carefully.
A = Attend to words that may suggest the process to use (for example, *share, altogether, less than*).
V = Visualize the problem, and perhaps make a sketch, diagram or table.
E = Estimate the possible answer.

The letters CCC suggest what to do next:

C = Choose the numbers to use.
C = Calculate the answer.
C = Check the answer against your estimate.

Once students have been taught a particular strategy, they must have an opportunity to apply the strategy themselves under teacher guidance and with feedback. Finally they must be able to use the strategy independently, and generalize its use to other problem contexts. The sequence for teaching problem solving to students with learning difficulties therefore begins with direct teaching, followed by guided practice, and ending with student-centred control and independent use.

Since there is evidence that students can be helped to become more proficient at solving problems (Montague and Dietz 2009), teachers of students with learning difficulties need to devote adequate time to this important aspect of mathematics. As mentioned above, perhaps the students' use of pocket calculators will enable teachers to spend more time on exploring problems, rather than restricting struggling students to a diet of mechanical arithmetic. Supplementary use of a calculator need not inhibit the development of students' computational skills;

and children who are permitted to use calculators often develop a better attitude towards mathematics.

Additional teaching points to consider when improving the problem-solving abilities of students with learning difficulties include:

- pre-teaching any difficult vocabulary associated with a specific word problem so that comprehension is enhanced;
- providing cues (such as directional arrows) to indicate where to begin calculations and in which direction to proceed;
- linking problems to the students' life experiences;
- providing more examples than usual to establish and strengthen the application of a particular strategy;
- giving children experience in setting their own problems for others to solve;
- stressing the value of self-checking and self-correction;
- using appropriate computer-aided instruction (CAI).

Students with specific talents in mathematics

Mathematics is one area of the curriculum where some gifted students may display a high degree of aptitude and achievement (QCDA 2009b). It is all too easy for these students to become bored and frustrated in mathematics lessons where the material is pitched at the average standard for the age group and the pace of progress is slow. Often too much time is devoted to routine problems involving concepts and skills that the student has already mastered. To meet the special needs of talented mathematicians some form of differentiation is absolutely essential to offer higher levels of challenge, enrichment and application (Taylor-Cox 2008). Such differentiation may be accomplished partly by selecting curriculum content, resource materials and computer software at a level appropriate for the student's higher abilities, and partly by grouping students by ability for mathematics. In both cases, teachers need to have a good depth of subject knowledge to be able to select relevant content to include in such programmes (OfSTED 2008).

Judging by the number of pleas for practical advice appearing in teachers' online chat-rooms and websites, many primary school teachers feel inadequately prepared for teaching mathematics to students of high ability. Without adequate depth of subject knowledge, teachers may simply put together a hotchpotch of cute activities and puzzles that lack real scope, purpose and wider application. What are needed instead are projects that require talented students to use initiative and advance their mathematical skills through investigation, application and problem solving in a meaningful and interesting context.

On the matter of organization, some schools with a sufficient number of students with talents in mathematics have found it valuable to withdraw them for special group work for certain periods each week or to offer extra-curricular activities with a focus on mathematics (QCDA 2009b). This arrangement works well because the students can interact with equally able peers and the teacher can operate a more advanced programme incorporating acceleration, extension and enrichment.

Of course, it must also be note that a few gifted and talented students, while high achievers in most school subjects, may actually exhibit a specific learning disability in the area of mathematics (*dyscalculia*). The advice on teaching presented in this chapter is applicable to these students. They may also need personal counselling and advice if their maths disability is causing them undue worry or anxiety.

Online resources

- In 2009–10, the Department for Children, Schools and Families (UK) published two useful documents titled *Moving on in mathematics: Narrowing the gaps*, and *Overcoming barriers in mathematics: Helping children move from Level 4 to Level 5*. These files are available to download from the National Strategies website (DCSF) at: http://nationalstrategies.standards.dcsf.gov.uk/primary/ (accessed 29 March 2010).

- *Misunderstood Minds* website presents excellent coverage of learning difficulties in the mathematics domain. Available online at: www.pbs.org/wgbh/misunderstoodminds/mathdiffs.html (accessed 29 March 2010).

- *About.com: Learning Disabilities* site discusses the difficulties some students have in mastering basic mathematics. Online at: http://learningdisabilities.about.com/od/learningdisabilitybasics/p/ldbasicmath.htm (accessed 29 March 2010).

Further reading

Hughes, A.M. (2009) *Problem Solving, Reasoning and Numeracy in the Early Years Foundation Stages*, London: Routledge.

Johnson, A. (2010) *Teaching Mathematics to Culturally and Linguistically Diverse Learners*, Boston: Pearson.

Posamentier, A.S. and Stepelman, J. (2010) *Teaching Secondary Mathematics: Techniques and Enrichment Units* (8th edn), Boston: Allyn and Bacon.

QCDA (Qualifications and Curriculum Development Agency: UK) (2009) *Teaching Gifted Students: Mathematics*, London: QCDA.

Riccomini, P.J. and Witzel, B.S. (2010) *Response to Intervention in Maths,* Thousand Oaks, CA: Corwin Press.

Taylor-Cox, J. (2009) *Math Intervention: Building Number Power with Formative Assessments, Differentiation and Games, Pre K-2*, Larchmont, NY: Eye On Education.

Van de Walle, J.A., Karp, K. and Bay-Williams, J.M. (2010) *Elementary and Middle School Mathematics: Teaching Developmentally*, Boston: Allyn and Bacon.

Chapter 14

Differentiating curriculum and instruction

Meeting students' special educational needs in mainstream classrooms usually requires that subject matter, learning activities, teaching procedures, resource materials and patterns of classroom organization must be adapted or modified to some extent. This strategy of adapting to students' needs and abilities to make classrooms more inclusive is known as *differentiated instruction* (e.g. Kluth and Danaher 2010; Little *et al.* 2009). In the simplest terms, differentiated instruction can be defined as teaching things differently according to observed differences among learners. In principle, effective differentiation means that the educational needs of children with disabilities, learning difficulties, language differences, and with gifts and talents can all be met in the regular classroom.

Although effective differentiated instruction has become the yardstick of best practice in inclusive schools, it must be acknowledged that implementing differentiation is never simple in practice. Maintaining a differentiated approach in mixed-ability classes invariably places heavy demands on teachers' time, knowledge, ingenuity and organizational skills. It is no easy task to teach and manage a class in which many types of activity are occurring simultaneously. In this chapter, some generic principles for differentiation are discussed, together with specific suggestions for adapting curriculum content, resources, teaching approaches and assessment procedures. Some problems associated with differentiation are also highlighted.

Keep it simple

From the beginning it is essential to stress the *simplicity* principle. Adaptations and modifications should not be made unless absolutely necessary. Whenever possible, a student with special needs should be helped to use mainstream materials and to participate in regular learning activities and tasks. Adaptations to curriculum are most effective and most easily sustained when they are simple, easy to design and implement, and based on typical assignments and activities. Differentiation should be less about drastically changing the content of the curriculum and more about providing alternative pathways and additional support to achieve common goals in learning a particular topic (e.g. Dettmer *et al.* 2009).

The process of applying differentiation in the classroom can sound very daunting for teachers because the professional literature describes many different and complicated ways of adapting and modifying instruction. Although in theory there are many strategies for differentiation, in practice it is not always feasible to apply more than one or two such strategies at the same time, particularly with large classes.

Basic principles for differentiation

Differentiated instruction for students with special needs necessitates tailoring some aspects of the classroom programme to take account of students' prior knowledge, strengths, weaknesses, learning preferences, interests and current levels of ability or disability in order to maximize their opportunities to learn. To implement this approach it is necessary to respond to individual differences among students by, for example:

- setting individualized objectives for learning;
- modifying curriculum content to match more closely the cognitive level of the students;
- providing different paths to learning to suit differing learning preferences;
- varying time allocation for classroom tasks to take account of students' differing rates of learning;
- adapting instructional materials;
- using assistive technology;
- encouraging students to produce work in different forms or through different media;
- organizing flexible groupings of students;
- varying the amount of direct guidance and assistance given to individuals.

Examples of differentiation

Adapting curriculum content

The curriculum content to be studied may be increased or decreased in terms of depth and complexity. Key aspects of the curriculum may be reduced to smaller units and presented in smaller steps for students with learning difficulties. Content may be extended and made more challenging for students of high ability. In both cases, lesson content may attempt to capitalize on students' own interests. Modifying curriculum content usually implies that students with learning difficulties may be required to cover less material in the lesson and the tasks or activities are usually easier to accomplish. In the case of gifted or more-able students, the reverse would be true – they might cover more content and in greater depth.

Several potential problems exist when modifying the curriculum. Reducing the complexity and demands of tasks and setting easier objectives for some students may sound like very good advice, but watering down the curriculum in this way can have the long-term effect of increasing the achievement gap between students with learning difficulties and other students. By reducing the demands placed on students of lower ability, we may be exaggerating the effect of individual differences and perpetuating inequalities among students. As stated above, differentiation is most easily implemented where it does not involve drastic changes to the curriculum. Obviously this argument cannot be extended to cover students with moderate to severe disabilities integrated in inclusive classrooms. In such cases, it will be necessary to modify significantly the demands of the mainstream curriculum to match more closely the students' cognitive level. In many countries, this is achieved through the medium of an individual education plan (IEP) and the provision of additional services.

Activities and learning tasks

The difficulty level of the tasks and activities that students are required to undertake in the lesson can be varied. Activities may also be completed via different pathways (e.g. computer programs, discussion, text books, videos). It is important that activities set for less-able students are not simply 'busy work' that is less demanding and less interesting.

One approach to differentiating activities and tasks is termed 'tiered assignments' with work planned and provided at three or four levels of challenge. Students are first allocated tasks at a level that matches their own ability and rate of learning. They can progress to higher levels over time.

Instructional materials

One area where modifications can be made to improve access to the curriculum is that of instructional resources (Janney and Snell 2004). The resource materials used within a lesson (texts, worksheets, exercises, blackboard notes, computer software) may need to be modified, and equipment may need to be provided for some students (e.g. blocks for counting in mathematics, a 'talking' calculator for a student with impaired vision, a pencil with a thick grip for a student with poor hand coordination). A variety of texts and instructional materials at various levels of complexity and readability should be made available for students to use. Some materials will be designed for use in cooperative learning situations, while other material may be for use for individual assignments.

When preparing print materials (worksheets, assignment cards, study notes, independent learning contracts) for students with learning difficulties the following strategies may be helpful:

- simplify the language – use short sentences, substitute simple words for difficult terms;
- modify sentence construction to facilitate comprehension – active voice is

easier to process than passive voice, 'The teacher read a story' rather than 'A story was read by the teacher';

- make printed instructions or questions clear and simple;
- present information in small blocks of text rather than dense paragraphs;
- use bullet points and lists rather than paragraphs;
- pre-teach any new vocabulary – if a difficult word cannot be simplified, ensure that it is introduced and discussed before students are expected to read it unaided;
- improve legibility of print and layout – if necessary, enlarge the size of print;
- highlight important terms or information – use underlining or print the words in bold type or colour;
- provide clear illustrations or diagrams;
- use cues or prompts where responses are required from the students – for example, provide the initial letter of the answer, or use dashes to show the number of words required in the answer.

Applying some of the strategies listed above will often be sufficient to allow a student with a mild disability or a literacy problem to access text without the need for further adaptation.

Differentiation through materials is often attempted merely by providing graded worksheets. The use of too many worksheet assignments in class can produce boredom. While there may be occasions where graded worksheets are appropriate and helpful, their frequent use can label a student as belonging to a particular ability group. Students do not like to be given simplified materials because this practice marks them out as 'different' and undermines their status in the peer group. Adolescents in particular are acutely sensitive to peer-group reactions and deeply resent being treated as if they are lacking in ability (Hall 1997).

Homework assignments

Differentiated homework assignments are an important way of meeting the needs of gifted and able students as well as those of students with difficulties. Some students may be given homework that involves additional practice at the same level of difficulty while others may have extension tasks involving more challenging applications, critical thinking and reflection.

Products from lessons

Often the output from students' efforts in a lesson will be tangible products such as written work, graphics, or models; but sometimes 'product' refers to other forms of evidence of learning, such as an oral report, a performance, a presentation to the group, participation in discussion, or the answering of oral questions. Differentiating the products of learning may mean that:

- each student is not expected to produce exactly the same amount or quality of work as every other student;
- a student may be asked to produce work in a different format – for example, an audio recording, a drawing or poster, scrapbook, a multiple-choice exercise rather than an essay;
- individual students may negotiate what they will produce and how they will produce it in order to provide evidence of their learning in a particular topic;

The potential danger in setting out from the start to accept less work from some students or of an inferior quality is that this strategy represents a lowering of expectations that can result in a self-fulfilling prophecy. The students produce less and less, and we in turn expect less and less of them. A different perspective suggests that teachers need to help students achieve more, not less, in terms of work output than they would have achieved without support. Differentiation of product should never be seen as offering a 'soft option'. It should never lead to a student consistently managing to avoid tasks he or she does not like to complete.

Classroom organization

At various times, the classroom can be set up to support more individualized projects or for group work. Use may be made of learning centres, computer-aided instruction, or resource-based learning (see Chapter 15). Teachers can use various ways of grouping students within the class to allow for different activities to take place, under differing amounts of teacher direction.

Teaching strategies

When teaching procedures and processes are differentiated some of the following strategies may be used:

- more use may be made of explicit and direct forms of instruction for certain groups within the classroom;
- re-teaching of some concepts or information to some students may be necessary, using simpler language and more examples;
- questions asked during a lesson may be pitched at different levels of difficulty for different individuals;
- closer monitoring of the work of some students may take place throughout the lesson;
- the teacher may use particular tactics to gain and maintain the interest of poorly motivated students;
- corrective feedback and descriptive praise may be given in more detail or less detail, according to the students' needs;
- the teacher may give more assistance or less assistance to individual students;

- extra practice may be provided for some students, often via differentiated homework assignments;
- extension work may be set for the most able students, requiring mainly independent study, investigation and application.

There is evidence to suggest that teachers are much better at using modifications to teaching process described above than they are at modifying curriculum content (Chan *et al.* 2002). They appear to find teaching process modifications more natural and much easier to accomplish within their personal teaching style. For example, skilled teachers already provide additional help to students when necessary by using prompting and cueing and advice. They differentiate their questioning and they make greater use of praise, encouragement and rewards during lessons. These are all strategies that can be applied while the teacher is still following a common curriculum with the whole class – and for this reason they are regarded as the most feasible adaptations for teachers to make.

Pace

The rate at which new information is presented, discussions are conducted and activities are pursued can be varied. The speed at which students are required to complete tasks, answer questions and produce outputs can be adjusted to individual needs. The nature of learning tasks set for students will be matched to their learning rate and abilities, with some tasks taking longer to complete than others.

Amount of assistance

Teachers can vary the amount of direct help given to individuals during a lesson. They may also encourage peer assistance and collaboration among students. The services of a classroom assistant can also be used. Giving extra individual assistance as and when necessary is one of the relatively easier strategies for teachers to employ to enable a mixed ability class to study the core curriculum.

Assessment

Assessment refers to any process used to determine how much learning, and what quality of learning, has occurred for each student in the class. Assessment provides an indication of how effective a particular episode of teaching and learning has been. The process of assessment also highlights anything that may need to be taught again, revised, or given additional practice time for some students.

Descriptions of differentiation usually include reference to modifying assessment procedures for a student with a disability or learning difficulty (Rieck and Wadsworth 2005). This form of differentiation is deemed necessary because these students may have problems demonstrating what they know (or can do) if the assessment method requires them to use language, literacy, numeracy or motor skills they do not possess. Modifications to assessment processes include such options as:

- simplifying the assessment task;
- shortening the task or test;
- allowing longer time for some students to complete the work;
- allowing a student with special needs to have some assistance in performing the task (e.g. questions read aloud to the student; student dictating answers to a scribe);
- enabling the student to present the work in a different format (e.g. notes rather than essay).

Classroom tests are one of the ways in which teachers routinely assess the progress of their students. Students with special needs may require modification to test formats or additional time allowed to complete the test. Some may need a variation in the mode of responding. Standard adaptations for test formats include:

- enlarging the print;
- leaving more space for the student to write the answer;
- using different types of question (e.g. short answer, multiple-choice, sentence completion, gapped paragraphs, matching formats);
- rewriting instructions in simple language and highlighting key points;
- keeping directions brief and simple;
- providing prompts such as *Begin the problem here. Answer in one sentence only.*

Modifications to test administration procedures include:

- using oral questioning and answering;
- using a scribe to write down a student's answers;
- giving short rest breaks during the test without penalty;
- allowing extra time to complete the test;
- avoiding penalties for poor spelling or handwriting;
- allowing a student to use a laptop computer to undertake the test;
- giving credit for drawings or diagrams if these help to indicate that the student knows the concept or information;
- for some students, administer the test in a quiet environment other than the classroom to reduce distractions (e.g. social worker's office, withdrawal room).

Starting points

An appropriate place to begin planning differentiated instruction is by identifying essential core information, concepts or skills associated with the topic to be taught.

All students in the class will be expected to master this core content to the best of their individual abilities. Planning and differentiating the topic then becomes a process of creating many different ways the students can achieve this goal through engaging in a variety of coherent experiences matched to their abilities. For example, some students may be led to encounter new ideas through reading about them in books; some may need to encounter them through direct experience or via video or role play; others will gain most from discussing the issues or problems with teacher and peers; and some will acquire the concepts most easily through direct teaching. *As a general rule, all students in the group will learn best if provided with a variety of activities and pathways.*

Planning needs to include consideration of strategies for delivering additional help to certain students during the lesson (e.g. via peer assistance, a learning support assistant, or from the teacher). It is also important to consider how students will be grouped, and how the available time will be used most effectively.

When planning the differentiated objectives for a lesson it is helpful to keep in mind the three stem statements:

- All students will . . .
- Some students will . . .
- A few students may . . .

In other words, *all students will* be expected to master the essential knowledge and skills, but possibly through engaging in different learning activities. *Some students will* achieve more than this core; and *a few students may* achieve one or two higher-order objectives through extension and enrichment activities.

Accommodations for students with disabilities

The term 'accommodation' usually conveys the notion of making sure that students with disabilities can participate fully or partially in a lesson by varying the type of activities or the method of instruction, providing additional human and technical resources, giving extra support, modifying the ways in which the student can respond, or changing the classroom environment. Janney and Snell (2004: 39) suggest: 'Accommodations are provided to enable the student to gain access to the classroom or the curriculum.'

Many of the modifications and adaptations already described above are equally appropriate for students with disabilities. For example, simplifying objectives and tasks, re-teaching important concepts and skills frequently, allowing more time for students to complete work, encouraging different outputs from students and facilitating peer assistance are all strategies that reduce or remove barriers to learning. Some students will also need additional support and modified equipment. The specific needs of students with disabilities are usually identified within their individual education plans (IEPs) and the IEP should be seen as the main source of advice for the types of differentiation and adaptation needed by these students.

Technological accommodations often involve the use of assistive devices to help a student communicate or to produce work (e.g. modified keyboard, computer with a visual display and touch screen or with voice synthesizer, braillers for blind students, enlarged text on computer screen for a student with partial sight, radio-frequency hearing aids for students with impaired hearing). Less sophisticated aids might include communication boards or picture-card systems for students without speech. It is beyond the scope of this book to discuss assistive technology in great detail, but some additional information is provided in Chapter 3 and Chapter 4.

Universal Design for Learning

In recent years, much has been written about the notion of Universal Design for Learning (UDL). The assumption behind UDL is that it should be possible to prepare and present information and skills to students in multiple ways that best match their aptitudes and engage them in activities that enable them to express themselves and demonstrate their learning. In principle, UDL caters for the needs of all students, ranging from those with difficulties through to those with gifts and talents. Under this principle, it should be possible for students of differing abilities in any classroom to have equal access to the curriculum and to achieve the planned learning objectives by taking different pathways tailored to their abilities and needs (Turnbull *et al.* 2010).

Gargiulo and Metcalf (2010) state that the three essential features of UDL that must be considered when designing curricula to meet the needs of all learners are: (i) *multiple means of representation* (e.g. via print medium, Braille, video, audio, ICT, concrete materials, diagrams, simulations); (ii) *multiple means of engagement* (looking, listening, hands on, participating, discussing, individual, group, independent, collaborative, interacting, peer tutoring); and (iii) *multiple means of expression* (e.g. oral, written, demonstration, creation, illustration, performance). It is also suggested that digital formats tend to be flexible enough to incorporate many of these features in ways that can adapt to individual differences among learners. Digital technology can build in many variations in modes of presentation, engagement and response, thus relieving the teacher of the massive burden of designing these alternate pathways in advance for each and every lesson.

UDL obviously has much in common with differentiated instruction, in the sense that barriers to learning are removed or reduced by offering multiple pathways to achievement. Unfortunately, up to this time UDL is a largely unfulfilled ideal: it remains a practice more written about than implemented. However, an increasing number of teachers are experimenting with ways of addressing individual differences and, for example, making more effective use of technology, multi-media study kits, peer tutoring, flexible grouping and tiered assignments.

Online resources

- An article by Susan Bashinski, Adapting the curriculum to meet the needs of diverse learners, is available on the PBS Teachers' website: www.pbs.org/teachers/earlychildhood/articles/adapting.html (accessed 30 March 2010).
- A summary and examples of adaptations and accommodations can be located online at: www.saskschools.ca/curr_content/adhs/adapting.htm (accessed 30 March 2010).
- South East Regional Clearinghouse website provides some practical advice on adaptations that can be made for students with disabilities: http://serch.cofc.edu/special/accessscience/AdaptingCurric_General.htm (accessed 30 March 2010).

Further reading

Athans, S.K. and Devine, D.A. (2010) *Fun-tastic Activities for Differentiating Comprehension Instruction, Grades 2-6,* Newark, DE: International Reading Association.

Glass, K.T. (2009) *Lesson Design for Differentiated Instruction, Grades 4-9,* Thousand Oaks, CA: Corwin Press.

Kryza, K., Duncan, A. and Stephens, S.J. (2010) *Differentiation for Real Classrooms: Making it Simple, Making it Work,* Thousand Oaks, CA: Corwin Press.

Peterson, J.M. and Hittie, M.M. (2010*) Inclusive Teaching: The Journey towards Effective Schools for All Learners* (2nd edn), Boston: Pearson.

Smutny, J.F. and Von Fremd, S.E. (2010) *Differentiating for the Young Child: Teaching Strategies across the Content Areas* (2nd edn), Thousand Oaks, CA: Corwin Press.

Walpole, S. and McKenna, M.C. (2009) *How to Plan Differentiated Reading Instruction: Resources for K-3,* New York: Guilford Press.

Chapter 15

Teaching methods for general and specific purposes

There are many ways of approaching the complex task of teaching children with special needs. A teacher's decision to select a particular approach for use at a particular time must depend upon the nature of the lesson content to be taught, the learning objectives and the salient characteristics of the students in the group. Learning difficulties may be caused or exacerbated for some students if an inappropriate teaching approach is used.

There is no single method that is superior to all other methods for all purposes. One particular method of teaching cannot possibly suit all types of learning or all ages and abilities of students, so methods must be selected according to their suitability of fit for achieving specific learning objectives with particular students.

Current evidence suggests that many problems associated with learning may be directly related to inappropriate methods of instruction (Farkota 2005; Pincott 2004; Pletka 2007). For example, unstructured and informal methods for teaching the beginning stages of reading and writing are unlikely to be entirely successful with every child; yet until recently they were the preferred approach advocated by many education authorities. As indicated in other chapters, studies have shown that most children make significantly better progress in literacy when directly taught the essential knowledge and skills required for decoding and comprehending (e.g. Brown and Colmar 2009; Rose 2009). Similarly, in the early stages of learning mathematics, some students experience greater success when directly instructed and given time to practice with feedback from the teacher, rather than being expected to discover number concepts and algorithms through investigative problem-solving activities alone (Kroesbergen *et al.* 2004).

This chapter provides an overview of teaching methods, ranging from those that may be regarded as 'teacher directed' (or *instructive*) to those that are clearly more 'learner oriented' (or *constructive*). The strengths and weakness in each method will be summarized, with particular reference to achieving particular types of learning objectives and their suitability for teaching students with learning difficulties or disabilities.

Teacher-directed approaches

Expository teaching

Expository teaching represents a method for presenting new information directly to learners in a form they can access and understand. Expository methods include demonstrating, lecturing, explaining, narrating, requiring students to read a textbook or manual, showing students an instructional video, or asking students to work through a computer program presenting information.

Expository teaching is used across the curriculum when introducing an overview of a new topic to a class, when clarifying a concept that has been misunderstood by students, when responding to issues raised by students, when setting out the steps in a new procedure or process, and when consolidating or reviewing learning at the end of a lesson or series of lessons. Expository teaching can be greatly enhanced by the use of appropriate visual support such as 'advance organizers', on-screen PowerPoint material, pictures, models, key points summarized on the whiteboard, by using bold type or colour to highlight textbook information, and providing students with supplementary notes. *The most essential skill for a teacher to possess for expository teaching is the ability to explain things simply and clearly.* This skill depends partly on the teacher's ability to appreciate a new topic from the perspective of a student learning it for the first time, partly on the ability to organize information into teachable and learnable units, and partly on the ability to express ideas in vocabulary that is understood by the learners.

Expository teaching has several potential weaknesses, particularly when used with students with learning difficulties. These weaknesses include:

* the method does not take account of individual differences among learners such as prior knowledge, language background, literacy skills, experience, attention span, or motivation;
* if used too frequently, or for long periods without active participation by the students, expository teaching can lead to boredom and disengagement;
* expository methods require learners to have adequate linguistic skills, particularly a good listening vocabulary, adequate reading comprehension and functional writing skills (e.g. for note-taking) – these prerequisites are often lacking in students with special needs;
* students with learning difficulties often lack confidence and assertiveness so they are unlikely ever to ask the teacher questions during the lesson, or seek clarification on a particular issue.

It would be rare indeed to find a primary or secondary teacher using expository teaching as their only approach. They realize that almost any lesson at any age level requires active participation and input from the students. During the course of a single lesson a teacher may switch several times between teacher-directed input and student-centred activity. The lesson may commence with instruction and explanation, but then change quickly to student-centred activity with the teacher adopting a more supportive and facilitative role. Then in the final stage of the lesson there is a return to teacher direction in order to consolidate learning and check for understanding. During a single lesson in a classroom, the instructional techniques will generally reflect the skilful integration of appropriate amounts of expository teaching together with student-centred learning activities.

Interactive whole-class teaching

Interactive whole-class teaching embodies some of the elements of expository teaching but facilitates very high levels of active participation and high response rates from the students. The lesson operates using a two-way process in which the teacher explains, ask questions and challenges students' thinking, but also responds to questions and ideas contributed frequently by the students. The students offer their own suggestions, express their opinions, ask questions of the teacher and each other, explain their thinking, or demonstrate their methods. However, inter-active whole-class teaching does not simply comprise verbal exchanges between teacher and students, the teacher also makes effective use of instructional media to gain and hold students' attention. Teaching strategies often incorporated into inter-active whole-class teaching with lower-ability students include *choral responding* (Cartledge *et al.* 2009) and the use of *response cards* (Munro and Stephenson 2009). Choral responding simply involves all (or several) students answering a question or repeating information together, rather than the traditional method of asking them to raise a hand and then calling upon one student. When response cards are used, the teacher provides all students in the class with a set of blank cards at the beginning of the session. At certain times during the lesson the teacher asks the students a particular question and each student immediately writes his or her response on the card and holds it up for the teacher to check. Both choral responding and response cards ensure a high rate of active participation by all students.

As mentioned in Chapter 13, in countries where students gain excellent results in international surveys of achievement, teachers seem to employ interactive whole-class teaching methods very effectively. In Britain, interactive whole-class teaching has been advocated as one way for improving literacy and numeracy standards in primary schools. The approach is seen as much more productive than individual programming or unstructured group work. It is claimed that effective use of interactive whole-class teaching helps to close the learning gap that usu-ally appears between higher-achievers and lower-achievers when individualized 'work at your own pace' methods are used.

Some potential problems associated with interactive whole-class teaching include:

* the teacher needs to be very skilled in drawing all students into discussion otherwise some students will not participate actively in the lesson;

- some teachers, particularly those who believe strongly in informal methods, appear to find this fast-paced, interactive approach difficult to implement and sustain;
- the pace of the lesson will be slowed unintentionally if teachers tell individual students to raise a hand if they wish to ask or answer a question;
- at the other extreme, if the pace of the lesson is too brisk, students with learning difficulties tend to opt out.

Direct instruction

Direct instruction is the term applied to all forms of active teaching that attempt to convey the curriculum to students in a reasonably structured and systematic manner. Direct instruction is characterized by precise learning objectives, clear demonstrations, explanations, modelling by the teacher, guided practice, corrective feedback and independent practice by the students. Teaching takes place at a brisk pace and learning is assessed regularly. Re-teaching and remediation are provided where necessary. Direct instruction of this type has proved to be very effective indeed in raising achievement levels in basic academic skills for all students, and is particularly beneficial for students with learning difficulties and those with intellectual disability (Mitchell 2008; Swaine *et al.* 2010; White 2005).

The most highly structured and carefully designed model using direct instruction is associated most closely with the work of Engelmann and others at the University of Oregon (e.g. Engelmann 1999). This highly teacher-directed form of curriculum delivery, based on behavioural learning principles, is usually referred to using the capitalized form *Direct Instruction* (DI). DI is a system for teaching basic academic skills such as reading, spelling and arithmetic through the provision of carefully sequenced and scripted lessons (Carnine *et al.* 2006). DI was originally associated with the published programme called DISTAR (*Direct Instructional System for Teaching and Remediation*) for teaching basic skills to disadvantaged and at-risk children in the US, but DI programmes now include materials covering writing, spelling, comprehension, mathematics and problem solving for a much wider age and ability range. Some elements of DI are highly appropriate for teaching students at Tier 3 (intensive remediation) in the Response to Intervention model.

In a typical DI session, young children are taught in small groups based on ability. Usually, they are seated in a semi-circle facing the teacher, who gains and holds their attention and follows the teaching steps clearly set out in the script. The scripted presentation ensures that all steps in the planned teaching sequence are followed, and that all questions and instructions are clear. Lessons are designed so that there is a very high rate of responding by all children in the group. The teacher gives immediate feedback, correction and encouragement. Choral responding by the whole group is used as a strategy for motivating students and maximizing participation.

Since DI is highly effective, one would expect to find the method being widely used for teaching the foundation stages of academic skills; but this is not the case. While DI has enjoyed some popularity in special education settings, it has had rather limited impact in mainstream schools. It appears that mainstream primary and early childhood teachers prefer to use methods that encourage children to learn at their own rate and in their own way. These teachers shy away from methods that appear prescriptive and structured. It is also clear that most teacher education institutions in the past twenty years have tended to omit coverage of DI in their methodology courses; instead, devoting their full attention to methods that are child-centred and guided by constructivist learning theory.

The difficulties or limitations associated with the use of DI relate mainly to the teachers, not to students or the method. They include:

- the fact that DI must be implemented on a daily basis, using small group instruction rather than a whole-class teaching can cause problems in scheduling and staffing;
- many teachers, particularly in Britain and Australia, react very negatively towards DI, claiming that it is too highly structured, too rapidly paced and allows no creativity on the part of teachers.

Student-centred approaches

Discovery learning

Discovery learning (DL) is based on constructivist learning theory. In DL, students construct knowledge about a topic largely through their interactions with materials and by accessing whatever human and other resources they may require. The emphasis is on the students being active investigators rather than passive recipients of information delivered to them by a teacher or textbook. In order to participate successfully in open discovery activities, learners must have adequate inductive reasoning ability to recognize principles or relationships emerging from their observations. In typical discovery situations in mathematics, science or social studies, examples and non-examples of specific concepts are available to the learners, and from these they must 'discover' the corresponding rule or relationship.

The two main forms of discovery learning are 'unstructured' discovery and 'guided' discovery. Unstructured discovery places learners in situations where they are given very little direction from the teacher and must decide for themselves the appropriate way to investigate a given topic or problem. At the end of the process, they must reach their own conclusions and develop their conceptual understanding from their observations and data. This unstructured approach (often under the guise of 'problem-based learning') is sometimes used in secondary school science, mathematics and for topics in social studies, but the outcome is not always good, particularly for students with poor literacy or study-skills, weak self-management and difficulties with inductive reasoning. Often students with learning difficulties do not have a clear idea of what they are expected to do, and do not believe in their own ability to engage successfully with a problem by thinking in an active way. Jacobsen *et al.* (2009) reviewed research on the effectiveness of discovery learning and concluded that some students develop serious misconceptions and can become confused and frustrated in unstructured discovery activities.

Guided discovery has a much tighter structure, and teachers have found that learning is more successful when skills required in the investigative process are explicitly taught and the students have the prerequisite understandings. The teacher sets clear objectives, provides initial explanation to help students begin the task efficiently, and may offer suggestions for a step-by-step procedure to find the target information or to solve the problem.

The major benefits of DL include the following:

- learners are actively involved in the process of learning and the topics studied are often intrinsically motivating;
- the activities used in authentic discovery contexts are usually more meaningful than classroom exercises and textbook study;
- it is claimed (but is by no means certain) that learners are more likely to remember concepts if they discover them;
- DL builds on learners' prior knowledge and experience;
- DL encourages independence in learning because learners acquire new investigative skills that can be generalized and applied in many other contexts;
- DL also fosters positive group-working skills.

The major problems associated with DL include:

- the approach can be a very time-consuming, often taking much longer for concepts to be acquired than would occur with direct teaching;
- DL relies on learners having adequate literacy, numeracy and independent study skills;
- students may learn little of value from discovery activities if they lack an adequate prior knowledge for interpreting their discoveries accurately;
- 'activity' does not necessarily equate with 'learning' – learners may be actively involved but may still not understand or recognize underlying concepts, rules or principles;
- children with learning problems have difficulty forming valid opinions, making predictions and drawing conclusions based on evidence;
- poor outcomes occur when teachers are not good at designing and managing discovery learning environments;
- some teachers do not monitor activities effectively so are not able to give individual guidance (scaffolding) that is frequently needed by learners.

Project-based and resource-based learning

The project approach has been used in primary and secondary schools for many years. It lends itself easily to curriculum areas such as social studies, environmental education, geography, history, civics, science, mathematics and the languages, enabling students to apply and extend their knowledge. Project work can help students integrate ideas and information from these different subjects. Information technology can be fully utilized in project work, resulting in students learning both ICT skills and specific content knowledge simultaneously (OTEC 2005). The extended timeframe usually provided for project work allows students to plan carefully, revise and reflect more deeply upon their learning.

There are many potential benefits from project work compared to traditional textbook teaching. Project-based learning has the following advantages:

- it is an inclusive approach in that all learners can participate to the best of their ability;
- projects promote meaningful learning, connecting new information to students' past experience and prior knowledge;
- the learning process involved in gathering data is valued as well as the product;
- students are responsible for their own learning, thus increasing self-direction;
- undertaking a project encourages decision-making and allows for student choice;
- researching the topic develops deeper knowledge of subject matter;
- learners use higher-order thinking and conceptual skills, in addition to acquiring facts;
- information collection, analysis and presentation encourages various modes of communication and representation;
- preparing the project helps students apply and improve basic reading, writing and ICT skills;
- assessment is performance based;
- if undertaken with a partner or in a group, project work increases teamworking and cooperative skills.

Potential difficulties associated with project-based learning include:

- some students lack adequate study skills for researching and collating information;
- when working on projects, some students may give the impression of productive involvement but may in fact be learning and contributing very little;
- when projects involve the production of posters, models, charts, recordings, photographs and written reports for display, there is a danger that these are actually 'window dressing' that hides a fairly shallow investigation and understanding of the topic;

- when different aspects of a topic are given to different group members to research, there is a danger that individual members never really gain an over-all understanding of the whole topic.

Resource-based learning (RBL) can be considered another form of inquiry method, closely associated with problem-based or issues-based learning, and underpinned by constructivist learning principles. In resource-based learning, as in project-based learning, students use books, community publications, reports, online information and other resources to obtain information, they must then ana-lyse and critique before organizing it in an appropriate form for presentation. RBL is best suited to most 'content' areas of the school curriculum (e.g. social studies, history, geography, science, environmental studies) and is said to be adaptable to students' different abilities.

The main aim of RBL is to foster students' autonomy in learning by providing opportunities for them to work individually or collaboratively while applying rel-evant study skills to investigate authentic topics. Typically, in RBL situations the teacher introduces an issue, topic or problem to be investigated through the use of relevant resources that are made immediately available. The teacher and students together clarify the nature the task and set goals for inquiry; then students work individually or in groups to carry out the necessary investigation over a series of lessons. In some cases, it may be necessary to pre-teach researching skills such as locating information, extracting relevant data, summarizing, locating websites and taking notes.

Some of the advantages claimed for RBL include:

- the method motivates students and encourages self-directed learning and reflection;
- students learn from their own active and creative processing of information using a range of authentic resources;
- RBL topics can stimulate higher-order thinking (problem solving, reasoning and critical evaluation);
- through the use of print and electronic media, students' independent study skills are strengthened and extended in ways that may easily generalize to other learning contexts;
- RBL can foster enthusiasm for learning and can increase academic engage-ment time.

Potential difficulties associated with RBL are similar to those identified for dis-covery learning, namely:

- RBL generally requires a resource-rich learning environment, including easy access to reference books and computers;
- effective engagement in RBL depends upon the students having adequate literacy, numeracy and independent study skills;

- students will learn little from RBL if they lack the prior knowledge necessary for interpreting new information;
- RBL demands motivation, initiative and self-management from the students;
- teachers may not monitor activities effectively, so are not able to give encouragement and support that is frequently needed by learners.

Problem-based and issues-based learning

Lee (2001: 10) has suggested that: 'Learning through problem-solving may be much more effective than traditional didactic methods of learning in creating in the student's mind a body of knowledge that is useful in the future.' This view sits well with constructivist theories of learning, and highlights the value of providing students with many genuine opportunities to apply knowledge and skills they may have been taught more directly. At the same time, they will acquire new information, skills and insights by engaging in the problem-solving process.

In problem-based learning (PBL), students are presented with a real-life situation or issue that requires a solution or a decision leading to some form of action. With older learners, the problems are often intentionally 'messy' (ill-defined) in the sense that not all of the information required for solution is provided in the problem, and there is no clear path or procedure to follow (Jacobsen *et al.* 2009).

Problem-based learning (PBL) and issues-based learning (IBL) are still not widely used in schools − other than in programmes for gifted students − but they have become popular in higher education. As discussed in Chapter 13, a problem-solving approach has also been recommended for application in mathematics teaching, but it is also necessary to supplement the approach by teaching students the essential computational skills.

The advantages of PBL and IBL are considered to be:

- the objectives are authentic and they can link school learning with the real world;
- the process of tackling problems and identifying, locating and using appropriate resources can be motivating for learners;
- PBL and IBL involve the active construction of new knowledge;
- solving problems usually requires the integration of information and skills from different disciplines;
- learning achieved through PBL and IBL is likely to be retained and can be transferred to other situations;
- the method encourages self-direction in learning and prepares students to think critically and analytically;
- problem solving usually requires cooperation and teamwork and can thus enhance communication and collaborative skills.

Donovan and Bransford (2005) have observed, in the context of mathematics, that to develop competence in investigative problem-solving students must have a deep foundation of factual knowledge, an understanding of facts and ideas in the context of a conceptual framework, and the ability to organize knowledge in ways that facilitate retrieval and application. It is a lack of these prerequisites among many children with learning difficulties that creates problems in using investigative or PBL approach with these students. Their most obvious weaknesses tend to include:

- lack of specific subject knowledge about the topic or content of the problem;
- limited experience in working collaboratively;
- lack of confidence in working through problems or tasks without teacher direction;
- inability to identify and separate irrelevant information from what is relevant for addressing the problem;
- lack of flexibility in thinking;
- a tendency to decide on a solution too early, and then resist change later.

Situated learning

Using authentic tasks and contexts as the medium for teaching information, skills and strategies is also the basis of the approach known as 'situated learning' (Vincini 2003). Situated learning takes place in a setting that is functionally identical to where the learning will be applied in real life – for example, a workshop, on a fieldtrip, in the supermarket, or on a bus. Within that setting, a range of instructional methods may be used, including direct teaching, practice with feedback, problem solving and enquiry.

Situated learning is an attempt to combat criticism that much of the teaching that goes on in schools is artificial because it is not reality-based and often learners do not recognize the functional value of what they are taught. This fact has always been recognized in special schools – and special schools can perhaps be credited with the original concept of situated learning in the form of reality-based and experiential curricula.

The advantages of situated learning include:

- learning opportunities are provided in real or simulated contexts in which new knowledge or skills must be acquired for immediate use;
- experts or mentors are available to provide learners with support;
- instructional scaffolding and direct coaching are provided as necessary;
- situated learning represents a motivating and active approach to learning;
- students are more likely to become confident and independent thinkers;
- learning is likely to generalize more easily to new contexts;
- collaboration among learners can be encouraged.

Difficulties in providing situated learning in school contexts include:

- the task of arranging and maintaining real-life learning situations over time adds considerably to teachers' workload;

- assembling the computer-simulated resources that are often needed demands technical expertise;
- some teachers are not confident in teaching in unusual settings and without clear lesson structures;
- class size can be a major obstacle;
- situated learning is most difficult to implement in schools following prescriptive curricula with an emphasis on examination results.

E-learning

The term e-learning now covers all technology-enhanced instructional approaches. The term includes computer-assisted learning (CAL), computer-aided instruction (CAI) and all web-based and online teaching and resources (Seale 2006). These and many other forms of technology and media can lead to improvements in the quality of educational programmes and can greatly enhance students' motivation and participation (Pletka 2007). The term *blended teaching* is often used to describe contexts in which face-to-face instruction is combined with use of web-based and resource-based independent study.

E-learning can be a self-paced approach that encourages maximum independence in seeking, using and communicating information. The computer-literacy skills that students acquire when engaged in e-learning are now regarded as essential life skills.

Unfortunately, while the topic 'computer studies' figures increasingly in primary and secondary school curricula, many general subjects teachers still do not integrate e-learning into their own subject. The reasons for this seem to include lack of equipment in the school or lack of technical expertise. Teaching is still mainly implemented through other forms of presentation and study such as group work, discussions, silent reading and independent or collaborative project work (Pletka 2007). Schools have yet to utilize the full potential of computers to deliver multi-media instructional programs covering virtually any curriculum area, and geared to any age or ability level.

In the beginning reading and remedial teaching domains, computer packages can provide motivating and engaging activities that involve abundant revision and practice of basic skills (e.g. Karemaker *et al.* 2010; Parette *et al.* 2009; Wild 2009). Combining e-learning with other forms of teaching has proved to be effective with blind students and others with disabilities (Freire *et al.* 2010; Izzo *et al.* 2009). Such programs can also improve students' confidence, motivation and attention to task. Polloway *et al.* (2008) report that students with learning difficulties and disabilities frequently display a positive attitude towards using computers, are eager to participate and show improved levels of on-task behaviour.

In general, the findings from research into the effectiveness of e-learning have been positive (e.g. Prideaux *et al.* 2005; US Department of Education 2010). The appropriate use of e-learning as a supplement within the classroom programme can exert positive influences on students' enthusiasm, motivation and engagement

– and these are important considerations when working with students who have learning difficulties (Pletka 2007; Seale 2006). However, while technology can certainly enhance students' initial learning, there is no strong evidence that the information and skills acquired by such means are retained and remembered more easily by students than through learning by other methods (Kose 2009).

CAL and CAI have the following benefits:

- the mode of presentation ensures that learners make active, self-initiated responses and are 'in charge' of the learning situation;
- software can be matched to student's ability level and rate of learning, and is therefore one way of individualizing or differentiating instruction;
- learners usually gain immediate knowledge of results after every response;
- reinforcement and corrective feedback can be provided immediately;
- students move towards greater independence and self-regulation in learning;
- working at a computer is challenging but non-threatening;
- CAL provides a private method of making errors and self-correcting;
- learners can engage in extra practice and overlearning to master basic skills;
- most (but not all) students enjoy working at a computer more than using text-books and print resources;
- students can extend their computer competencies;
- teaching subjects such as science, social studies, mathematics, environmental education and the arts can be enhanced by documentary or simulation pro-grams and by giving access to Internet resources.

Difficulties associated with the use of CAI and CAL include:

- students with literacy problems may have difficulty comprehending verbal information on the screen;
- some students lack prerequisite computer skills;
- some teachers lack expertise in integrating e-learning into the curriculum;
- there may be a shortage of computers in the school, or computers are only available in a computer lab at limited times each week;
- technical failures occur resulting in lost time and frustration;
- a few students prefer group interactions with peers and the teacher, rather than using technology and media.

In the methods described in this chapter, the potential problems that may be encountered by children with learning difficulties have been identified. With this information in mind, teachers are in a better position to select methods that match their teaching objectives and are compatible with students' learning characteris-tics.

Online resources

- ADPRIMA 2010 website lists the uses, advantages and disadvantages of several teaching methods. Online at: www.adprima.com/teachmeth.htm (accessed 30 March 2010).
- Special Education Resources for General Educators (SERGE) website provides basic information on selecting methods for SEN students, together with links to sources on related issues: http://serge.ccsso.org/question_2_1.html (accessed 30 March 2010).
- Information on problem-based learning can be found at: www.studygs.net/pbl.htm (accessed 30 March 2010).
- Interactive whole-class teaching in the context of mathematics is described at: www.ncetm.org.uk/mathemapedia/Whole+class+interactive+te aching (accessed 30 March 2010).
- Comments on the effectiveness of Direct Instruction (DI) can be located at: www.jefflindsay.com/EducData.shtml (accessed 30 March 2010).
- The theory underpinning discovery learning is explained at: www.learning-theories.com/discovery-learning-bruner.html (accessed 30 March 2010).
- Updates and news on e-learning can be found at: www.elearninglearning.com/wpblog/organizational-learning-oer/ (accessed 30 March 2010).

Further reading

Boyle, J. and Scanlon, D. (2010) *Methods and Strategies for Teaching Students with Mild Disabilities,* Belmont, CA: Wadsworth-Cengage Learning.

Burden, J. and Byrd, D.M. (2010) *Methods for Effective Teaching* (5th edn), Boston: Allyn and Bacon.

Danielson, C. (2010) *Teaching Methods*, Upper Saddle River, NJ: Pearson-Merrill.

Goeke, J.L. (2009) *Explicit Instruction: A Framework for Meaningful Direct Teaching,* Upper Saddle River, NJ: Merrill.

Hollingsworth, J. (2009) *Explicit Direct Instruction: The Power of the Well-crafted, Well-taught Lesson,* Thousand Oaks, CA: Corwin Press.

Jacobsen, D.A., Eggen, P. and Kauchak, D. (2009) *Methods for Teaching: Promoting Student Learning in K-12 classrooms* (8th edn), Upper Saddle River, NJ: Pearson-Merrill.

Lemlech, J.K. (2010) *Curriculum and Instructional Methods for the Elementary and Middle School* (7th edn), Boston: Allyn and Bacon.

References

Abar, B. and Loken, E. (2010) 'Self-regulated learning and self-directed study in a pre-college sample', *Learning and Individual Differences*, 20, 1: 25–9.

Abrams, F. (2010) *Learning to Fail: How Society Lets Young People Down*, London: Routledge.

Alberto, P.A. and Troutman, A.C. (2009) *Applied Behavior Analysis for Teachers* (8th edn), Upper Saddle River, NJ: Pearson-Merrill.

Alfassi, M., Weiss, I. and Lifshitz, H. (2009) 'The efficacy of reciprocal teaching in fostering the reading literacy of students with intellectual disability', *European Journal of Special Needs Education*, 24, 3: 291–305.

Allen, K.E. and Cowdrey, G.E. (2009) *The Exceptional Child: Inclusion in Early Childhood Education* (6th edn), Clifton Park, NY: Thomson-Delmar.

Allington, R.L. (2005) *What Really Matters for Struggling Readers?* (2nd edn), New York: Longman.

Antia, S.D., Reed, S. and Kreimeyer, K.H. (2005) 'Written language of deaf and hard-of-hearing students in public schools', *Journal of Deaf Studies and Deaf Education* 10, 3: 244–55.

APA (American Psychiatric Association) (2000) *Diagnostic and Statistical Manual of Mental Disorders: Text Revised (DSM–IV–TR)*, Washington, DC: APA.

Ashcroft, W., Argiro, S. and Keohane, J. (2010) *Success Strategies for Teaching Kids with Autism,* Waco, TX: Prufrock Press.

Assouline, S.G., Nicpon, M.F. and Whiteman, C. (2010) 'Cognitive and psychosocial characteristics of gifted students with written language disability', *Gifted Child Quarterly*, 54, 2: 102–15.

Baker, S.K., Chard, D.J., Ketterlin-Geller, L., Apichatabutra, C. and Doabler, C. (2009) 'Teaching writing strategies to at-risk students: the quality of evidence for self-regulated strategy development', *Exceptional Children*, 75, 3: 303–19.

Bardin, J.A. and Lewis, S. (2008) 'A survey of the academic engagement of students with visual impairments in general education classes', *Journal of Visual Impairment and Blindness,* 102, 8: 472–9.

Baroody, A., Eiland, M. and Thompson, B. (2009) 'Fostering at-risk preschoolers' number sense', *Early Education and Development*, 20, 1: 80–128.

Bates, J. and Munday, S. (2005) *Able, Gifted and Talented,* London: Continuum.

Batshaw, M.L., Shapiro, B. and Farber, M.L.Z. (2007). 'Developmental delay and intellectual disability', in M.L. Batshaw, L. Pellegrino and N.J. Roizen (eds) *Children with Disabilities* (6th ed. pp. 245–61), Baltimore, MD: Brookes.

Beane, A.L. (2008) *Protect Your Child from Bullying*, San Francisco, CA: Jossey-Bass.

Bellert, A. (2009) 'Narrowing the gap: a report on the *QuickSmart* mathematics intervention', *Australian Journal of Learning Difficulties*, 14, 2: 171–83.

Bender, W.N. (2007) *Learning Disabilities: Characteristics, Identification and Teaching Strategies* (6th edn), Boston, MA: Allyn and Bacon.

Berninger, V.W., Vaughn, K., Abbot, R.D., Begay, K., Coleman, K., Curtin, G., Hawkins, J.M. and Graham, S. (2002) 'Teaching spelling and composition alone and together: implications for the simple view of writing', *Journal of Educational Psychology*, 94, 2: 291–304.

Best, S.J., Heller, K.W. and Bigge, J.L. (2010) *Teaching Individuals with Physical or Multiple Disabilities* (6th edn), Upper Saddle River, NJ: Pearson-Merrill.

Betts, G. (1985) *The Autonomous Learner Model for the Gifted and Talented*, Greeley, CO: ALPS Publishing.

Bissex, G. (1980) *GYNS AT WRK: A Child Learns to Write and Read*, Cambridge, MA: Harvard University Press.

Bixler, J. (2009) *Negotiating Literacy Learning: Exploring the Challenges and Achievements of Struggling Readers*, Boston: Pearson-Allyn and Bacon.

Bowen, J. (2010) 'Visual impairment and its impact on self-esteem', *British Journal of Visual Impairment*, 28, 1: 47–56.

Brissiaud, R. and Sander, E. (2010) 'Arithmetic word problem solving: a situation strategy first framework', *Developmental Science*, 13, 1: 92–107.

Browder, D., Ahlgrim-Delzell, L., Spooner, F., Mims, P.J. and Baker, J.N. (2009) 'Using time delay to teach literacy to students with severe developmental disabilities', *Exceptional Children*, 75, 3: 343–65.

Brown, G. and Colmar, S. (2009) 'Historical and current perspectives on the necessary and sufficient components for effective classroom instruction', *Special Education Perspectives*, 18, 1: 47–60.

Cadima, J., McWilliam, R.A. and Leal, T. (2010) 'Environmental risk factors and children's literacy skills during transition to elementary school', *International Journal of Behavioral Development*, 34, 1: 24–33.

Calculator, S.N. (2009) 'Augmentative and alternative communication (AAC) and inclusive education for students with the most severe disabilities', *International Journal of Inclusive Education*, 13, 1: 93–113.

Caldwell, P. (2006) *Finding you, Finding me: Using Intensive Interaction*, London: Jessica Kingsley.

Carnine, D.W., Silbert, J., Kameenui, E.J. and Tarver, S.G. (2004) *Direct Instruction Reading* (4th edn), Upper Saddle River, NJ: Pearson-Prentice Hall.

Carnine, D.W., Silbert, J., Kameenui, E.J., Tarver, S.G. and Jongjohann, K. (2006) *Teaching Struggling and At-risk Readers: A Direct Instruction Approach*, Upper Saddle River, NJ: Pearson-Merrill-Prentice Hall.

Cartledge, G. (2005) 'Learning disabilities and social skills: reflections', *Learning Disability Quarterly* 28, 2: 179–81.

Cartledge, G., Gardner, R. and Ford, D.Y. (2009) *Diverse Learners with Exceptionalities*, Upper Saddle River, NJ: Merrill.

Catts, H.W., Hogan, T.P., Adlof, S.M. and Barth, A.E. (2003) *The simple view of reading: Changes over time.* Online document from Society for the Scientific Study of Reading: www2.ku.edu/~splh/Catts/poster7.pdf (accessed 31 March 2010).

Cekaite, A. (2009) 'Collaborative corrections with spelling control: digital resources and peer assistance', *International Journal of Computer-supported Collaborative Learning*, 4, 3: 319–41.

Chalk, J.C., Hagan-Burke, S. and Burke, M.D. (2005) 'The effects of self-regulated strategy development on the writing process for high school students with learning disabilities', *Learning Disability Quarterly* 28, 1: 75–87.

Chambers, B., Slavin, R.E., Madden, N., Abrami, P.C., Tucker, B., Chueng, A. and Gifford, R. (2008) 'Technology infusion in Success for All: Reading outcomes for First Graders', *Elementary School Journal*, 109, 1: 1–15.

Chan, C., Chang, M.L., Westwood, P.S. and Yuen, M.T. (2002) 'Teaching adaptively: how easy is "differentiation" in practice? A perspective from Hong Kong', *Asian-Pacific Educational Researcher* 11, 1: 27–58.

Chan, L. and Dally, K. (2000) 'Review of literature', in W. Louden, L. Chan, J. Elkins, D. Greaves, H. House, M. Milton, S. Nichols, M. Rohl, J. Rivalland and C. van Kraayenoord (eds) *Mapping the Territory: Primary Students with Learning Difficulties in Literacy and Numeracy*, Canberra: Department of Education, Training and Youth Affairs.

Checker, L.J., Remine, M.D. and Brown, P.M. (2009) 'Deaf and hearing impaired children in regional and rural areas: parent views on education services', *Deafness and Education International*, 11, 1: 21–38.

Chitiyo, M. and Wheeler, J.J. (2009) 'Challenges faced by school teachers in implementing positive behavior support in their schools', *Remedial and Special Education*, 30, 1: 58–63.

Christian, B.T. (2008) *Outrageous Behaviour Modification* (2nd edn), Austin, TX: ProEd.

Clark, B. (2008) *Growing up Gifted* (7th edn), Upper Saddle River, NJ: Pearson-Merrill-Prentice Hall.

Clark, L. (2009) 'Record one in five pupils has special educational needs but are schools fiddling the numbers?' *Mail-Online*, 8 May 2009. Online: www.dailymail.co.uk/news/article-1178450/Record-pupils-special-educational-needs--schools-fiddling-numbers.html (accessed 31 March 2010).

Colangelo, N. and Assouline, S. (2009) 'Acceleration: meeting the academic and social needs of students', in T. Balchin, B. Hymer and D.J. Matthews (eds) *The Routledge International Companion to Gifted Education* (pp. 194–202), London: Routledge.

Coleman, L.J. (2005) *Nurturing Talent in High School*, New York: Teachers College Press.

Coltheart, M. and Prior, M. (2007) 'Learning to Read in Australia. Occasional Paper 1/2007', Canberra: Academy of the Social Sciences in Australia.

Commonwealth of Australia Senate Committee on Employment, Workplace Relations, Small Business and Education (2001) *The Education of Gifted and Talented Children*, Canberra: Commonwealth of Australia.

Conroy, M., Marchand, T. and Webster, M. (2009) *Motivating Primary Students to Write Using Writers' Workshop*. Action Research Project for MA Degree: Saint Xavier University, Chicago, Illinois.

Cooney, K. and Hay, I. (2005) 'Internet-based literacy development for middle school students with reading difficulties', *Literacy Learning: The Middle Years* 13, 1: 36–44.

Cotugno, A.J. (2009) 'Social competence and social skills training and intervention for children with autism spectrum disorders', *Journal of Autism and Developmental Disorders*, 39, 9: 1268–77.

Court, D. and Givon, S. (2007) 'Group intervention: Improving social skills of adolescents with learning disabilities', in K.L. Freiberg (ed.) *Educating Exceptional Children* (17th edn, pp. 63–7), Dubuque, IA: McGraw Hill-Duskin.

Coyne, M.D., Zipoli, R.P., Chard, D.J., Faggella-Luby, M., Ruby, M., Santoro, L.E. and Baker, S. (2009) 'Direct instruction of comprehension: Instructional examples from intervention research on listening and reading comprehension', *Reading and Writing Quarterly*, 25, 2–3: 221–45.

Cripps, C. (1990) 'Teaching joined writing to children on school entry as an agent for catching spelling', *Australian Journal of Remedial Education* 22, 3: 11–15.

Cullen-Powell, L., Barlow, J. and Bagh, J. (2005) 'The Self-discovery Programme for children with special educational needs in mainstream primary and secondary schools', *Emotional and Behavioural Difficulties* 10, 3: 189–201.

Cuvo, A.J., May, M.E. and Post, T.M. (2001) 'Effects of living room, Snoezelen room, and outside activities on stereotypic behaviors and engagement by adults with profound mental retardation', *Research in Developmental Disabilities* 22, 3: 183–204.

Davies, A. (2006) *Teaching THRASS*, Chester: THRASS UK.

DCSF (Department for Children, Schools and Families: UK). (2006) *The new conceptual framework for teaching reading: the 'simple view of reading' – Overview for literacy leaders and managers in schools and early years settings.* Online document from Primary National Strategy, UK: http://nationalstrategies.standards.dcsf.gov.uk/node/19504?uc%20=%20force_uj> (accessed 31 March 2010).

DCSF (Department for Children, Schools and Families: UK) (2009a) *Special Educational Needs in England: January 2009.* Online: www.dcsf.gov.uk/rsgatDB/SFR/s000852/SFR14_2009.pdf (accessed 26 March 2010).

DCSF (Department for Children, Schools and Families: UK) (2009b) *Special Educational Needs and Disability: Data Collection by Type of SEN.* Online: www.teachernet.gov.uk/wholeschool/sen/datatypes/ (accessed 26 March 2010).

DCSF (Department for Children, Schools and Families: UK). (2009c) *Gifted and Talented Education: Guidance on Addressing Underachievement.* Online: http://publications.dcsf.gov.uk/eOrderingDownload/00378–2009BKT-EN.pdf (accessed 23 March 2010).

DCSF/TeacherNet (2009) *Data collection by type of SEN.* Online: www.teachernet.gov.uk/wholeschool/sen/datatypes/ (accessed 26 March 2010).

de Lemos, M. (2005) 'Effective strategies for the teaching of reading: what works, and why', *Australian Journal of Learning Disabilities*, 10, 3/4: 11–17.

DEECD (Department of Education and Early Childhood Development: Victoria) (2009) *Gifted Education: Learning and Teaching.* Online: www.education.vic.gov.au/studentlearning/programs/gifted/learnteach/default.htm (accessed 31 March 2010).

Delisle, J.R. (2006) *Parenting Gifted Kids*, Waco, TX: Prufrock Press.

Dempsey, I. and Foreman, P. (2001) 'A review of educational approaches for individuals with autism', *International Journal of Disability, Development and Education* 48: 103–16.

DEST (Department of Education, Science and Training [Australia]) (2005) Teaching Reading: National Inquiry into the Teaching of Literacy, Canberra: Government Printing Service, Commonwealth of Australia.

DET [NSW] (Department of Education and Training, New South Wales) (2009) *Literacy Teaching Guide: Phonics*, Sydney: DET.

Dettmer, P., Thurston, L. Knackendoffel, A. and Dyck, N. (2009) *Consultation, Collaboration and Teamwork for Students with Special Needs* (6th edn), Boston: Pearson-Merrill.

DfES (Department for Education and Skills: Britain) (2004) *Removing Barriers to Achievement,* Annersley: DfES Publications.

DfES (Department for Education and Skills: Britain) (2005) *Targeting Support:*

Implementing Interventions for Children with Significant Difficulties in Mathematics, Norwich: HMSO.

Diederichs, L. (2009) 'Pioneering the use of cued speech and THRASS for communication and literacy for the deaf and hearing impaired'. Online: www.changemakers.com/en-us/node/24488 (accessed 31 March 2010).

Dixon, R. and Englemann, S. (2006) *Spelling Through Morphographs*, Desoto, TX: SRA-McGraw Hill.

Dixon, R.M., Marsh, H.W. and Craven, R.G. (2004) 'Interpersonal cognitive problem-solving intervention with five adults with intellectual impairment', in H.W.Marsh, J.Baumert, G.Richards and U.Trantwein (eds) *Self-concept, Motivation and Identity: Where to From Here?* Proceedings of 3rd International Biennial *SELF* Research Conference, Berlin, 4–7 July, 2004.

Dombey, H. (2009) The Simple View of Reading. Online: www.ite.org.uk/ite_readings/simple_view_reading.pdf (accessed 31 March 2010).

Donovan, M.S. and Bransford, J.D. (2005) 'Introduction', in National Research Council, *How Students Learn: Mathematics in the Classroom* (pp. 1–26), Washington, DC: The National Academies Press.

Dowker, A. (2005) 'Early identification and intervention for students with mathematics difficulties', *Journal of Learning Disabilities* 38, 4: 324–32.

Downing, J.E. (2008) *Including Students with Severe and Multiple Disabilities in Typical Classrooms* (3rd edn), Baltimore, MD: Brookes.

Duffy, C. (2009) 'Numbers count', *Mathematics Teaching,* 216: 3–4.

Dybdahl, C.S. and Ryan, S. (2009) 'Inclusion for students with Fetal Alcohol Syndrome: classroom teachers talk about practice', *Preventing School Failure,* 53, 3: 185–96.

Dymond, S.K. and Orelove, P. (2001) 'What constitutes effective curriculum for students with severe disabilities?' *Exceptionality* 9, 3: 109–22.

Ehri, L., Dreyer, L., Flugman, B. and Gross, A. (2007) 'Reading Rescue: an effective tutoring intervention model for first-grade struggling readers', *American Educational Research Journal*, 44: 414–48.

Elliott, A. (2009) *Challenge Me™, Speech and Communication Cards*, London: Jessica Kingsley.

Ellis, L. (2005) *Balancing Approaches: Revisiting the Educational Psychology Research on Teaching Students with Learning Difficulties*, Melbourne: Australian Council for Educational Research.

Ellis, L., Wheldall, K. and Beaman, R. (2007) 'The research locus and conceptual basis for MULTILIT: why we do what we do', *Australian Journal of Learning Disabilities,* 12, 2: 61–5.

Engelmann, S. (1999) 'The benefits of direct instruction: affirmative action for at-risk students', *Educational Leadership* 57, 1: 77–9.

Erion, J., Davenport, C., Rodax, N., Scholl, B. and Hardy, J. (2009) 'Cover-Copy-Compare: one versus three repetitions', *Journal of Behavioral Education,* 18, 4: 319–30.

Etscheidt, S. and Clopton, K. (2008) 'Behaviour intervention plans', in E.L. Grigorenko (ed.), *Educating Individuals with Disabilities* (pp. 361–79), New York: Springer.

Evans, D. (2009) 'Shocking attainment gap between hearing-impaired pupils and their peers revealed,' *Times Educational Supplement (Cymru),* 16 October.

Farkota, R. (2005) 'Basic math problems: the brutal reality!' *Learning Difficulties Australia Bulletin* 37, 3: 10–11.

Feeley, K. and Jones, E. (2008) 'Strategies to address challenging behavior in young children with Down syndrome', *Down Syndrome Research and Practice,* 12, 2: 153–63.

Fielding-Barnsley, R. and Twaddell, P. (2009) 'Report on informal seminar with Sir Jim Rose', *LDA Bulletin,* 41, 3/4: 6.

Firth, G. (2009) 'A dual aspect process model of Intensive Interaction', *British Journal of Learning Disabilities,* 37, 1: 43–4.

Fisher, B., Bruce, M. and Greive, C. (2007) 'Look-Say-Cover-Write-Say-Check and Old Way/New Way Mediational Learning: a comparison of the effectiveness of two tutoring programs for children with persistent spelling difficulties', *Special Education Perspectives,* 16, 1: 19–38.

Fisher, K. and Haufe, T. (2009) *Developing social skills in children who have disabilities through the use of social stories and visual supports.* ERIC Online document ED504818: www.eric.ed.gov/ERICDocs/data/ericdocs2sql/content_storage_01/0000019b/80/43/dc/73.pdf (accessed 30 March 2010).

Flood, J., Lapp, D. and Fisher, D. (2005) 'Neurological Impress Method Plus', *Reading Psychology* 26: 147–60.

Foorman, B.R., Schatschneider, C., Eakin, M.N., Fletcher, J.M., Moats, L.C. and Francis, D.J. (2006) 'The impact of instructional practices in Grades 1 and 2 on reading and spelling achievement in high poverty schools', *Contemporary Educational Psychology* 31, 1: 1–29.

Foreman, P. (2009) *Education of Students with Intellectual Disability: Research and Practice,* Charlotte, NC: Information Age Publishing.

Foss, J.M. (2001) *Nonverbal Learning Disability: How to Recognise It and Minimise its Effects.* ERIC Digest ED 461238. Online: http://eric.ed.gov/ERICDocs/data/ericdocs2sql/content_storage_01/0000019b/80/29/cd/fa.pdf (accessed 26 March 2010).

Frederickson, N. and Cline, T. (2009) *Special Educational Needs, Inclusion and Diversity* (2nd edn), Maidenhead: Open University and McGraw Hill.

Freire, A.P., Linhalis, F., Bianchini, S.L., Fortes, R. and Pimentel, M.C. (2010) 'Revealing the whiteboard to blind students: an inclusive approach to provide mediation in synchronous E-learning activities', *Computers and Education,* 54, 4: 866–76.

French, L.R. and Shore, B.M. (2009) 'A reconsideration of the widely held conviction that gifted students prefer to work alone,' in T. Balchin, B. Hymer and D.J. Matthews (eds), *The Routledge International Companion to Gifted Education* (pp. 176–82), London: Routledge.

Friedlauder, D. (2009) 'Sam comes to school: including students with autism in your classroom', *The Clearing House,* 82, 3: 141–4.

Friend, M. and Bursuck, W.D. (2009) *Including Students with Special Needs: A Practical Guide for Classroom Teachers* (5th edn), Upper Saddle River, NJ: Pearson Educational.

Fuchs, L.S. and Fuchs, D. (2005) 'Enhancing mathematical problem solving for students with disabilities', *Journal of Special Education* 39, 1: 45–57.

Fuchs, L.S., Compton, D., Fuchs, D., Paulsen, K., Bryant, J. and Hamlett, C.L. (2005) 'Responsiveness to intervention: preventing and identifying mathematics disability', *Teaching Exceptional Children* 37, 4: 60–3.

Gagné, F. (2009) 'Talent development as seen through the differentiated model of giftedness and talent,' in T. Balchin, B. Hymer and D.J. Matthews (eds) *The Routledge International Companion to Gifted Education* (pp. 32–41), London: Routledge.

Gardner, H. (1983) *Frames of Mind: The Theory of Multiple Intelligences,* New York: Basic Books.

Gargiulo, R.M. (2009) *Special Education in Contemporary Society* (3rd edn), Los Angeles, CA: Sage.

Gargiulo, R.M. and Metcalf, D. (2010) *Teaching in Today's Inclusive Classrooms: A Universal Design for Learning Approach*, Belmont, CA: Wadsworth.

Geake, J. (2009) 'Neural interconnectivity and intellectual creativity: giftedness, savants and learning styles,' in T. Balchin, B. Hymer and D.J. Matthews (eds) *The Routledge International Companion to Gifted Education* (pp. 10–17), London: Routledge.

Gibson, L. (2009) 'The effects of a computer-assisted reading program on the word reading fluency and comprehension of at-risk urban 1st Grade students', PhD thesis, Ohio State University. Online: http://etd.ohiolink.edu/view.cgi?acc_num=osu1249578049 (accessed 5 February 2010).

Gillingham, A. and Stillman, B. (1960) *Remedial Teaching for Children with Specific Disability in Reading, Spelling and Penmanship*, Cambridge, MA: Educators Publishing Service.

Gilman, B. (2008) *Challenging Highly Gifted Learners,* Waco, TX: Prufrock Press.

Glanzman, M.M. and Blum, N.J. (2007) 'Attention deficits and hyperactivity', in M.L. Batshaw, L. Pellegrino and N.J. Roizen (eds) *Children with Disabilities* (6th edn, pp. 345–65), Baltimore, MD: Brookes.

Graham, L., Pegg, J. and Alder, L. (2007) 'Improving the reading achievement of middle-years students with learning difficulties', *Australian Journal of Language and Literacy*, 30, 3: 221–34.

Graham, S. and Harris, K. (2005) 'Improving the writing performance of young struggling writers: theoretical and programmatic research from the center on accelerating student learning', *Journal of Special Education* 39, 1: 19–33.

Graves, D.H. (1983) *Writing: Teachers and Children at Work*, Exeter, NH: Heinemann.

Gross, M. (2004) *Exceptionally Gifted Children*, London: RoutledgeFalmer.

Groth-Marnat, G. (2009) *Handbook of Psychological Assessment* (5th edn), Hoboken, NJ: Wiley.

Guerin, G. and Male, M.C. (2006) *Addressing Learning Disabilities and Difficulties* (2nd edn), Thousand Oaks, CA: Corwin Press.

Gyles, P.D.T., Shore, B.M. and Schneider, B.H. (2009) 'Big ships, small ships, friendships and competition', *Teaching for High Potential,* Spring Issue: 3–19.

Haggerty, N.K., Black, R.S. and Smith, G.J. (2005) 'Increasing self-managed coping skills through social stories and apron storytelling', *Teaching Exceptional Children* 37, 4: 40–7.

Hall, S. (1997) 'The problem with differentiation', *School Science Review* 78, 284: 95–8.

Hallahan, D.P., Kauffman, J.M. and Pullen, P.C. (2009) *Exceptional Learners* (11th edn), Boston: Allyn and Bacon.

Hamilton, B. (2009) 'Making the most of a teaching partner', *Reading Teacher*, 63, 3: 245–8.

Hampton, S., Murphy, S. and Lowry, M. (2009) *Using Rubrics to Improve Student Writing, Grade 1,* Newark, DE: International Reading Association.

Haqberg, B.S., Miniscalco, C. and Gillberg, C. (2010) 'Clinic attenders with autism or attention-deficit hyperactivity disorder: cognitive profile at school age and its relationship to preschool indicators of language delay', *Research in Developmental Disabilities,* 31, 1: 1–8.

Heller, K.W. and Bigge, J.L. (2010) 'Augmentative and alternative communication', in S.J.

Best, K.W. Heller and J.L. Bigge (eds) *Teaching Individuals with Physical or Multiple Disabilities* (6th edn), Upper Saddle River, NJ: Pearson-Merrill.

Henley, M. (2010) *Classroom Management: A Proactive Approach* (2nd edn), Upper Saddle River, NJ: Merrill.

Herer, G.R., Knightly, C.A. and Steinberg, A.G. (2007) 'Hearing: Sounds and silences', in M. Batshaw, L. Pelligrino and N.J. Roizen (eds), *Children with Disabilities* (6th edn, pp.157–84), Baltmore, ND: Brookes.

Heron, T.E., Villareal, D.M., Yao, M., Christianson, R.J. and Heron, K.M. (2006) 'Peer tutoring: applications in classrooms and specialized environments', *Reading and Writing Quarterly* 22, 1: 27–45.

Hertberg-Davis, H. (2009) 'Myth 7: Differentiation in the regular classroom is equivalent to gifted programs and is sufficient', *Gifted Child Quarterly*, 53, 4: 251–3.

Heward, W.L. (2009) *Exceptional Children* (9th edn), Columbus, OH: Pearson-Merrill.

Hooper, S.R. and Umansky, W. (2009) *Young Children with Special Needs* (5th edn), Upper Saddle River, NJ: Pearson-Merrill.

Hoover, W.A. and Gough, P.B. (1990) 'The simple view of reading', *Reading and Writing,* 2: 127–60.

House of Commons Education and Skills Committee (Britain) (2005) *Teaching Children to Read*, London: HMSO.

Howard, M. (2009) *RTI from All Sides*, Portsmouth, NH: Heinemann.

Howard, V.F., Williams, B.F. and Lepper, C. (2010) *Very Young Children with Special Needs* (4th edn), Boston: Pearson Education.

Howarth, R. (2008) *100 ideas for Supporting Pupils with Social and Behavioural Difficulties*, London: Continuum.

Howlin, P., Magiati, I. and Charman, T. (2009) 'Systematic review of early intensive behavioural interventions for children with autism', *American Journal on Intellectual and Developmental Disabilities,* 114, 1: 23–41.

Hue, M.T. and Li, W.S. (2008) *Classroom Management: Creating a Positive Learning Environment,* Hong Kong: Hong Kong University Press.

Humphrey, N. (2009) 'Including students with attention-deficit hyperactivity disorder in mainstream schools', *British Journal of Special Education,* 36, 1: 19–25.

Humphrey, N. and Brooks, A.G. (2006) 'An evaluation of a short cognitive-behavioural anger management intervention for pupils at risk of exclusion', *Emotional and Behavioural Difficulties* 11, 1: 5–23.

IES (Institute of Education Sciences: US Department of Education) (2009a) *Assisting Students Struggling with Reading: Response to Intervention (RTI) and Multi-tier Intervention in the Primary Grades*. Online. Online: http://ies.ed.gov/ncee/wwc/pdf/practiceguides/rti_reading_pg_021809.pdf (accessed 26 March 2010).

IES (Institute of Education Sciences: US Department of Education) (2009b) *Assisting Students Struggling with Mathematics: Response to Intervention (RTI) for Elementary and Middle Schools*. Online: http://ies.ed.gov/ncee/wwc/pdf/practiceguides/rti_math_pg_042109.pdf (accessed 26 March 2010).

IES (Institute of Education Sciences, US Department of Education) (2009c) *Success for All*. What Works Clearinghouse online: www.eric.ed.gov/ERICDocs/data/ericdocs2sql/content_storage_01/0000019b/80/44/d4/ec.pdf (accessed 04 February 2010).

Ingram, F. (2010) *Using Computers to Improve Reading Skills*. Online: http://kids-educational-activities.suite101.com/article.cfm/using_computers_to_improve_reading_skills (accessed 01 April 2010).

Iversen, S., Tunmer, W. and Chapman, J.W. (2005) 'The effects of varying group size on the Reading Recovery approach to preventive early intervention', *Journal of Learning Disabilities* 38, 5: 456–72.

Izzo, M.V., Yurick, A. and McArrell, B. (2009) 'Supported E-text: Effects of Text-to-Speech on access and achievement for high school students with disabilities', *Journal of Special Education Technology*, 24, 3: 9–20.

Jacobsen, D.A., Eggen, P. and Kauchak, D. (2009) *Methods for Teaching: Promoting Student Learning in K-12 Classrooms* (8th edn), Upper Saddle River, NJ: Pearson-Merrill.

Janney, R. and Snell. M.E. (2004) *Modifying Schoolwork* (2nd edn), Baltimore, MD: Brookes.

Joseph, L.M. and Konrad, M. (2009) 'Teaching students with intellectual or developmental disabilities to write: a review of the literature', *Research in Developmental Disabilities: A Multidisciplinary Journal,* 30, 1: 1–19.

Kaiser, A.P. and Grim, J.C. (2006) 'Teaching functional communication skills', in M.E. Snell and F. Brown (eds) *Instruction of Students with Severe Disabilities* (6th edn), Upper Saddle River, NJ: Pearson-Merrill-Prentice Hall.

Karemaker, A., Pitchford, N.J. and O'Malley, C. (2010) 'Enhanced recognition of written words and enjoyment of reading in struggling beginning readers through Whole-Word Multimedia software', *Computers and Education*, 54, 1: 199–208.

Kats-Gold, I. and Priel, B. (2009) 'Emotion, understanding and social skills among boys at risk of attention deficit hyperactivity disorder', *Psychology in the Schools,* 46, 7: 658–78.

Kauffman, J.M., Landrum, T.J., Mock, D.R., Sayeski, B. and Sayeski, K.L. (2005) 'Diverse knowledge and skills require a diversity of instructional groups: a position statement', *Remedial and Special Education* 26, 1: 2–6.

Kimball, J.W., Kinney, E.M., Taylor, B.A. and Stromer, R. (2004) 'Video enhanced activity schedules for children with autism: a promising package for teaching social skills', *Education and Treatment of Children,* 27, 3: 280–98.

Kirby, A., Davies, R. and Bryant, A. (2005) 'Do teachers know more about specific learning difficulties than general practitioners?' *British Journal of Special Education* 32, 3: 122–26.

Kitano, M., Montgomery, D., Van Tassel-Baska, J. and Johnsen, S.K. (2008) *Using the National Gifted Education Standards for Pre-K to 12 Professional Development*, Thousand Oaks, CA: Corwin Press.

Kluth, P. and Danaher, S. (2010) *From Tutor Scripts to Talking Sticks: 100 Ways to Differentiate Instruction in K-12 Inclusive Classrooms*, Baltimore, MD: Brookes.

Koegel, R.L. and Koegel, L.K. (2006) *Pivotal Response Treatments for Autism: Communication, Social and Academic Development*, Baltimore, MD: Brookes.

Kohnen, S., Nickels, L. and Castles, A. (2009) 'Assessing spelling skills and strategies: a critique of available resources', *Australian Journal of Learning Difficulties,* 14, 1: 113–50.

Konings, K., Wiers, R., Wiel, M. and Schmidt, H. (2005) 'Problem-based learning as a valuable educational method for physically disabled teenagers? The discrepancy between theory and practice', *Journal of Developmental and Physical Disabilities* 17, 2: 107–17.

Kose, E. (2009) 'Assessment of the effectiveness of the educational environment supported by computer-aided presentation at primary school level', *Computers and Education*, 53, 4: 1355–62.

Kostelnik, M.J., Whiren, A.P., Soderman, A.K. and Gregory, K.M. (2009) *Guiding Children's Social Development and Learning* (6th edn), Clifton Park, NY: Delmar.

Kroeger, S.D., Burton, C. and Preston, C. (2009) 'Integrating evidence-based practices in middle science reading', *Teaching Exceptional Children,* 41, 3: 6–16.

Kroesbergen, E.H., Van Luit, J.E.H. and Maas, C.J.M. (2004) 'Effectiveness of constructivist mathematics instruction for low-achieving students in The Netherlands', *Elementary School Journal* 104, 3: 233–51.

Kulik, J. (2004) 'Meta-analytic studies of acceleration,' in N. Colangelo, S. Assouline and M. Gross (eds) *A Nation Deceived: How Schools Hold Back America's Brightest Students* (pp. 13–22), Iowa City, IO: University of Iowa.

Kyriacou, C. (2005) 'The impact of daily mathematics lessons in England on pupil confidence and competence in early mathematics: a systematic review', *British Journal of Educational Studies* 53, 2: 168–86.

Lan, Y.J., Sung, Y.T. and Chang, K.E. (2009) 'Let Us Read Together: Development and evaluation of a computer-assisted reciprocal early English reading system', *Computers in Education,* 53, 4: 1188–98.

Lane, K.L., Kalberg, J.R. and Menzies, H.M. (2009) *Developing School-wide Programs to Prevent and Manage Problem Behaviors,* New York: Guilford Press.

Larrivee, B. (2009) *Authentic Classroom Management* (3rd edn), Upper Saddle River, NJ: Pearson-Merrill.

Latterell, C.M. (2005) *Math Wars: A Guide for Parents and Teachers*, Westport, CT: Praeger.

Leaf, J.B., Taubman, M., Bloomfield, S., Palos-Rafuse, L., Leaf, R., McEachin, J. and Oppenheim, M. (2009) 'Increasing social skills and pro-social behavior for three children diagnosed with autism through the use of a teaching package', *Research in Autism Spectrum Disorders,* 3, 1: 275–89.

Lee, C. (2001) 'Problem-based learning: a personal view', *Planet* (Special Edition 2): 10.

Lee, M. (2009) *Annual Monitoring of Reading Recovery: Data from 2008.* Online: www. educationcounts.govt.nz/publications/series/1547/56099/7 (accessed 01 April 2010).

Lerner, J. and Kline, F. (2006) *Learning Disabilities and Related Disorders* (10th edn), Boston: Houghton Mifflin.

Levin, J. and Nolan, J.F. (2010) *Principles of Classroom Management* (6th edn), Upper Saddle River, NJ: Pearson Educational.

Levy, S.E. and Hyman, S.L. (2005) 'Novel treatments for autistic spectrum disorders', *Mental Retardation and Developmental Disabilities Research Reviews* 11, 2: 131–42.

Li, W.S. (2008) 'Managing misbehaviour', in M.T. Hue and W.S. Li (eds) *Classroom Management: Creating a Positive Learning Environment* (pp. 63–83), Hong Kong: Hong Kong University Press.

Liboiron, N. and Soto, G. (2006) 'Shared story book reading with a student who uses alternative and augmentative communication: a description of scaffolding procedures', *Child Language Teaching and Therapy* 21, 1: 69–95.

Lindberg, J.A., Ziegler, M.F. and Barczyk, L. (2009) *Common-sense Classroom Management,* Thousand Oaks, CA; Corwin Press.

Ling, D. and Ling, A. (1978) *Aural Habilitation: The Foundations of Verbal Learning in Hearing Impaired Children.* Washington, DC: Alexander Graham Bell Association.

Little, C.A., Hauser, S. and Corbishley, J. (2009) 'Constructing complexity for differentiated learning', *Mathematics Teaching in Middle School,* 15, 1: 34–42.

Lloyd, S. and Lib, S. (2000) *The Phonics Handbook: Jolly Phonics*, Chigwell: Jolly Learning Ltd.

Lonigan, C.J. and Shanahan, T. (2008) *Developing Early Literacy: Report of the National Early Literacy Panel (Executive Summary)*, Washington, DC: National Institute for Literacy.

Lovaas, O.I. and Smith, T. (2003) 'Early and intensive behavioral interventions in autism', in A.E. Kazdin and J. R. Weisz (eds) *Evidence-based Psychotherapies for Children and Adolescents* (pp. 325–40), New York: Guilford Press.

Lyndon, H. (1989) 'I did it my way: an introduction to Old Way–New Way', *Australasian Journal of Special Education* 13: 32–7.

MacArthur, C.A. (2009) 'Reflections and research on writing and technology for struggling writers', *Learning Disabilities Research and Practice,* 24, 2: 93–103.

Maccini, P. and Gagnon, J. (2006) 'Mathematics instructional practices and assessment accommodations made by secondary special and general educators', *Exceptional Children*, 72: 217–35.

MacConville, R. and Palmer, J. (2007) 'Including pupils with hearing impairment', in R. MacConville (ed.) *Looking at Inclusion: Listening to the Voices of Young People* (pp. 99–126), London: Paul Chapman.

MacConville, R. and Rhys-Davies, L. (2007) 'Including pupils with visual impairment', in R. MacConville (ed.) *Looking at Inclusion: Listening to the Voices of Young People* (pp. 39–55), London: Paul Chapman.

Manning, M. and Underbakke, C. (2005) 'Spelling development research necessitates replacement of weekly word lists', *Childhood Education* 81, 4: 236–38.

Mannix, D. (2009) *Social Skills Activities for Secondary Students with Special Needs* (2nd edn), San Francisco, CA: Jossey-Bass.

Martin, L.C. (2009) *Strategies for Teaching Students with Learning Disabilities,* Thousand Oaks, CA: Corwin Press.

Martin, L.T., Burns, R.M. and Schonlau, M. (2010) 'Mental disorders among gifted and non-gifted youth', *Gifted Child Quarterly,* 54, 1: 31–41.

Martin, M. (2007) *Helping Children with Nonverbal Learning Disabilities to Flourish,* London: Jessica Kingsley.

Mason, L.H., Benedek-Wood, E. and Valasa, L. (2009) 'Teaching low-achieving students to self-regulate persuasive quick write responses', *Journal of Adolescent and Adult Literacy,* 54, 4: 303–312.

Masters, G.N. (2009) *A Shared Challenge: Improving Literacy, Numeracy and Science in Queensland Primary Schools*, Melbourne: Australian Council for Educational Research.

Mastropieri, M.A. and Scruggs, T.E. (2010) *The Inclusive Classroom: Strategies for Effective Differentiated Instruction* (4th edn), Upper Saddle River, NJ: Merrill.

Mayfield, K.H., Glenn, I.M, and Vollmer, T.R. (2008) 'Teaching spelling through prompting and review procedures using computer-based instruction', *Journal of Behavioral Education*, 17, 3: 303–12.

McDonnell, J. (2010) 'Employment training', in J. McDonnell and M. L. Hardman (eds) *Successful Transition Program* (2nd edn, pp.241–56), Thousand Oaks, CA: Sage.

McDougall, M., Evans, D. and Spandagou, I. (2009) 'Teaching phonics and sight words to Year 1 through the medium of "working with words" and "games"', *Special Education Perspectives*, 18, 1: 35–46.

McGuire, J. (2010) 'Promoting self-determination', in J. McDonnell and M. L. Hardman (eds) *Successful Transition Programs* (2nd edn, pp.101–14), Thousand Oaks, CA: Sage.

McInerney, D.M. and McInerney, V. (2009) *Educational Psychology: Constructing Learning* (5th edn), Frenchs Forest, NSW: Pearson Australia.

McMaster, K.L., Fuchs, D. and Fuchs, L.S. (2006) 'Research on peer-assisted learning strategies: the promise and the limitations of peer-mediated instruction', *Reading and Writing Quarterly* 22, 1: 5–25.

McMurray, S., Drysdale, J. and Jordan, G. (2009) 'Motor processing difficulties: guidance for teachers in mainstream classrooms', *Support for Learning*, 24, 3: 119–25.

Meadow, K.P. (2005) 'Early manual communication in relation to the deaf child's intellectual, social and communicative functioning', *Journal of Deaf Studies and Deaf Education* 10, 4: 321–9.

Medwell, J., Strand, S. and Wray, D. (2009) 'The links between handwriting and composition for Year 6 children', *Cambridge Journal of Education*, 39, 3: 329–44.

Mercer, C.D. and Pullen, P.C. (2009) *Students with Learning Disabilities* (7th edn), Upper Saddle River, NJ: Merrill-Pearson.

Mesibov, G.B., Shea, V. and Schopler, E (2005) *The TEACCH Approach to Autism Spectrum Disorders,* New York: Kluwer Academic-Plenum.

Miller, S.P. (2009) *Validated Practices for Teaching Students with Diverse Needs and Abilities* (2nd edn), Upper Saddle River, NJ: Pearson Education.

Mitchell, D. (2008) *What Really Works in Special and Inclusive Education: Using Evidence-based Teaching Strategies*, London: Routledge.

Montague, M. and Dietz, S. (2009) 'Evaluating the evidence base for cognitive strategy instruction and mathematical problem solving', *Exceptional Children,* 75, 3: 285–303.

Montgomery, D. (2008) 'Cohort analysis of writing in Year 7 following two, four and seven years of the National Literacy Strategy', *Support for Learning*, 23, 1: 3–11.

Montgomery, D. (2009) 'Special educational needs and dual exceptionality,' in T. Balchin, B. Hymer and D.J. Matthews (eds) *The Routledge International Companion to Gifted Education* (pp. 218–25), London: Routledge.

Moon, T.R., Brighton, C.M., Callahan, C.M. and Jarvis, J.M. (2008) 'Twice-exceptional students: being gifted and learning disabled', in E.L. Grigorenko (ed.) *Educating Individuals with Disabilities* (pp. 295–317), New York: Springer.

Mooney, P., Ryan, J.B., Uhing, B.M., Reid, R. and Epstein, M.H. (2005) 'A review of self-management interventions targeting academic outcomes for students with emotional and behavioral disorders', *Journal of Behavioral Education* 14, 3: 203–21.

Moore-Hart, M.A. (2010) *Teaching Writing in Diverse Classrooms K-8*, Boston: Pearson-Allyn and Bacon.

Moran, D.J. (2004) 'The need for research-based educational methods', in D.J. Moran and R.W. Malott (eds) *Evidence-based Educational Methods*, San Diego, CA: Elsevier Academic.

Moscardini, L. (2009) 'Tools or crutches? Apparatus as a sense-making aid in mathematics teaching with children with moderate learning difficulties', *Support for Learning,* 24, 1: 35–41.

Mueller, V. and Hurtig, R. (2010) 'Technology-enhanced shared reading with deaf and hard-of-hearing children: the role of a fluent signing narrator', *Journal of Deaf Studies and Deaf Education,* 15, 1: 72–101.

Munro, D.W. and Stephenson, J. (2009) 'Response cards: an effective strategy for increasing student participation, achievement and on-task behaviour', *Special Education Perspectives*, 18, 1: 16–34.

Myrbakk, E. and von Tetzchner, S. (2008) 'Psychiatric disorders and behaviour problems in people with intellectual disability', *Research in Developmental Disabilities: A Multidisciplinary Journal*, 29, 4, 316–32.

National Association for Gifted Children (2003) *Ability Grouping*, Washington, DC: The Association.

National Council of Teachers of Mathematics (US) (2005) *Overview: Principles for School Mathematics*. Online: http://standards.nctm.org/document/chapter2/index.htm (accessed 1 April 2010).

National Dissemination Centre for Children with Disabilities (US) (2010) *Intellectual Disability (*formerly *Mental Retardation)*. Online: www.nichcy.org/Disabilities/Specific/pages/IntellectualDisability.aspx (accessed 26 March 2010).

National Literacy Trust (2009a) *The Poverty Trap*. Online: www.literacytrust.org. / news/665_the_poverty_trap (accessed 26 March 2010).

National Literacy Trust (UK) (2009b) 'Why is literacy important?' Online document available from: www.literacytrust.org.uk/About/FAQs.html (accessed 20 January 2010).

National Reading Panel (US) (2000) *Teaching Children to Read: An Evidence-based Assessment of the Scientific Research Literature on Reading and its Implications for Reading Instruction*, Washington, DC: National Institute of Child Health and Human Development.

NCSiMERRA (National Centre of Science, Information and Communication Technology, and Mathematics Education for Rural and Regional Australia) (2009) *QuickSmart Intervention Research Program Data 2001–2008: Full Report*, Armidale, NSW: University of New England.

Neufeld, P. (2006) 'Comprehension instruction in content area classes', *The Reading Teacher* 59, 4: 302–12.

Norwich, B. and Kelly, N. (2004) 'Pupils' views on inclusion: moderate learning difficulties and bullying in mainstream and special schools', *British Educational Research Journal*, 30, 1: 43–65.

O'Connor, R.E. (2007) *Teaching Word Recognition: Effective Strategies for Students with Learning Difficulties*, New York: Guilford Press.

OECD (Organization for Economic Cooperation and Development) (2006) *Starting Strong II: Early Childhood and Care*, Paris: OECD.

OECD (Organization for Economic Cooperation and Development) (2007) *Students with Disabilities, Learning Difficulties and Disadvantages: Policies, Statistics, and Indicators*, Paris: OECD.

Oeseburg, B., Jansen, D., Groothoff, J.W., Dijkstra, G. and Reijneveld, S.A. (2010) 'Emotional and behavioural problems in adolescents with intellectual disability with and without chronic diseases', *Journal of Intellectual Disability Research*, 54, 1: 81–9.

OfSTED (Office for Standards in Education: UK) (2001) *Providing for Gifted and Talented Pupils: Evaluation of Excellence in Cities and Other Grant-funded Programmes*, London: Office for Standards in Education.

OfSTED (Office for Standards in Education: UK) (2008) *Mathematics: Understanding the Score*, London: Office for Standards in Education.

Olson, J.L., Platt, J.C. and Dieker, L.A. (2008) *Teaching Children and Adolescents with Special Needs* (5th edn), Upper Saddle River, NJ: Pearson-Merrill-Prentice Hall.

OTEC (Oregon Technology in Education Council) (2005) *Learning Theories and Transfer of Learning.* Online: http://otec.uoregon.edu/learning_theory.htm#Situated%20Learning (accessed 1 April 2010).

Pajares, F. and Urdan, T. (eds) (2006) *Self-efficacy Beliefs of Adolescents*, Greenwich, CT: Information Age Publishing.

Parette, H., Blum, C., Boeckmann, N. and Watts, E. (2009) 'Teaching word recognition to young children who are at risk using Microsoft PowerPoint™ coupled with direct instruction', *Early Childhood Education Journal*, 36, 5: 393–401.

Pawelski, C.E. (2007) 'Conductive Education', in A.M. Bursztyn (ed.) *The Praeger Handbook of Special Education* (pp. 84–8). Westport, CT: Praeger.

Pentimonti, J.M. and Justice, L.M. (2010) 'Teachers' use of scaffolding strategies during read alouds in the preschool classroom', *Early Childhood Education Journal*, 37, 4: 241–8.

Peterson, J.M. and Hittie, M.M. (2010) *Inclusive Teaching: The Journey toward Effective Schools for All Learners* (2nd edn), Boston: Pearson-Merrill.

Phillipson, S.N. and Cheung, H.Y. (2007) 'Giftedness within the Confucian-heritage cultures,' in S.N. Phillipson (ed.) *Learning Diversity in the Chinese Classroom* (pp. 205–47), Hong Kong: Hong Kong University Press.

Piaget, J. (1963) *Origins of Intelligence in Children,* New York: Norton.

Pickering, S.J. and Gathercole, S.E. (2004) 'Distinctive working memory profiles in children with special educational needs', *Educational Psychology* 24, 3: 393–408.

Piirto, J. and Heward, W.L. (2009) 'Giftedness and talent,' in W.L. Heward (ed.) *Exceptional Children* (9th edn, pp. 490–529), Columbus, OH: Pearson-Merrill.

Pincott, R. (2004) 'Are we responsible for our children's maths difficulties?' in B.A. Knight and W. Scott (eds) *Learning Difficulties: Multiple Perspectives* (pp.129–140), Frenchs Forest, NSW: Pearson.

Pletka, B. (2007) *Educating the Net Generation*, Santa Monica, CA: Santa Monica Press.

Polkinghorne, J. (2004) 'Electronic literacy: Part 1 and Part 2', *Australian Journal of Learning Disabilities* 9, 2: 24–7.

Polloway, E.A., Patton, J.R. and Serna, L. (2008) *Strategies for Teaching Learners with Special Needs* (9th edn), Upper Saddle River, NJ: Pearson-Merrill-Prentice Hall.

Prater, M.A. (2007) *Teaching Strategies for Students with Mild to Moderate Disabilities,* Boston: Allyn and Bacon.

Prideaux, A., Marsh, K.A. and Caplygin, D. (2005) 'Efficacy of the Cellfield Intervention for reading difficulties: an integrated computer-based approach targeting deficits associated with dyslexia', *Australian Journal of Learning Disabilities* 10, 2: 51–62.

Prizant, B.M., Wetherby, A.M., Rubin, E., Laurent, A. and Rydell, P. (2006) *The SCERTS Manual: A Comprehensive Educational Approach for Children with Autism Spectrum Disorders* (Vol. 1 and Vol. 2), Baltimore: Brookes.

QCDA (Qualifications and Curriculum Development Agency: UK) (2009a) *Engaging Mathematics for all Learners.* Online: www.qcda.gov.uk/libraryAssets/media/Engaging_mathematics.pdf (accessed 1 April 2010).

QCDA (Qualifications and Curriculum Development Agency: UK) (2009b) *Teaching Gifted Students: Mathematics.* Online: www.qcda.gov.uk/2120.aspx (accessed 1 April 2010).

Quirmbach, L.M., Lincoln, A.J., Feinberg-Gizzo, M.J., Ingersoll, B.R. and Andrews, S.M. (2009) 'Social Stories: mechanisms of effectiveness in increasing game play in children diagnosed with autism spectrum disorders', *Journal of Autism and Developmental Disorders,* 39, 2: 299–321.

RCP (Royal College of Psychiatrists) (2009) 'The child with general learning disability'. Online: www.rcpsych.ac.uk/mentalhealthinfo/mentalhealthandgrowingup/learningdisability.aspx (accessed 26 March 2010).

Reed, M., Peternel, G., Olszewski-Kubilius, P. and Lee, S.Y. (2009) 'Project EXCITE: implications for educators of gifted minority students', *Teaching for High Potential*, Spring Issue: 4–6.

Renzulli, J.S. (1976) 'The enrichment triad model: a guide for developing defensible programs for the gifted and talented', *Gifted Child Quarterly*, 20: 303–26.

Renzulli, J.S. (2003) 'Conception of giftedness and its relationship to the development of social capital,' in N. Colangelo and G. Davis (eds) *Handbook of Gifted Education* (3rd edn, pp. 75–87), Boston: MA: Allyn and Bacon.

Renzulli, J.S. and Reis, S.M. (1997) *The Schoolwide Enrichment Model: A How-to Guide for Educational Excellence*, Mansfield Center, CT: Creative Learning Press.

Reynolds, M., Wheldall, K. and Madelaine, A. (2007) 'Meeting Initial Needs in Literacy (MINILIT): a ramp to MULTILIT for younger low-progress readers', *Australian Journal of Learning Disabilities*, 12, 2: 67–72.

Reynolds, M., Wheldall, K. and Madelaine, A. (2009) 'The devil is in the detail regarding the efficacy of Reading Recovery: a rejoinder to Schwartz, Hobsbaum, Briggs, and Scull', *International Journal of Disability, Development and Education*, 56: 17–35.

Riddick, B. (2010) *Living with Dyslexia: The Social and Emotional Consequences of Specific Learning Difficulties*, London: Routledge.

Rieck, W.A. and Wadsworth, D.E. (2005) 'Assessment accommodations: helping students with exceptional learning needs', *Intervention in School and Clinic*, 41, 2: 105–9.

Rimm, S.B. and Lovance, K.J. (2004) 'The use of subject and grade skipping for the prevention and reversal of underachievement', in L. Brody (ed.) *Grouping and Acceleration Practices in Gifted Education* (pp. 33–45), Thousand Oaks, CA: Corwin Press.

Ritchey, K.D., Coker, D.L. and McCraw, S.B. (2010) 'A comparison of metrics for scoring beginning spelling', *Assessment for Effective Intervention*, 35, 2: 78–88.

Robertson, L. (2009) *Literacy and Deafness*, San Diego, CA: Plural Publishing.

Rose, J. (2005) *Independent Review of the Teaching of Early Reading: Interim Report*, London: Department for Education and Skills.

Rose, J. (2009) *Identifying and Teaching Children and Young People with Dyslexia and Literacy Difficulties*, Nottingham: DCSF Publications. Online: http://publications.teachernet.gov.uk/default.aspx?PageFunction=productdetails&PageMode=publications&ProductId=DCSF-00659-2009& (accessed 26 March 2010).

Rosenshine, B. and Meister, C. (1994) 'Reciprocal teaching: a review of research', *Review of Educational Research* 64, 4: 479–530.

Ross, R.H. and Roberts-Pacchione, B. (2007) *Wanna Play: Friendship Skills for Preschool and Elementary Grades*, Thousand Oaks, CA: Corwin Press.

Rouse, P. (2009) *Inclusion in Physical Education*, Champaign, IL: Human Kinetics.

Rowe, K. (2006) 'Effective teaching practices for students with and without learning difficulties', *Australian Journal of Learning Disabilities*, 11, 3: 99–115.

Salend, S.J. (2007) *Creating Inclusive Classrooms: Effective and Reflective Practices for All Students* (6th edn), Upper Saddle River, NJ: Prentice Hall.

Salisbury, R. (ed.) (2008) *Teaching Pupils with Visual Impairment*, Abingdon: Routledge.

Scharer, P.L. and Zutell, J. (2003) 'The development of spelling', in N. Hall, J. Larson and J. Marsh (eds) *Handbook of Early Childhood Literacy*, London: Sage.

Scheffler, R.M., Brown, T.T., Fulton, B.D., Hinshaw, S.P., Levine, P. and Stone, S. (2009) 'Positive association between attention deficit-hyperactivity disorder medication use and academic achievement during elementary school', *Pediatrics,* 123, 5: 1273–9.

Scull, J.A. and Lo Bianco, J. (2008) 'Successful engagement in an early literacy intervention', *Journal of Early Childhood Literacy*, 8, 2: 123–50.

Seale, J. (2006) *E-Learning and Disability in Higher Education*, New York: Routledge.

Seale, J. and Nind, M. (2010) *Understanding and Promoting Access for People with Learning Difficulties,* London: Routledge.

Sheakoski, M. (2008) 'Language Experience Approach: a teaching strategy to increase decoding and reading comprehension'. Online: http://primary-school-curriculum. suite101.com/article.cfm/language_experience_approach (accessed 4 February 2010).

Shepherd, T.L. (2010) *Working with Students with Emotional and Behavior Disorders,* Upper Saddle River, NJ: Pearson Education.

Simpson, R.L. (2005) 'Evidence-based practices and students with autism spectrum disorders', *Focus on Autism and Other Developmental Disabilities* 20, 3: 140–9.

Sipe, R.B. (2008) 'Teaching challenged spellers in high school English classrooms', *English Journal*, 97, 4: 38–44.

Sisk, D.A. (2009) *Making Great Kids Greater: Easing the Burden of Being Gifted,* Thousand Oaks, CA: Corwin Press.

Slavin, R., Lake, C. and Groff, C. (2009) 'Effective programs in middle and high school mathematics: a best-evidence synthesis', *Review of Educational Research*, 72, 2: 839– 911.

Slavin, R., Madden, N.A., Chambers, B. and Haxby, B. (2009) *Two Million Children: Success for All* (2nd edn), Thousand Oaks, CA: Corwin Press.

Smith, D.D. and Tyler, N.C. (2010) *Introduction to Special Education: Making a Difference* (7th edn), Upper Saddle River, NJ: Pearson Educational.

Smith, P. (2007) 'Have we made any progress? Including students with intellectual disabilities in regular classrooms', *Intellectual and Developmental Disabilities,* 45: 297–309.

Snowling, M.J. (2008) *State-of-the Science Review SR-D2: Dyslexia,* London: Government Office for Science. Online: www.foresight.gov.uk/Mental%20Capital/SR-D2_MCW_ v2.pdf (accessed 26 March 2010).

Stainthorp, R. and Stuart, M. (2008) *The Simple View of Reading and evidence-based practice.* Online: www.ucet.ac.uk/downloads/1511.pdf (accessed 1 April 2010).

Staudt, D.H. (2009) 'Intensive word study and repeated reading improves reading skills for two students with learning disabilities', *Reading Teacher*, 63, 2: 142–51.

Steer, A. (2009) *Learning Behaviour: Lessons Learned. A Review of Behaviour Standards and Practices in our Schools*, Annesley: DCSF Publications. Online: http://publications.teachernet.gov.uk/eOrderingDownload/DCSF-Learning-Behaviour.pdf (accessed 1 April 2010).

Stevens, M. (2009) *Challenging the Gifted Child*, London: Jessica Kingsley.

Strichart, S.S. and Mangrum, C.T. (2010) *Study Skills for Learning Disabled and Struggling Students, Grades 6 -12* (4th edn), Upper Saddle River, NJ: Merrill.

Supalo, C.A., Mallouck, T., Rankel, L., Amorosi, C. and Graybill, C. (2008) 'Low cost laboratory adaptations for pre-college students who are blind or visually impaired', *Journal of Chemical Education,* 85, 2: 243–7.

Svensson, C. (2010) 'Specific learning difficulties in writing', in J. Graham and A. Kelly (eds) *Writing under Control* (3rd edn, pp. 228–41), London: Routledge.

Swain, K., Bertini, T and Coffey, D. (2010) 'The effects of folding-in of basic mathematical facts for students with disabilities', *Learning Disabilities: A Multidisciplinary Journal,* 16, 1: 23–9.

Swainston, T. (2007) *Behaviour Management: Ideas in Action,* London: Continuum International.

Swanson, H.L. (2000) 'What instruction works for students with learning disabilities?' in R. Gersten, E. Schiller and S. Vaughn (eds) *Contemporary Special Education Research,* Mahwah, NJ: Erlbaum.

Sword, L.K. (2003) *Preschool Characteristics of Giftedness: Checklist.* Online: www.gift-edservices.com.au/handouts/Preschool%20Characteristics%20of%20Giftedness%20Ch ecklist.doc (accessed 1 April 2010).

Tan, K.H., Wheldall, K., Madelaine, A. and Lee, L.W. (2007) 'A review of the simple view of reading: decoding and linguistic comprehension skills of low-progress readers', *Australian Journal of Learning Disabilities,* 12, 1: 19–30.

Taylor, R.L., Smiley, L.R. and Richards, S.B. (2009) *Exceptional Students: Preparing Teachers for the 21st Century,* Boston: McGraw Hill.

Taylor-Cox, J. (2008) *Differentiating in Number and Operations,* Portsmouth, NH: Heinemann.

TeacherNet (2010) *Quality Standards in Education: Support Services for Children and Young People with Visual Impairment.* Online: www.teachernet.gov.uk/_doc/6576/ quality%20standards%20-%20visual%20impair.htm (accessed 19 February 2010).

Templeton, S. (2010) *Vocabulary their Way: Word Study with Middle and Secondary Students,* Boston: Allyn and Bacon.

Tomazin, F. (2009) 'Stemming the tide of cyber bullying', *The Age,* 13 October. Online: www.theage.com.au/national/stemming-the-tide-of-cyber-bullying-20091012-gu1x. html (accessed 1 April 2010).

Tomlinson, C.A., Kaplan, S.N., Purcell, J.H., Leppien, J.H., Burns, D.E., Renzulli, J.S., Imbeau, M.B. and Strickland, C.A. (2008) *The Parallel Curriculum* (2nd edn), Thousand Oaks, CA: Corwin Press.

Tompkins, G.E. (2007) *Teaching Writing: Balancing Process and Product* (5th edn), Upper Saddle River, NJ: Pearson.

Torgerson, C., Brooks, G. and Hall, J. (2006) 'A systematic review of the research literature on the use of phonics in the teaching of reading and spelling. Research Report 711'. London: Department for Education and Skills.

Treffinger, D.J., Young, G.C., Nassab, C.A., Selby, E.C. and Wittig, C.V. (2008) *The Talent Development Planning Handbook,* Thousand Oaks, CA: Corwin Press.

Trezek, B.J. and Malmgren, K.W. (2005) 'The efficacy of utilizing a phonics treatment package with middle school deaf and hard-of-hearing students', *Journal of Deaf Studies and Deaf Education* 10, 3: 256–71.

Trezek, B.J., Wang, Y. and Paul P.V. (2010) *Reading and Deafness: Theory, Research and Practice,* Clifton Park, NY: Delmar.

Turnbull, A., Turnbull, R. and Wehmeyer, M.L. (2010) *Exceptional Lives* (6th edn), Upper Saddle River, NJ: Merrill.

UKLA/ PNS (United Kingdom Literacy Association/ Primary National Strategy) (2004) *Raising Boys' Achievements in Writing,* Royston, Hertfordshire: UKLA.

University of Kansas (2010) 'Learning Strategies'. Online: www.ku-crl.org/sim/strategies. shtml (accessed 16 January 2010).

Urbanski, J. and Permuth, S. (2009) *The Truth about Bullying,* Lanham, MD: Rowman and Littlefield.

US Department of Education (2008) *Reading Recovery*. What Works Clearinghouse Intervention Report, ERIC Document ED 503466. Online: www.eric.ed.gov/ERICDocs/data/ericdocs2sql/content_storage_01/0000019b/80/41/d5/e4.pdf (accessed 31 January 2010).

US Department of Education (2009) *Students with Disabilities: Fast Facts*. Online: http://nces.ed.gov/fastfacts/display.asp?id=59 (accessed 26 March 2010).

US Department of Education (2010) 'WWC quick review of the article "Technology's edge: the educational benefits of computer-aided instruction"', *What Works Clearinghouse Report ED 508123*, Washington, DC: Institute of Educational Sciences.

Viel-Ruma, K., Houchins, D. and Fredrick, L. (2007) 'Error self-correction and spelling: improving the spelling accuracy of secondary students with disabilities in written expression', *Journal of Behavioral Education*, 16, 3: 291–301.

Vincini (2003) *The Nature of Situated Learning*. Online: http://uit.tufts.edu/at/downloads/newsletter_feb_2003.pdf (accessed 1 April 2010).

Wang, P. and Spillane, A. (2009) 'Evidence-based social skills interventions for children with autism: a meta-analysis', *Education and Training in Developmental Disabilities*, 44, 3: 318–42.

Waters, H.S. and Schneider, W. (eds) (2010) *Metacognition, Strategy Use and Instruction*, New York: Guilford Press.

Watson, A., Kehler, M. and Martino, W. (2010) 'The problem of boys' literacy underachievement: raising some questions', *Journal of Adolescent and Adult Literacy*, 53, 5: 356–61.

Webb, J.T., Gore, J.L., Amend, E.R. and DeVries, A.R. (2007) *A Parent's Guide to Gifted Children*, Scottsdale, AZ: Great Potential Press.

Wehmeyer, M.L. and Field, S.L. (2007) *Self-determination: Instructional and Assessment Strategies*, Thousand Oaks, CA; Corwin Press.

Wendling, B.J. and Mather, N. (2009) *Essentials of Evidence-based Academic Interventions*, Hoboken, NJ: Wiley.

Wendon, L. (2006) *Letterland*, Barton, Cambridge; Letterland International. Online: www.letterland.com/Teachers/Teachers_1.html (accessed 1 April 2010).

Westwood, P. (2009a) *What Teachers Need to Know About Students with Disabilities*, Melbourne: Australian Council for Educational Research.

Westwood, P. (2009b) 'Arguing the case for a simple view of literacy assessment', *Australian Journal of Learning Difficulties*, 14, 1: 3–15.

Wheeler, J.J. and Richey, D.D. (2010) *Behavior Management* (2nd edn), Columbus, OH: Merrill.

Wheldall, K. (2009a) 'A non-categorical approach to teaching low-progress readers', *LDA Bulletin*, 41, 4: 13–15.

Wheldall, K. (2009b) 'Effective instruction for socially disadvantaged low-progress readers: the Schoolwise Program', *Australian Journal of Learning Difficulties*, 14, 2: 151–70.

White, S. (2005) 'Education that works in the Milwaukee public schools: benefits from phonics and direct instruction', *Wisconsin Policy Research Institute Report* 18, 4: 1–23.

Wild, M. (2009) 'Using computer-aided instruction to support the systematic practice of phonological skills in beginning readers', *Journal of Research in Reading*, 32, 4: 413–32.

Williams, P. (2009) *Social Work with People with Learning Difficulties* (2nd edn), Exeter: Learning Matters.

Wilson, L., Andrew, C. and Below, J. (2006) 'A comparison of teacher-pupil interaction within mathematics lessons in St Petersburg, Russia and the North-East of England', *British Educational Research Journal* 32, 3: 411–41.

Wolsey, T.D. and Fisher, D. (2009) *Learning to Predict and Predicting to Learn: Cognitive Strategies and Instructional Routines*. Boston: Pearson-Allyn and Bacon.

Wood, S. (2010) 'Best practices in counselling the gifted in schools: what's really happening?' *Gifted Child Quarterly*, 54, 1: 42–58.

Wright, C., Shelton, D. and Wright, M. (2009) 'A contemporary review of the assessment and treatment of ADHD', *Australian Journal of Learning Difficulties,* 14, 2: 199–214.

Wright, R. (2003) Mathematics Recovery: a program of intervention in early number learning, *Australian Journal of Learning Disabilities* 8, 4: 6–11.

Yell, M.L., Meadows, N.B., Drasgow, E. and Shriner, J.G. (2009) *Evidence-based Practices for Educating Students with Emotional and Behavioral Disorders,* Upper Saddle River, NJ: Pearson-Merrill.

Yu, S.V. and Murik, J. (2008) 'Teaching mathematics to secondary students who experience learning difficulties: a report on the interventions used by ten teachers', *Special Education Perspectives,* 17: 1: 49–66.

Index

Main entries are in **bold**